David Vizard's
HOW TO Super Tune and Modify
HOLLEY
CARBURETORS

David Vizard

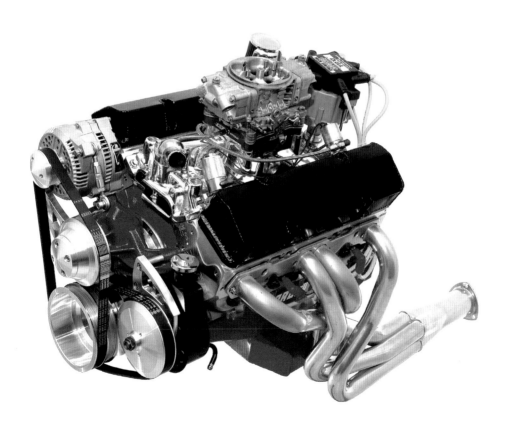

CarTech®

CarTech®, Inc.
838 Lake Street South
Forest Lake, MN 55025
Phone: 651-277-1200 or 800-551-4754
Fax: 651-277-1203
www.cartechbooks.com

Edit by Paul Johnson
Layout by Monica Seiberlich

ISBN 978-1-934709-65-8
Item No. SA216

Library of Congress Cataloging-in-Publication Data

Vizard, David.
  David Vizard's how to super tune and modify Holley carburetors / by David Vizard.
    p. cm.
  ISBN 978-1-934709-65-8
  1. Holley carburetors. 2. Automobiles–Motors–Carburetors. I. Title.

  TL212.V39 2013
  629.25'330288–dc23

              2013012931

Written, edited, and designed in the U.S.A.
Printed in China
10 9 8 7 6 5 4 3

Title Page:
This 580-hp Chevy 355 is visually stunning engine. The polished surface on the intake manifold contributes to the overall production of horsepower and can be an aid to your vehicle's on-track performance.

Back Cover Photos

Top Left:
Holley's big-CFM Dominator was only a viable wide-band power proposition because of its intermediate cruise circuit and the use of high-gain annular discharge boosters.

Top Right:
The stepped dog-leg booster (arrow) has only marginally more gain than the regular dog-leg booster, but the step brings about better fuel atomization. This style of booster is about the most versatile currently in use and is a good choice if fuel atomization appears to be inadequate.

Middle Left:
Holley's Ultra models have an adjustable idle air bypass screw (yellow arrow). Air for the bypass goes through the holes indicated by the blue arrows.

Middle Right:
Until the main jets come into play, the engine relies on the transition slot for calibration. Here, the baseplate has been removed from the carb body to better show the butterfly position for the slot's best operation. The amount of slot remaining above the butterfly is shown by the red arrow. The amount of slot as viewed from the underside is shown by the yellow arrow. The slot is open about 1½ turns of the idle-speed adjusting screw.

Bottom Left:
This is the business end of the accelerator pump system. These pump jets, commonly called squirters, are available in a wide range of sizes.

Bottom Right:
In a home workshop, you can use a die grinder and some 100-grit emery rolls to do all the work on this body. The points of note are the detailed boosters with a sharp edge (yellow arrows), the rounding of the edges leading into the secondary barrels (blue arrows), and the radiusing of the edges on the choke horn (green arrows).

OVERSEAS DISTRIBUTION BY:

PGUK
63 Hatton Garden
London EC1N 8LE, England
Phone: 020 7061 1980 • Fax: 020 7242 3725
www.pguk.co.uk

Renniks Publications Ltd.
3/37-39 Green Street
Banksmeadow, NSW 2109, Australia
Phone: 2 9695 7055 • Fax: 2 9695 7355
www.renniks.com

CONTENTS

ACKNOWLEDGMENTS

The author of any book worth its salt pulls information from many sources. I am no exception. Since my first real immersion in the world of Holley carbs in 1976, there have been literally hundreds of people who have taught me something about these carbs. I am sorry that I don't remember the faces and names of everybody who helped along the way over the years between 1976 and now. To all I am grateful for your contribution to my education. However, as is so often the case, there is inevitably some person or persons who turn out to be pivotal as far as routing one's life down a given path. For me, that was David Braswell of Braswell Carburetion in Tucson, Arizona.

My good friend Denny Wycoff introduced me to David. Denny was a racer and drove for several years, with great success, for J. D. Braswell,

David's dad. Denny was a very innovative racer and teaming up with J. D. was a natural, as J. D. was also a highly innovative character. Well, the apple, as they say, never falls far from the tree. Not unexpectedly, David Braswell inherited his father's mental agility as well as a love for racing. David's life focus was on carburetion in general and Holley carbs in particular.

From 1976 to 1980, I lived in Tucson just a few miles from Braswell Carburetion. If I had a question, David always had the time to answer in detail. If I had a question David could not answer with his extensive and definitive experience, he went out of his way to help out on whatever tests were needed to generate a detailed answer. Nothing was ever too much trouble or took too much time. So, in the production of this book, a great deal of credit must go

to David Braswell. Thanks, David.

To David's great input I also want to add that of Holley's engineering staff, past and present. Occasionally I get to work with them and for me it has always been a learning event.

Having the technical know-how at hand is only a good start in the production of a book. There are many administrative chores that need to be handled. Over the 35-plus years I have been dealing with Holley I have worked with a number of very helpful PR people within the company. I want to thank all of them. But in the last few years, and when production of the book was at its most intense, I had to rely heavily on Holley's current PR person, Bill Tichnor, and his assistant, Blaine Burnett. Every time I had an issue or problem, these guys came through. Thanks guys, your efforts are much appreciated.

INTRODUCTION

I well remember my first efforts at "hopping up" carburetors. I was 14 years old and living in England. The hop-up exercise involved flowing air through the tiny carb on a 35-cc bicycle-assist engine. In stock form the engine had just enough power to push a 90-pound kid at just under 26 mph on the flat. That was faster than I could pedal, but I wanted more.

The concept of making power from an internal combustion engine was, even at this age, relatively clear to me. Although there wasn't much to draw on at the time, I read all I could find on the subject of increasing output. Using an electric drill, emery rolls, and grind stones I ported the cylinder barrel's intake and exhaust.

A look at the carb instantly revealed that the butterfly and its shaft blocked a lot of air coming into the carb. So I stripped the carb and, with files as my only tools, proceeded to do an extensive streamlining job on the carb's shaft and butterfly. I never flow tested the carb to see what improvements were made but in light of many years of subsequent experience I guess it was at least 50 percent better in terms of flow.

While I was busy doing this a friend of mine was having his dad skim the head for more compression. After about 30 hours of work on the engine I reinstalled it on my bike. What a difference. Speed increased by a solid 10 mph. I could also climb typical main road gradients with minimal loss of speed if I also pedaled. For a 14-year-old, I was flying along!

Following this was a blank period of about a year as far as hopping up anything, but by early 1958 things changed for the better. I built a crude but highly effective flow bench and started porting heads in serious fashion.

The Austin A30

Just before my seventeenth birthday I managed to acquire a very tidy three-year-old Austin A30. It was powered by a very anemic 803-cc A-series engine that cranked out about 25 flywheel hp. Even though the car weighed only about 1,400 pounds, the power available still meant it was barely faster than the cheapo 100-cc two-stroke motorcycles of the day. At best it went about 65 mph. But salvation was at hand; about a year earlier Austin had introduced the A35, which came with a much stronger 948-cc (30 hp) version of the engine in my A30.

A short while after that the Austin-Healey Sprite (of Frog Eye fame) was introduced with a twin SU carb version of the A35 engine. This unit cranked out about 40 hp. As it happened, a local guy bought one of these little AH Sprites (a few years later I owned one and what a fun car it was). This is where events turned in my favor. After about 7 miles, he stopped to go in a store situated on a busy road. While the car was parked, an out-of-control 10-ton truck totaled it. Upon hearing this my brother

I have just timed in the cam on a Ford 302 small-block engine for a Mustang. With a well-calibrated single 4-barrel carb on a single-plane intake, the engine produced 475 streetable horsepower on the dyno.

and I put together all our savings and made an offer for the complete and undamaged engine. We got it for about $80 in 1960 money. The outlay left my brother and me just about broke. We installed the AH Sprite engine "as is" and boy what a difference there was in performance.

Testing

With the acquisition of the Sprite engine we had something to work with as far as engine mods go. My brother and I baselined the A30 on a main road that went over a local 1,000-foot-high hill. This was basically our dyno. With the stock

The "Bug Eye" Austin-Healey Sprite weighed very little, so with a hopped-up 100-hp A-series engine, it was very much a little rocket ship! As a collector car these days, a Sprite fetches big bucks.

engine the tach read right on 5,000 rpm in third gear and that was it. Next we installed one of my ported heads and this time the tach topped out at 6,200 rpm. What an improvement that was.

Next we ported the twin carb intake. Although the flow increased quite a lot there was very little difference in speed on the test hill. Pulling everything back apart and taking a good look at the inside of a 1¼-inch SU I realized that these carbs, as good as they were, had been designed for speed of production as a priority.

What I did then was to repeat the airflow exercise I had done on the little 35-cc bike engine. In this instance it was not just the butterflies that were given the treatment but the whole interior of the carb. At this juncture I did have my simple airflow bench to check results. (If you're interested, this bench build is detailed in my book *How to Port & Flow Test Cylinder Heads*.) With no real increase in cross-sectional area that pair of 1¼-inch SUs flowed about the same as a pair of 1½-inch SUs.

Doing the airflow work proved to be the easy part. What was far from easy was getting the mixture right. This involved needles with different taper angles. It was almost a nightmare but finally things came right after a dozen or more attempts. On the test hill, the Austin A30's RPM rose to 6,500. Some rough-and-ready cal-

culations indicated that the engine's power had gone up by 10 hp with the substitution of the standard cylinder head and about another 5 from the carb mods. With zero cost involved that seemed to be a pretty good value. With these results in hand modifying SU carbs became almost the norm.

By 1963, and with about 65 hp, the A30, which saw about half a dozen races, was replaced with an 850 Mini (another A–series variant). This seemed so slow compared to what I was used to driving that I pounced on the engine about two days after taking possession of it.

Chassis Dynos

At this juncture a chassis dyno came into the picture. So, after modifying the head, intake, and carb plus a muffler change I went to the dyno to see what had been achieved. A *really* good stock 850 Mini made 20 horses at the front wheels. After calibrating the carb and ignition mine made 32 to 33 hp. I did not do any real races that year, only a couple of driving test (slalom) events.

The following year I shared the driving in a 1,000-cc Cooper S. This was my introduction to Weber carbs. When it comes to fixed-jet carbs (which was what the Weber was) I really learned the ropes on those big Webers. But what I learned was more in the way of how to utilize

all the calibration components that Weber offered to allow these carbs to deliver the correct air/fuel ratio. Also at this time, side-draft Dell'Ortos came into my life. In 1966 I started my own performance engineering shop and just about every engine conversion or build that I did went on the dyno for final calibration of carb and ignition.

From 1967 to 1971 I mostly raced Minis, either 1,000- or 1,293-cc models. I managed a few wins and podium places but found it difficult to counter the lack of money. As fast as my five-port all-iron carbureted engines were, they were still no match for the guys with 1,000-cc overhead-cam fuel-injected Cosworth-powered cars and 1,300 twin cams in the bigger class. However, when track conditions deteriorated I very much came into my own.

One of my last forays in my lightweight and highly modified 1,293-cc Mini proved to be a somewhat epic event. At the tight twist-and-turn Prescott track in Gloucestershire, UK, on a wet track (wet but not running wet) I proceeded to annihilate even the Formula 1 cars. The fastest F1 car being 0.19 second slower than I was.

The Avenger Era

In 1972, with Chrysler backing, I started developing and racing the "new from the ground up" Chrysler (UK) Avenger; a four-seat sedan that was built tough by any standards. It also had a great deal of hidden potential. The carb work I had done to date served me well in this quarter. I soon found that the Avenger's less-than-conventional short-stroke two-valve pushrod engine was hyper critical as far as mixture droplet size was concerned. What I learned here won me a drag race championship by winning every event that year.

Much to my amazement it seemed that few engine builders, including the factory team, actually realized the need for superfine atomization for the Avenger engine. For my following year's road racer, which had to use the original carbs (though they could be modified), I spent a lot of time reengineering the Strombergs. By about halfway through the season I had my Stromberg-carbed Avenger up to scratch and it was truly unassailable. At the last race at Mallory Park in Cheshire, England, I could put between 200 and 300 yards per lap lead over my strongest competitors, both former champs for the class. That meant I could lap the second-place guy in less than nine laps. All this came about because I understood carburetion and the engine's requirements better than the engine builders building the other guys' engines.

The following year was my debut in the British Touring Car Championship (BTCC) with the Avenger. The rules allowed any modification to the carburetion that affected fuel but the air side was fixed. I had to use 30-mm main venturis. Armed with the knowledge that this engine was really (I mean *really*) fussy when

it came to fuel atomization, I reengineered the entire Weber DCOE internals. I made up new main venturis and high-gain auxiliary venturis (referred to as boosters in a Holley carb), which delivered far finer fuel atomization than the Webers. Along with this, the internals were more aerodynamic than the Webers so, with the same size venturis, the airflow was up by about 9 percent.

One day I got a call from Dez O'Dell, Chrysler's competition manager. He explained that a couple of Weber factory engineers were coming over with a truckload of parts to optimize the carbs on the Avenger race engine they were running in the factory cars. He asked if I could bring my carbs along for a comparative test. "Sure," I said, and on the appointed day arrived at the test venue.

With much of the internals reengineered, I went to do battle with the Weber engineers at a factory dyno test.

My experience with Italians has all been really good except for these Weber engineers, who treated me like some ignoramus who had just crawled out from under a rock, and that a dyno cell where real tech was being practiced was no place for a journalist. I bit my tongue and put

up with this for a day and a half.

By early afternoon on the second day they boastfully announced that there was absolutely no more power to be had from the carburetion on the test engine. I was in no mood to be tactful, so I picked up my modified Webers and walked over to the engine. I said, "Reasonable for a pair of beginners; now watch and learn."

The very first pull on my carbs netted 5 ft-lbs and 6 hp more than their best efforts and I felt no remorse about rubbing it in. For the following two years the number-one factory car used my carbs (and heads for that matter) and won the BTCC twice.

Holley Carbs Enter the Scene

In 1977 I was living in Tucson, Arizona. There was a great racing community in Tucson and I fit right in. This is also where I received an introduction to Holley carbs. Let me set the scene: I was over at Braswell Carburetion, and David Braswell, at that time the number-one supplier to NASCAR's top teams, was showing me his new alcohol carb. To get the amount of fuel flow required for alcohol, the float bowl was injected. Whenever the throttle went to the wide-open position, a switch activated two solenoids and fuel via a metering jet was then directly injected into each float bowl. The reason for this was that the stock float bowl needle and seat did not flow enough fuel no matter how big it was made.

I asked David if I could see a stock needle-and-seat assembly. I looked at it and announced that it was made wrong. I whipped out my calculator, and after a few moments, told him that if the needle were made with a spherical end instead of a conical end it would flow more than

This is the 1293 Mini I beat all the F1 cars with at Prescott. Daphne, the young lady also seen here, typed my first dozen or so books from dictation at speeds up to 90 words a minute!

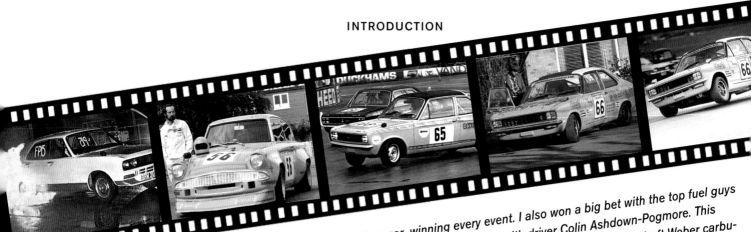

From Left to Right: I thoroughly beat the competition with this Avenger, winning every event. I also won a big bet with the top fuel guys that I could do a flame burnout just as well as they could. • Here is my 1-liter Ford Anglia with driver Colin Ashdown-Pogmore. This pushrod two-valve 61-ci screamer turned almost 12,000 rpm and cranked out 138 hp on a pair of dual-barrel, downdraft Weber carburetors. What is not apparent here is that the car is a tunnel design and could out corner the Formula Ford 2000 single seaters of the day (1972). • Here, I am putting on a race-winning performance in my Stromberg-equipped Avenger. In the wet, I was almost unbeatable regardless of what the other guys were driving. • My ultra-fast BTCC Avenger. Here I am at Thruxton on the way to a class track record. • Knowledge of carburetor design and the engine's needs really paid off with my BTCC Avenger.

enough fuel for the job at hand. David and his chief engineer/foreman where totally taken aback by a person they perceived as a journalist who could even spot, let alone resolve, engineering problems that fast. I had to explain to them that first and foremost I was a research and development engineer and trailing that by a very lengthy margin a partially competent writer. I charged David $25 for my time as an engineer. As for the needle and seat, it went on to sell in the tens of thousands, and to this day, this is what is most often sold for alcohol-fueled Holley carbs.

Boosters Again

At the 1977 SEMA show I met Mike Urich, who was Holley's chief engineer. Naturally we got to talking carbs and the subject got around to boosters. I asked Mike what research Holley had done on fuel atomization. Much to my surprise he said that they had done no direct investigations into what made for good atomization

and to what degree it affected part- and full-throttle performance.

When I got back to Tucson I made a mental note to look into fuel atomization as it applied to Holley carbs. David Braswell's facility was right here in town and I knew he was always looking to learn more about Holleys to make his custom ones even better. With David's extensive assistance I made a healthy start on my investigation of fuel atomization and how various characteristics interacted with the rest of the engine.

The tests done at this time (see Chapter 7) put me in good stead for later tests with other carb specialists such as the Carb Shop in Ontario, California. At this point my Holley R&D snowballed into an increasingly bigger and more educational deal.

Long Introduction

So why, in this introduction, have I gone to such lengths to explain where I am coming from? Two reasons. First it shows that I'm not a journalist writing about a subject where most of the info is

gleaned from a third party. Most of the "super tuning" info you are going to read within these pages is a result of my own personal experience. I am an engineer first and foremost, who just happens to be writing about the subject.

The second reason answers another question often asked, "Why do you persist with carbs when fuel injection is the way of the future?" The answer is simple. Because I am known to be a problem-solver in this area, I am regularly approached with carburetor-oriented projects. This book is just such an example. Ask yourself this question: If you were a speed equipment manufacturer, who would you rather have test your parts? Someone known for top-notch carb calibration or someone who needed to rely on a third and possibly disinterested party for the carb set up? I love fuel injection, but 19 out of 20 of my clients are carb users.

I almost forgot; there is a third and very compelling reason for my carb-centered existence. Get that carb right and it can match or even exceed the dyno figures seen by a comparable design of fuel-injected induction, but at a third or less of the cost!

A CARB'S TRUE FUNCTION

There are a lot of myths and misconceptions surrounding the subject of carburetion. Let's first look at what a well-designed and calibrated carb can do, then at what a carb cannot do.

Functions of a Carburetor

What a carburetor is supposed to do can be described in a few simple sentences. Getting it to do just that, though, can be more difficult. Let's start with a list of required functions.

• Airflow
• Mixture ratio
• Fuel atomization

On the face of it that short list does not sound like much of a challenge but a reality check reveals this is far from the real world. However, what we are trying to achieve is far from impossible. If you are of an older generation you may have heard a quote bandied about that sounds really neat but is in fact not true. The name of the professor responsible escapes my mind but the quote has stuck for 40 years and it goes like

this: "A carburetor is a wonderfully ingenious device for giving the incorrect mixture at all engine speeds."

It sounds pat, and coming from a learned person it tends to have all the makings of the truth. The truth of the matter is that a Holley (or any other good carb) can be calibrated to deliver a very precise mixture so as to produce excellent results under wide-open-throttle (WOT) conditions. In other words, let's assume at some RPM your engine is capable of delivering 300, 400, and 500 hp at three points going up the RPM range. Get your carburetion right, on the circuits applicable to WOT, and your results will hit the mark at each point within one or two horsepower or bet-

ter. That's well into fuel injection territory but at a fraction of the cost.

Let's look at the three functions in a little more detail.

Airflow

The carb must flow an adequate amount of air to meet the required needs for the engine's intended purpose. For most humdrum applications, such as lawn mowers and common street machines, maximum output takes a distant second place to cost. If you are reading this book you probably want more power for greater speed and acceleration. That means knowing just how much airflow is enough, and, as it happens, not falling into the trap of supposing

Fig. 1.1. One of Holley's Dominator series of carbs helps produce big power and this carb's 1,250-cfm flow capability is good for up to 1,200 or so horses.

Fig. 1.2. Holley carbs have won more races than just about all other carb manufacturers put together. If you have the know-how to make the most of these carbs, they can deliver outstanding performance.

that a little too much is okay. With some carbs, such as an SU, a little too much is okay because the carb only opens as much as required to satisfy the engine's airflow demand. This type of carb is called a constant-vacuum carb.

Most Holleys are a type of carb known as a fixed-jet/choke carb. Although there are many advantages to this type of design, as we shall see, there is a downside because too big a carb produces inferior results. Throughout this book it becomes apparent why this is so and how best to avoid the negative issues of too big a carb.

Mixture Ratio

It is important for a carb to mix the appropriate amount of fuel for its current operating conditions. This means a full-power rich mixture when maximum output is called for and a suitably lean mixture when economy is required. I already stated that getting the full-power mixture right over a wide range is entirely possible. While getting reasonable economy is doable it is a lot more difficult to get super economy without losing drivability. Chapter 5 delves into the practicalities of super-lean operation

for maximum economy; but remember that achieving it is not easy.

Fuel Atomization

On the face of it, the subject of fuel atomization seems simple enough. The better the fuel is atomized, the better the engine performs. Well, once again, the real world is not quite that simple. In practice there is a best atomization process for economy and a best process for full power. In each case the goal is to maximize cylinder pressure for the amount of fuel used. Chapter 7 goes into much detail on carb, venturi, and booster design parameters in relation to intake manifold design and operating conditions.

The Impossible

Unless you are really into carb design, the inner workings of a carb look like a collection of parts for executing a little black magic. Don't feel bad about that; most of today's top carb designers were there once. The trick race Holley carb you see in Figure 1.1 is complex but not unfathomable.

In reality, the function of any carb can be reduced to two simple functions that it must perform. The first of these functions is to deliver a certain ratio of fuel and air to the engine. The second is to atomize and distribute the fuel so that a significant portion is vaporized and the remaining wet fuel is sufficiently well atomized to turn to a vapor as the piston reaches top dead center (TDC) on the compression stroke. (See Chapter 3 for more detail.)

Economy Air/Fuel Ratios

Here I want to talk about air/fuel ratios and the much-rumored

100-mpg carb that the fuel companies supposedly brought out and then buried to not lose profits. Let's start with the fact that any respectable carb can be calibrated to deliver whatever air/fuel ratio you want to the extent that it can range from way too lean (insufficient fuel for the air) to way too rich (too much fuel). However, you must never loose sight of the fact that it's not what *you* may want to see in the way of mixture ratio that counts; it's what the *engine* wants.

At the lean end of the scale, the most important for fuel economy, most engines run into lean misfire at about 18:1 to 19:1 air/fuel ratio. However, with enough high-tech R&D and components put into the engine it is possible, as was found on my EconoMin project to run effectively at just over a 22:1 air/fuel ratio. I may have summed this up in a sentence but be assured there was more to it than just leaning out the mixture—a lot more, in fact.

Now consider this: If you can get any decent carb to deliver an air/fuel ratio significantly leaner than, say, 30:1, the problem of finding fuel mileage must not be constrained by that carb's ability to deliver a lean enough mixture. In other words, any decent carb (and there are dozens out there) delivers an economy mixture far leaner than any current (2012) engine can burn.

Fuel Atomization

Some carbs, such as the constant-vacuum SU and Stromberg carbs, can atomize fuel better than a 45-psi fuel injection nozzle, so the question of whether or not fuel can be adequately atomized is answered: Yes, it can. Not all carbs are as good as these at atomization, but there is a fix.

If a carb fails to atomize the fuel well enough, a little manifold heat fixes the problem. Fuel-economy driving takes place at part throttle, so it also means that there is, if the right cam events are used, a lot of intake manifold vacuum present. This also has a strong influence on vaporization.

Mileage Improvement

Any decently designed and correctly sized carb can cover a far wider range of fuel mixture conditions than the engine can actually deal with, so what is the rumored 100-mpg carb going to do that the ones we currently have available cannot already do? Answer: absolutely nothing! The engine is the limiting factor, not the carb. So you see the argument for the existence of a 100-mpg carb is starting to become somewhat tenuous. But I have not finished yet.

We don't need to consider the 100-mpg carb in terms of a 50-cc moped because that is not in context with what is so often referred to. When discussing the possibility of a 100-mpg carb, the context is a midsize sedan and speeds at which we could reasonably expect people to drive.

Let's say such a vehicle is a typical 2,300-pound sedan (and that's on the small side) and the speed is, say, 50 mph (and that's on the slow side). By picking these conservative numbers I'm giving the benefit of the doubt to the 100-mpg carb. Powering such a car at a steady 50 mph typically takes about 15 hp. With brake specific fuel consumption (BSFC) figures of a modern engine being what they are at part throttle, such a car would turn in right around 50 mpg at that speed. Also it would be

utilizing the fuel's energy at close to 25 percent (that is, the engine's thermal efficiency is 25 percent). If this hypothetical engine converted 100 percent of the fuel's heat into mechanical energy the mileage would increase to about 200 mpg.

Those numbers indicate a lot of room for improvement in engine design. The problem is not with the carb's design so much as the typical engine's inability to convert the fuel's total heat value into power. The carb has the ability to deliver any suitable mixture the engine may require. The carb is already nearly 100 percent effective, meaning the 100 mpg comes from engine development, not from fuel-delivery development (i.e., the carb). This means that long ago carburetors had already reached nearly maximum potential and there is little room left for improvement. From that, we can safely conclude that the 100-mpg carb never has existed and never will!

By now you should be convinced that as long as the carb is suitably calibrated, at least 98 percent of any mileage improvement comes mostly from engine development and maybe a little extra from fuels.

If you want easy-to-get mileage you could drive more carefully, avoid passing, drive slower, and back into the driveway at night. But if you are anything approaching a type-A personality, like me, the very fact there is a car in front means that some overtaking is due!

I have to race something and the only way I have been able to consistently drive for economy is to race a trip computer that reads out in mileage to date and instantaneous mileage. The bottom line is: I need to get there now, not five minutes later. All this adds up to one thing for me: The

vehicle I drive better be able to go fast on next to no fuel.

You can read my other CarTech books (*How to Build Max-Performance Chevy Small-Blocks on a Budget*, *How to Build Max-Performance Chevy Big-Blocks on a Budget*, and *David Vizard's How to Build Horsepower*) for more detail on how to increase the output of a typical Detroit-built street V-8 engine. The principles apply to all engines and explain how to increase output by as much as 100 percent. While focusing mostly on power a lot of the power-improving techniques bring about an increase in mileage due to better fuel usage and the reduction of losses by friction and exhaust system inefficiencies.

Yes, this book is about carbs, and Holley carbs in particular. To get mileage, select a carb that has features that favor part-throttle usage (see Chapter 6 for more detail). But to make the most of your econ-carb choice be aware of many engine modifications (some minor others not so minor) that complement what your carb can do.

The questions you may want answered and the fuel-saving modifications are in alphabetical order on the following list:

- Big-bore short stroke or small-bore long stroke?
- Big valves or small?
- Camshafts for mileage
- Carb calibration
- Cold-air intake
- Compression ratio effect
- Exhaust system length and diameter
- Fuel
- Gearing
- Ignition timing
- Intake port dimension and finish
- Intake-to-exhaust size ratio

- Internal friction
- Mixture preparation
- Nitrous?
- Oil and lube (how to go 750,000 miles before a rebuild)
- Optimum valve size
- Piston speed for optimum mileage

- Swirl and tumble
- Supercharger and turbocharger
- Thermal barrier
- Two-valve head versus four-valve head; which is more fuel efficient?

With a list this long you can see that getting better fuel mileage is just a little more than super-tuning your Holley. So, next time you hear about the 100-mpg carb you can rightly scoff at it.

Holley Dominator Versus Fuel Injection

Over the years small refinements in carbs and manifolds have resulted in close optimization of such factors as fuel atomization and distribution within the intake manifold. Good vaporized to wet fuel flow ratios as the charge enters the cylinder so as to promote effective combustion and so on.

The salient point is that if you experiment with an EFI system long enough you will end up most likely exceeding the best that can be done with a carb. But let me make it clear: It won't come easy. Output aside, an EFI setup has a number of advantages if the overall function of the fuel delivery system is considered. The biggest is part-throttle drivability. When cams are short, a carbureted engine drives just as well as an EFI-equipped engine. When cams get radical, the advantage drops squarely into EFI's favor. When intake vacuum is low, a carb experiences difficulty delivering an accurate and well-atomized air/fuel mix.

An EFI system does not rely on vacuum for calibration or delivery purposes. It is programmed to deliver a well-atomized amount of fuel that is often determined by throttle position and RPM alone. The result is far better low-speed drivability when big cams are used.

The bottom line is: The decision to use either carburetion or EFI is dependent on application and budget.

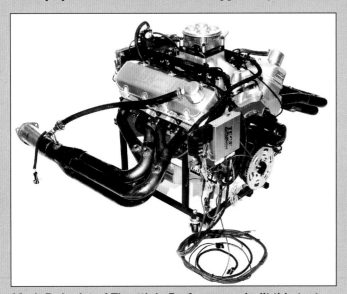

Mark Dalquist of Throttle's Performance built this test engine. It was an all-aluminum 565-inch big-block Chevy intended for street use that finally made a couple of horsepower shy of 900.

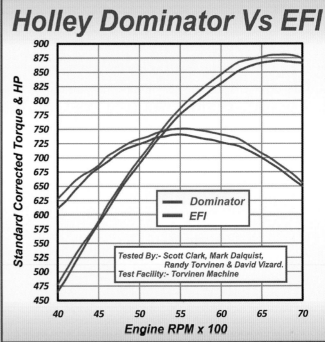

The test results delivered by our 565-inch Chevy show that a good carb can match or even exceed the output of a typical quality EFI system.

OPERATING PRINCIPLES

By about 1975 it looked as if fuel injection was about to spell the demise of the carb as a prime performance fuel delivery system. But, even today, the carb is a dominant feature of engines used for street performance and racing. So why are they still here and, if my guess is right, for at least the next 25 years? Because they work extremely well.

A gasoline mechanical fuel injection system was always an expensive

and usually finicky deal. Then along came the microchip and electromagnetic injectors and everything supposedly got easier. That was probably the case if you were computer savvy, but in the mid 1970s most car nuts were very much mechanically oriented and computers just did not figure into their engine building plans. However, mainstream soothsayers predicted the nearly total demise of the carburetor for pretty much all

applications other than lawn mowers and classic cars.

As we know, it did not happen. Instead, carburetor manufacturers upped the ante with new, more refined designs. In terms of power potential, what small gap there might have been, put them ahead when raw power was the only criterion. Today, the carb is still very much alive and well for one simple reason: For all its underlying simplicity, a correctly sized and calibrated carb can make horsepower numbers as big as any more complex fuel injection system and do so on a lot less money.

So why has fuel injection almost universally taken over on OE production lines? Primarily because a computer controls it, and therefore fuel injection lends itself to solving emissions-related problems. Outside of having socially acceptable tailpipe emissions, a carb supplies a means to performance, which ranks about equal to any fuel injection, but without the complexity and cost. But tapping into that performance potential requires you to understand the basic operating principles to enable optimal calibration.

Fig. 2.1. This AED-modified Holley Dominator may be expensive, but it drives like a $2,500 fuel-injection unit and makes more power without the complexity of fuel injection.

Fig. 2.2. The dyno shows that an SU carb is a very precise means of delivering a well-atomized mixture under all driving conditions, from idle to maximum RPM.

Basic Function

Correct calibration of the carb is mandatory in order for power to be made from a carbureted engine. To acquire any great proficiency at this, a sound understanding of the function of the carb is required. Most carbs fall into one of two groups: constant-vacuum and fixed-jet or choke ("choke" here refers to the venturi not the cold-start system). An SU carb such as used on many British cars from the early 1900s through the mid 1980s is a prime example of a constant-vacuum carb. However, more than 90 percent of all carbs used on American V-8 engines are the fixed-jet/choke type, such as typified by a regular Holley carb or the fixed-choke primary paired with a vacuum secondary such as with a Quadrajet.

Fig. 2.3. Unlike most carbs, opening the butterfly does not directly allow more air into the engine. When the butterfly opens, it communicates engine vacuum to the piston (see Figure 2.4), and thus opens it to supply just the amount of air the engine needs.

Exploring Venturi Properties

All fixed-choke carbs depend on the properties of a venturi for their function. As air is drawn through a venturi, it speeds up and the pressure drops at the venturi's minor diameter. (See Figure 2.5) This suction effect draws the fuel up from a reservoir, which, in the case of a carb, is the float bowl, and discharges it into the airstream. The greater the airflow, the greater the amount of fuel drawn into the venturi.

At this point you may wonder why the pressure drops as the velocity increases. In essence, any given volume of air possesses a finite amount of energy in various forms. These are temperature, pressure, and kinetic

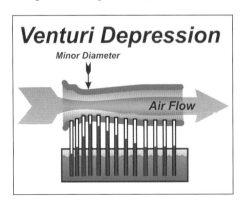

Venturi Depression

Minor Diameter

Air Flow

Fig. 2.4. Here you can see the SU's vacuum-actuated piston. As the piston rises, it pulls a tapered needle out of a jet.

energy from any velocity involved. When the velocity increases, the kinetic energy increases as dictated by the formula:

$$\text{Kinetic Energy} = 1/2 \, MV^2$$

Where:
M = mass
V = velocity

Note that the kinetic energy goes up as the square of the speed (V^2). This means that unless some other form of energy drops, the volume of air contains more energy than it started with. In reality this cannot happen, so for a given mass to have only the same energy, the pressure drops. It is just that pressure drop caused by the air passing through the venturi that we use to draw fuel out of whatever reservoir it is stored in and deliver it to the engine's induction system.

Fig. 2.5. As the air speeds up at the venturi's minor diameter, the pressure drops. This drop in pressure draws fluid from the reservoir source.

Applying the Venturi Effect

If ever there was a misused term it is "venturi effect." I have heard it misused in relation to intake ports, rocket nozzles, and a ton of other stuff. When I ask what might be meant by it, I usually get nothing more than a blank look or a "Don't exactly know" response. The venturi effect is illustrated in Figure 2.5. It is a suction caused by the reduced pressure in the high-speed section of the necked-down section of a tube.

Next, we must look at how to translate this basic venturi effect into something resembling the main jet circuit (as opposed to idle, cruise, acceleration, and cold start) of a simple carb. Doing so results in what is seen in Figure 2.6. This also shows what is potentially the first calibration problem associated with a simple carb. Ideally, the fuel level in the reservoir needs to be at the same level as the point of discharge in the venturi. This means that as soon as air starts to flow so does the fuel.

Unfortunately such a setup would mean that any movement of the carb as a whole would spill fuel

Main Jet and Air Corrector Function

Main Jet

Air Corrector Jet

AIRFLOW

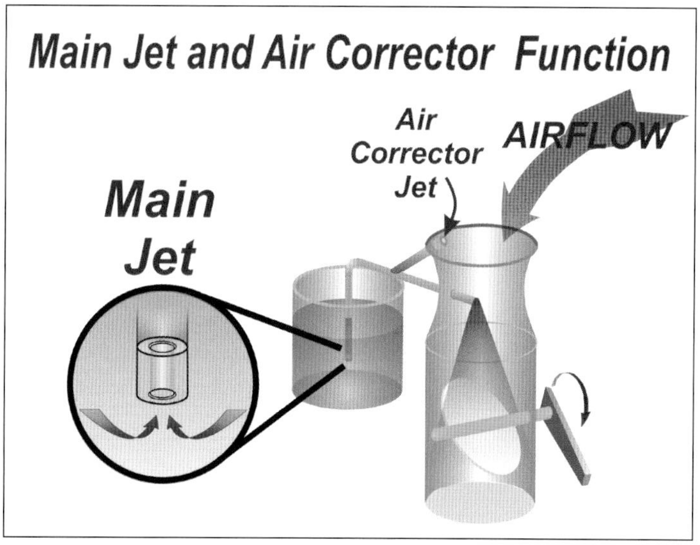

Fig. 2.7. Here air is shown in red and fuel is shown in blue. A mixture of air and fuel is shown in purple. The main jet restricts the amount of fuel delivered along the passage to the discharge point in the venturi. As RPM and air demand increase, the main jet becomes more effective at delivering fuel so the air/fuel mixture becomes too fuel rich to burn effectively. To compensate, air is leaked into the system through an air corrector jet. Allowing air into the system prior to the venturi discharge point bleeds off some of the suction (signal) to the main jet, thus eliminating the tendency to become overly rich. It also dilutes the fuel delivered from the main jet with air. This not only helps correct a mixture problem but also contributes to better fuel atomization.

into the engine whether it were running or not. To avoid this, the level of the fuel is set below that of the discharge point. This is called the "spill height" and is usually between 1/4 and 3/8 inch. Also, fuel flow (drawn into the venturi by the depression it creates) increases faster than the airflow; so a simple jet/venturi system produces a mixture that becomes progressively richer. The basic fix for this is called "air correction."

Air Correction Function

Air correction works by introducing air into the fuel prior to it reaching the point of discharge in the venturi. In simple terms the fuel is being diluted with air prior to exiting the discharge point in the main venturi. While most of the world calls these "air correction jets" Holley and most Holley users refer to them as "air bleeds." Their function, in its simplest form, is shown in Figure 2.7. The air corrector jet (or air bleed) becomes more effective as engine speed (RPM) and air demand increases so, under steady-state airflow conditions, it can, for most practical purposes, cancel out the main jet's tendency to deliver an increasingly richer mixture.

In the real world the air demand created by an engine is anything but

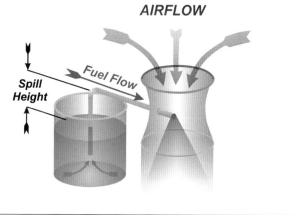

Venturi/Fuel Flow Function

AIRFLOW

Fuel Flow

Spill Height

Fig. 2.6. This is a functioning carb in its most basic form. It might be barely functional for a stationary engine running at one speed, but that's about all. To deal with a typical engine many fuel-to-air calibration fixes are required. The main jet is situated just where the fuel enters the delivery tube in the fuel reservoir.

steady state, even in a V-8. Because of this, the air-corrected main jet may still not supply the desired ratio of air to fuel at all points of operation. To compensate, engineers devised an ingenious system that not only addressed the reshaping of the fuel curve that would otherwise exist, but also fuel atomization. This is called the emulsion well or emulsion tube.

On an engine employing a single barrel of carburetion connected to each cylinder the emulsion tube design is critical for the accurate delivery of the carb's air-to-fuel ratio. As more cylinders are connected to the carb so the airflow gets nearer to steady state and the emulsion tubes function as a fuel mixture curve trimming device becomes less critical. Figure 2.9 shows how the emulsion tube works.

Although it has never been a big issue with the type of carbs traditionally used on V-8s, getting the emulsion tube right for a one-barrel-per-cylinder installation, such as a set of Webers or Dell'Ortos, is often considered to be a black art or a trial-and-error process. The good news here is you are about to get the Viz-

ard method for complete and simple emulsion tube "reading."

Calibration Considerations

Calibration components considered so far were the main jet, emul-

sion tube (or in the case of a Holley, the emulsion well), and air corrector. A larger main jet makes the mixture richer, just as a smaller main jet makes the mixture leaner. With the air corrector the reverse is true. The bigger it gets, the weaker or leaner the mixture

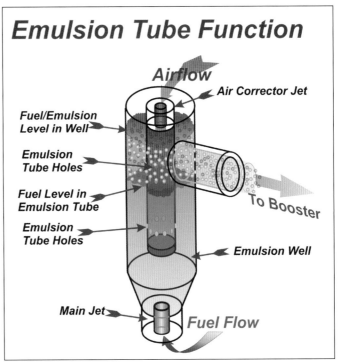

Fig. 2.9. The booster in the carb's main venturi develops suction and draws fuel (blue) up through the main jet into the emulsion well. In addition, air is drawn in through the air corrector jet into the emulsion tube within the well. This air then percolates out through the holes in the emulsion tube into the fuel in the emulsion well. The fuel, which now contains many small air bubbles, is emulsified.

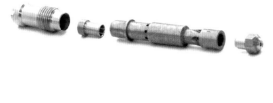

Fig. 2.8. Exotic carbs, such as Webers and Dell'Ortos, usually have the main jet/emulsion tube/air corrector jet as a single assembly. The main jet (far right) plugs Into the end of the emulsion tube as does the air corrector (second from far left). The holder (far left) screws into the carb body emulsion well and holds everything in place.

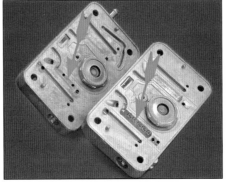

Fig. 2.10. The emulsion tube/well for a typical Holley metering block (left) is very simple, and it usually takes the form of one or two holes drilled into a passage connecting the emulsion well to the air corrector passage. The high-performance versions of most Holley-style carbs have emulsion tube/well holes (left), which are calibrated with brass screw-in jets (right).

Fig. 2.11. The air corrector jets for Holley-style carbs are positioned on either side of the booster leg. This carb has replaceable air correctors, but most run-of-the-mill Holleys have press-in ones. The outer ones are for the idle circuit and the inner ones are for the main jet circuit.

becomes, with the effect being more pronounced at higher RPM.

The effect the emulsion tube has on the mixture curve depends on the "hole" pattern. Here is how to read it. First, hold the emulsion tube upside down and inspect the hole pattern. Holes at the top of the emulsion tube affect the top end of the rev range. Holes in the middle trim the mid-RPM range. Holes at the bottom affect the low-RPM range. Where there are no holes, the mixture is rich.

Where there are holes, the mixture is leaned out. Just how much the mixture is leaned out by the presence of holes depends on how many there are and how big they are. The more holes, the more the mixture is leaned out at that point. Because it is fed with air from the air correction jets, the emulsion tube's overall function is influenced by the air corrector size. A larger air corrector leans out the mixture, but at low RPM, and small throttle openings, the air correction has little influence over the mixture. As the engine's demand for air increases, due to an increase in throttle opening and RPM, the air corrector's influence increases. At high RPM, just a few thousandths change in the air corrector size can have a significant affect on mixture ratio.

As mentioned earlier, one other aspect of the emulsion tube and its well is that it acts not only as a means of calibration but also as a control element for fuel atomization. By emulsifying the fuel prior to it reaching the booster located in the venturi the fuel is easier to shear into fine droplets at the point of discharge. Generally the more it is emulsified with air in the emulsion well/tube, the easier it is to atomize at the venturi.

With an understanding of how calibration is achieved let us now look at what the main circuit needs to deliver in the way of air-to-fuel ratios.

Mixture Requirements

To achieve optimal operation under all normal circumstances, a carburetor must deliver an air/fuel ratio appropriate for the prevailing conditions. For maximum power on gasoline, an air/fuel ratio of around 13:1 is needed. Under part-throttle cruise conditions, fuel economy (rather than outright power) is the major issue. During cruise, the engine's fuel efficiency can be improved considerably by leaning out the mixture. Typically, air/fuel ratios are quoted in terms of pounds of air per pound of fuel. Figure 2.12 shows the physical dimensional proportions of the range of air/fuel ratios you're likely to be dealing with.

If maximum power is the goal, the mixture ratio required must fall within certain well-defined limits. Figure 2.13 shows how the power changes as the mixture is varied. You can see that power drops off faster on the lean side of the graph than it does on the rich side. Also, to achieve better than 99 percent of the power

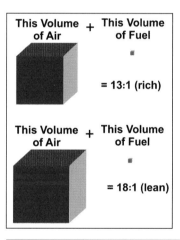

Fig. 2.12. Air/fuel ratios are typically quoted by weight, but this drawing shows the typical weights of fuel and air, and what they look like in terms of their volume. The fuel occupies a relatively small space compared to the air space. If the air-to-fuel ratio is "chemically correct," all the oxygen in the air plus the fuel are 100 percent utilized during the combustion process. For gasoline, this mixture is typically around 14.7:1. A rich mixture has too much fuel for the amount of air and a mixture that is lean has too little fuel. The ratios shown here are typical for maximum power and lean cruise.

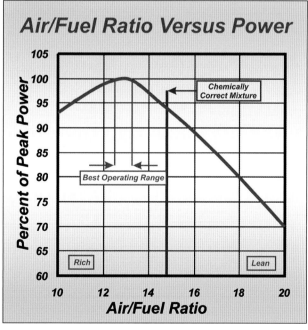

Fig. 2.13. The mixture must fall into the narrow operating range shown here to achieve maximum horsepower. This requires precise calibration of the carburetor over a wide range of RPM and airflow situations.

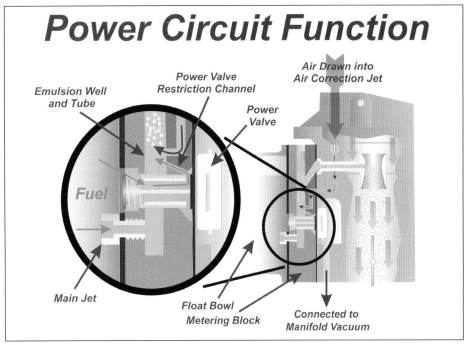

Power Circuit Function

Emulsion Well and Tube

Power Valve Restriction Channel

Air Drawn into Air Correction Jet

Power Valve

Fuel

Main Jet

Float Bowl Metering Block

Connected to Manifold Vacuum

Fig. 2.14. This cutaway shows the functions of all components (main jet, air corrector, emulsion well, etc.) that interact during WOT operation. The enlarged section shows the open power valve in greater detail. The power valve's chamber is connected to the intake manifold on the downstream side of the butterfly, so it experiences manifold vacuum. When the throttle is opened wide, the manifold vacuum drops and allows the spring on the power valve to lift the valve off its seat. This allows fuel to flow from the float bowl into the power valve and out of the PRVC into the emulsion well.

Power valves are available at various vacuum actuation values. For most street and street/strip uses, the power valve needs to actuate at between 4 and 7 inches of manifold vacuum.

Fig. 2.15. The arrow indicates one of the two PVRCs, which feed extra fuel into the main jet well to enrich the full-throttle mixture. This particular metering block is from a high-performance Holley carb, and utilizes screw-in jets for optimum calibration.

potential of the engine, the mixture delivered needs, for typical gasoline, to fall between 12.5 and a 13.4:1.

When the vehicle is cruising down the highway the mixture needs to lean out considerably if good mileage is to be achieved. Most of the carbs you are likely to be dealing with use a power-enrichment circuit activated by a vacuum-sensitive "power valve." This is usually a vacuum diaphragm, which senses how much intake manifold vacuum is present. Opening the throttle causes the intake manifold vacuum to decrease to near zero. This allows the power valve to open and operate as an additional main jet, which supplies the extra mixture-enriching fuel. This additional main

jet in any Holley style carb is commonly known as the power valve restriction channel (PVRC).

Traditionally, a Holley-style carb is calibrated with the main jet, but the introduction of a power valve in the circuit means that the main jet now calibrates the cruise mixture. The size of the power valve jet dictates the full-throttle mixture. In practice this is rarely done because most PVRCs are a fixed size. Many high-performance Holley carbs now have most circuits, including the emulsion tube/wells, easily calibratable with small replaceable jets.

Boosters

Maximum-output carburetion must have sufficient airflow to completely satisfy the engine's demand at peak power RPM and a little beyond. This calls for a carb that is bigger than if low- and mid-speed power were a primary goal. When a fixed-jet/choke and venturi carb is sized with high output in mind the booster design becomes more critical for operation over a typically acceptable range of 5,000 rpm.

Before delving into advanced booster design, review Figure 2.16. It details the basics of how this aptly named carb component works.

Before Holley introduced the high-flow Dominator series of carbs, it had to come up with booster designs with far more gain than had been previously used. The new design needed to take a relatively small signal generated at the minor diameter of the main venturi and amplify it into a strong, useable signal for the purpose of metering and atomization.

What you see today are booster forms that can cover a wide range of applications. Figure 2.18 shows, in the

Booster Action

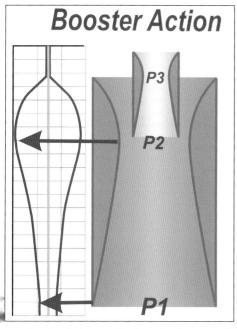

P3

P2

P1

Fig. 2.16. A booster allows the signal (pressure drop) at the minor diameter of the main venturi to be increased as measured at the minor diameter of the booster venturi. Here, the blue line shows the pressure drop through the main venturi; the red line shows the velocity.

The engine's suction (P1) causes a pressure drop, which dictates the amount and velocity of the air flowing through the main venturi. This is not true for the booster. The air flowing through the booster is actually dictated by the much greater pressure drop occurring at the minor diameter of the main venturi (P2). This brings about a much higher pressure drop and velocity at P3.

In simple terms, the booster has amplified the signal generated at the main venturi. A high-gain booster can increase the main venturi signal by as much as 400 percent.

Booster Styles

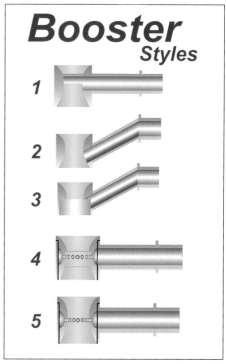

1

2

3

4

5

Fig. 2.18. Booster 1 is primarily used for street applications. Booster 2 is commonly used in high-performance carbs as is booster 3, which is a dog-leg booster as is booster 2 with a step machined into the underside. This enhances fuel atomization. Booster 4 is a stepped annular discharge design and booster 5 is a similar annular discharge style but without the step. Booster 4 and booster 5 are high-gain types, which are most often used in big-CFM carbs.

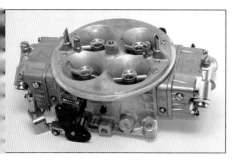

Fig. 2.17. Holley's big-CFM Dominator was only a viable wide-band power proposition because of its intermediate cruise circuit and the use of high-gain annular discharge boosters.

order of gain, the characteristic form of the main variants. For instance, at a typical WOT pressure drop, the number-1 booster amplifies the main venturi signal by about 1.8 while a number-5 with all the casting flash removed and a cleanup on the entry and exit delivers an amplified signal about four times that of the main venturi. Figure 2.19 provides a good perspective of the difference in signal strengths of the five booster styles tested in one barrel of an 850 Holley carb.

Booster Gain—How Much?

For a high-CFM carb to deliver over a wide RPM range, the booster gain must be high.

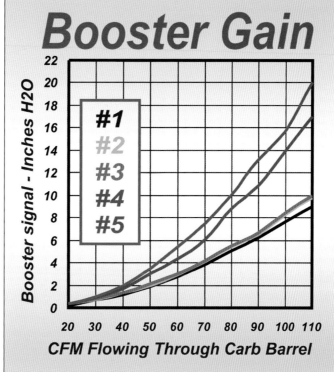

Booster Gain

#1
#2
#3
#4
#5

Booster signal - Inches H2O

22 20 18 16 14 12 10 8 6 4 2 0

20 30 40 50 60 70 80 90 100 110

CFM Flowing Through Carb Barrel

Fig. 2.19. This graph shows the signal strength for each of the booster styles depicted in Figure 2.18. Note the big difference between the lowest and highest.

But it can be too high. If the fuel is too finely atomized too much of it vaporizes in the intake manifold, which reduces the engine's volumetric efficiency (breathing efficiency) and consequently reduces power.

Getting the booster's characteristics just right for the application is a key factor in making torque and horsepower from any carbureted engine. That is why the relationship between sizing and booster selection is so important.

Idle and Transition System

As important as the WOT power circuits are, none of the assets are worth a nickel if the idle and transition circuits don't work as they should. Figure 2.21 shows the basic function of these two circuits in a Holley-style carb.

Although they may look quite different this mode of function is common to most types of carbs, whether Holley or an exotic carb such as a Weber. Some carbs, such as the Weber and Dell'Orto carbs, use a series of holes rather than a slot for the transition circuit. The mode of function, however, is the same.

Because the idle/transition circuits are most frequently used during normal driving, time spent calibrating them pays big dividends in producing good street drivability and fuel economy. Although idle circuit adjustment is a prime criterion, the first step toward achieving a good idle and subsequent low-speed cruise performance is to first select a suitable carb. For a short-cammed street machine, the idle circuit of a Holley-style carb need only be on the primary side of a 4-barrel carb. This works fine when there is plenty of intake vacuum (12 or more inches),

but when bigger cams are used it takes a larger butterfly opening to supply the engine's idle needs. (See Chapter 8 for details on how idle and low-speed vacuum are affected by cam selection and the type of intake manifold.)

Anything that reduces vacuum (such as a bigger cam) means that the butterfly needs to be open wider to supply the idle airflow called for by the engine because the vacuum (suction) by the engine is less. To meet airflow requirements under these conditions the butterfly must be opened wider. In this position, less of the transition slot length is available for doing its job. The first fix is to use a four-corner idle system where

Fig. 2.20. The idle discharge port is the hole in the throttle-body wall.

the primary and secondary barrels supply the engine's idle air demand. This leaves more total transition slot

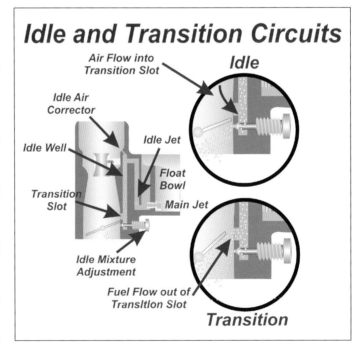

Fig. 2.21. The idle/transition circuit relies on the high vacuum at small throttle openings. This vacuum draws fuel from the float bowl through the idle jet. It then communicates with a passage that goes from the idle air corrector jet to the idle mixture adjustment screw.

In the passage, air from the air corrector and fuel mix to form an emulsion. In addition to air from the air corrector, air is also drawn in through the transition slot. This, at idle, is above the butterfly where it experiences typical air pressure. The idle mixture screw, when appropriately adjusted, meters sufficient fuel emulsion into the intake airstream to meet the idle needs.

As the throttle opens beyond the idle position, the butterfly begins to uncover the transition slot. The slot then begins to experience the intake manifold vacuum. As a result the slot progressively stops drawing in extra air and instead discharges extra fuel emulsion from the idle circuit to meet the needs of the extra incoming air from opening the throttle.

length to do what it is supposed to do: deal with the engine's transition needs.

At a certain point, the cam may be so big that even four idle circuits are not enough to smooth the transition. Under these circumstances, it may also be necessary to put one or more holes in the butterflies to allow further closing of the butterflies in an effort to gain more transition slot use.

Accelerator Pump System

Under idle and cruise conditions, a considerable amount of vacuum exists in the intake manifold. This vacuum reduces the boiling point of the fuel causing it to vaporize much easier under the prevailing high-vacuum conditions than under low vacuum. This useful characteristic considerably helps fuel distribution under idle and cruise situations. When driving down the freeway at 2,000 to 3,000 rpm with 15 or so inches of vacuum most, if not all, of the fuel being drawn into the engine

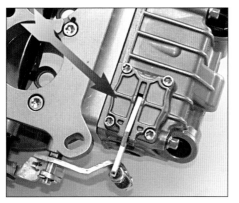

Fig. 2.22. For Holley-style carbs, an accelerator pump diaphragm is located at the bottom of the float bowl. Jet size, pump stroke, and pump capacity set the calibration.

is vaporized well before it reaches the cylinders.

Standing on the gas pedal completely changes the situation. When the vacuum almost instantly transitions from a high value to near zero, fuel that was held in vapor form condenses into liquid on the manifold walls. Although a fresh charge of air is entering the engine and carrying its associated fuel, the engine

momentarily goes very lean. This is due to the fuel that was contained in the air within the manifold condensing on the manifold walls, and for a moment at least, going nowhere. This causes an enormous lean-mixture flat spot that the engine simply does not drive through.

To offset fuel condensing on the walls of the intake manifold an accelerator pump system is added. This physically squirts additional fuel into the intake to cover the would-be hole in the carburetion. Figure 2.23 shows a basic schematic of a typical pump system. In this example, a piston is shown injecting the fuel, but most often, the function of the piston is carried out by a spring-loaded diaphragm, such as in a typical Holley carburetor. Calibration of the accelerator pump system is not only by means of jets to control the rate at which the fuel goes in. The system also uses various springs, cams, and diaphragm sizes to control the amount of fuel injected by virtue of the duration of the injection phase.

Carb Sizing

Although Holley makes choosing carbs appear easy in the literature, there is actually a lot more to it. Also, Holley's carburetor selection methods produce results on the conservative side. The reason for this is that they are in the carb business to sell you a functional carburetor, not to teach you how to be a carburetor engineer. Still, be aware that Holley has a useful interactive website. It not only helps you effectively choose the carb size but also goes through a list of carbs that meet the criteria called for. It deals with the decision-making process in terms of mechanical or vacuum secondaries very well.

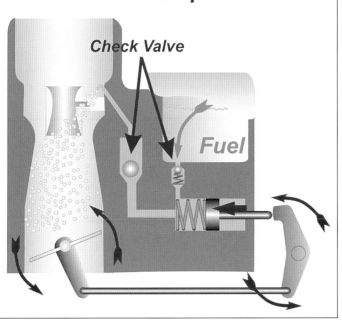

Accelerator Pump Circuit

Check Valve

Fuel

Fig. 2.23. Fuel for the accelerator pump is drawn in from the float bowl via a non-return valve. When the throttle is rapidly opened fuel is injected through the discharge passage, past the check valve, and out through the jet located just above the venturi.

That is the Holley selection method. If you want to tighten up on the accuracy of the CFM selection a little more, maybe the Vizard method as detailed in Chapter 6 is for you. Though still slightly on the conservative side, it is a lot more sophisticated than you are likely to find anywhere else.

Carb Options

Until the fuel-injection era, the most commonly seen performance carb on a GM vehicle was the Quadrajet. This carb was designed with both fuel economy and power output in mind. It featured small primary barrels with a multiple high gain booster system and very large secondary barrels that opened progressively as the engine's airflow requirement increased. In all, these carbs worked well, but compared to a Holley they are a little more difficult to calibrate and set up for modi-

fied engines used in competition. A number of Quadrajet issues, such as float-bowl fuel surge, must be dealt with, especially if cornering at high gs. There are still several million of these carbs in use. If you are restoring an older muscle car and want to stick with the Q-Jet, a good option is a rebuild by a specialist shop.

Rather than diminish the variety of carbs available, the onset of the fuel-injection era did almost the reverse. If you are looking to replace an older carb of a different type, it helps to know both the strong and weak points of what you may be replacing compared with whatever you may feel is a worthy replacement.

Edelbrock

These are a cost-conscious, evolutionary version of the now-discontinued Carter Thermo-Quads and are available from 500 to 800 cfm. They use the same functional flow-on-demand and needle/jet calibration

method that the Quadrajets have. As such they can be accurately calibrated for good all-round performance.

Unlike a Holley-style carb, many of the principal circuits can be calibrated without removing the float bowl. The main-circuit calibration needles can be removed without touching much else. For the most part these carbs come with the calibration pretty close for most normal applications. If some calibration adjustments are needed, simply visit Edelbrock's website. With cutaway drawings and simple instructions they make it practical for even a first-timer to calibrate this carb.

Holley

For anyone younger than 110 years old, Holley seems to have been around forever and to offer an incredibly wide range of carbs. If your engine is a relatively short cammed unit you can use a very basic Holley carb to

Fig. 2.24. From mild to wild. The Edelbrock carb (left) is a 500-cfm street driver. The Endurashine (right) is a finished 800-cfm unit.

Fig. 2.25. This Chevy small-block has an Edelbrock 2x4 carb setup with essentially a dual plane manifold. It delivers the strong low-end output typically seen with this type of manifold. By utilizing two carbs instead of one, Edelbrock has given this manifold a top-end potential similar to a single-plane, street 4-barrel manifold.

Fig. 2.26. Holley's 600 cfm (model 0-80457C) is a vacuum secondary carb. It features primary-only idle circuit, metering plate on the secondary, and electric choke. This carb is a low-cost option that works great on short-cammed engines up to about 350 hp.

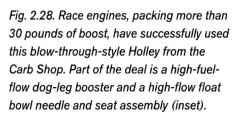

Fig. 2.28. Race engines, packing more than 30 pounds of boost, have successfully used this blow-through-style Holley from the Carb Shop. Part of the deal is a high-fuel-flow dog-leg booster and a high-flow float bowl needle and seat assembly (inset).

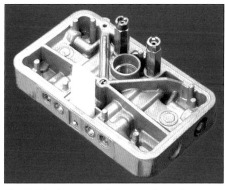

Fig. 2.29. Jet extensions, such as these hexagonal ones, are a good investment for the rear-metering block because they compensate for fuel migrating to the back of the float bowl under hard acceleration.

good effect. One great aspect here is the cost. The model 0-80457C 600-cfm vacuum secondary carb in Figure 2.26 not only looks good on a hot rod but also delivers good mileage and power output at a very friendly price. Many hot rodders opt for a mechanical secondary carb because that's what racers use.

For the street, a vacuum secondary is usually better. The often-perceived reduction in performance because of secondaries that do not open right away is mostly a myth. Apart from improving street drivability, it is often possible to use a vacuum secondary carb of about 50 cfm more than with a mechanical secondary.

Concessions need to be made when the use is more radical. First, with a cam of more than about 275 degrees of seat duration you should consider using a metering block (as opposed to a vastly cheaper metering plate) on the secondary as well as on the primary, plus a four-corner idle system. To get the transition circuit working properly, you may have to drill a small hole in each butterfly or open up the holes that are already there. If the carb is a Holley high-end model, this chore may not be needed because the carb can have an idle air bypass adjuster situated under the

Fig. 2.30. On this draw-through, Holley-carbed, Weiand-supercharged small-block, the carbs operate almost as they do on a naturally aspirated engine. The power valve is accessible from the intake manifold and not from the underside of the carb. This type of installation makes for easier calibration.

Fig. 2.27. The introduction of Holley's HP series put the company squarely into the value-plus race carb market. This series proved to be very versatile with a comprehensive range of calibration options, including PVRC and emulsion well jetting.

filter hold-down stud. (See Chapter 8 for more details on the idle and transition circuit setup.)

Braswell Carburetion

The Braswell carb comes from a name that has been associated with high-performance carbs for nearly 40 years. David Braswell, who has an enviable cup car win record, is best known in the industry for his design contributions to Holley's HP series of carbs. Having designed just about every aspect of a Holley at one time or another, he felt he was ready

to produce a carb from scratch. His creation embodies all the features of a new-millennium carb, and its all-aluminum construction about halves the weight compared to the usually used zinc-based alloy. I did a quick but hardly spot-on flow test of one of Dave Braswell's bigger 4150-style carbs and it indicated well over 1,000 cfm. Models for drag, road race, and oval track are available.

Barry Grant, Inc.

Barry Grant is another carb manufacturer that came out of the ranks

of Holley specialists. I am including the brand here because its carbs are still available on the used market. Production started in the early 1990s and progressively built to an extensive line ranging from small 2-barrel carbs to the monster King Demon 4-barrels, which can flow 1,300 cfm. Before the company's demise its most popular style of carb was the Demon, which was available in various models from a regular street version with a choke and vacuum secondary to a race Demon. These carbs were intended as a direct replacement for a 4150-series Holley.

The RS version of this carb and its bigger brother, the King Demon, have replaceable venturis. This adds an extra element in the tuning procedure because it allows the carb to be optimally sized for the job. In addition, race Demons also have replaceable boosters. This means that just about any aspect that can benefit from fine tuning can be fine tuned.

Among the last offerings from the Barry Grant stable was the vacuum secondary King Demon. Mounted on a dual-plane intake (such as Edelbrock's Air Gap Performer), it may just be what is needed for a really streetable high-output big-block. It has enough flow to supply an air-hungry big-block at the top end while having the potential to retain the ability to deliver the required characteristics for a strong off-idle performance.

I once started a big-block project intending to use the vacuum secondary King Demon and made some promising progress. The unfortunate demise of the company also brought an end to that line of investigation.

Like Holley and several other fuel system companies, Barry Grant made some high-volume race fuel pumps.

Fig. 2.31. The newest Braswell carb comes with a whole load of desirable features, including positive throttle stops and billet base plate and metering blocks.

Fig. 2.32. Repitched throttle bores, skinnier but larger-diameter butterflies, flow-developed boosters, and main venturis contribute to the Braswell carb's high flow.

Production pumps are sized to feed production engines, not the high-output ones we are striving to build. As of 2013 you can still find Barry Grant pumps in good used condition at swap meets. Very often you can get two used ones really cheap and rebuild them into one good one. That said, Holley's latest range of high-output fuel pumps do come at a very reasonable price.

Supercharged Applications

Superchargers have escalated in popularity since 1990 to the extent that there are now millions on the road in the United States. Most are being used with fuel injection, but that is because most blowers are factory-installed units with the Eaton blower topping the list.

When thinking about superchargers, most understandably think in terms of fuel injection for the fuel delivery system. Going to fuel injection does solve a lot of problems carbs can have when paired with a supercharger. But the sheer volume of blowers out there means that developing carbs specifically for use with blowers has become a viable business proposition in terms of cost to the consumer and production volumes.

There are two distinctly different ways a carb can be used in a supercharged application. The easiest to calibrate is a draw-through system, in which the carb operates in almost the same manner as it does on a naturally aspirated application.

The other option is the blow-through setup, in which the carb is pressurized. This can make for some radical spec changes if accurate mixture ratios are to be delivered under all circumstances. It is easier to get good calibration when using

Fig. 2.33. Although rated at 850 cfm, this Barry Grant race Demon actually flows about 930 cfm. In about 2005, I built a pump-gas-burning stroked, 351 Windsor with an 850 Demon that's actually punched out to 418 ci. After fine tuning using the dyno's oxygen mixture measuring system, the Demon proved its worth. Output was 563 ft-lbs and 610 hp. All this was done with a hydraulic-roller street cam. As this carb is no longer available, a Holley 950 HP Ultra carb makes an excellent substitute.

Fig. 2.34. The Barry Grant Demon and the King Demon carbs were available in an RS version, which featured replaceable venturi sleeves. Because the company is no longer in business, you may have to make your own venturis if you plan on experimenting in this area.

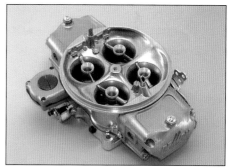

Fig. 2.35. One of the last carbs Barry Grant introduced was the vacuum secondary King Demon. It is just about the perfect carb for a true street, high-output big-block engine.

Fig. 2.36. Reminiscent of high-performance Pontiacs of the late 1960s, the Barry Grant six-shooter uses the center 2-barrel carb for everything up to cruise. If you stand on the throttle, the front and rear carbs kick in. If you are into the nostalgia of three 2-barrel carburetors, check out Holley's latest offerings.

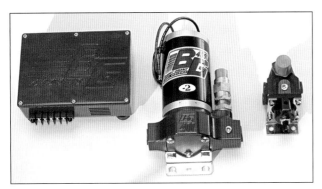

Fig. 2.37. This represents a top-of-the-line pump, pressure regulator, and output controller from Barry Grant. The controller cuts voltage to the pump during part-throttle use, thereby reducing pump wear and tear, and delivers a steadier fuel level for economy.

Fig. 2.38. The HP series opened the door to specialist carb shops and made an excellent basis for custom-prepped carbs. This 1,030-cfm unit from AED is a prime example. A lot of precision detail work has delivered extra airflow with no low-speed penalty, compared to a stock 950.

a turbine-type supercharger such as a Vortec or Pro-Charger. Part of the advantage of a blow-through system is that it can be much easier to build and a more compact installation.

Exotics

Most of the carbs discussed so far are used to feed a plenum-style manifold. There are some exotic carbs such as Webers, Dell'Ortos, and a few others that are designed to run one isolated barrel per cylinder. This sort of setup is known as an independent runner (IR) system. All the basics covered for a typical 4-barrel carb also apply to these seemingly more complex carbs. Although making the manifolds for exotic carbs is more complex and costlier, there are definite advantages to an IR setup, particularly if the carb has the required airflow.

First, mixture distribution is spot on. Second, there is no inter-cylinder robbing so the negative effect of a long cam on the idle vacuum and idle quality is reduced. This type of setup also makes significantly more low-speed torque so a bigger cam can be used before the loss of low-speed output becomes unacceptable.

Last, they have an awesome induction power roar when the throttles are wide open. All this power potential might make you think they must be gas guzzlers. Not so. You are paying for a carb installation that is about the same cost as a fuel injection setup. As such these carbs, when correctly calibrated, deliver an accurately metered and well-atomized mixture to the engine. I had four 2-barrel downdraft 48 IDA Webers (3,300-cfm in all) on my 350 Chevy work truck. It had stump-pulling torque from 800 rpm on and, even with a 1970s-style 3-speed automatic, it got 18 mpg overall!

Fig. 2.39. In the 1960s, a set of Weber carburetors on a side-draft manifold on a Pierce setup was one of the key aspects to making the Grand Sport Corvettes into the road race conquerors of the time.

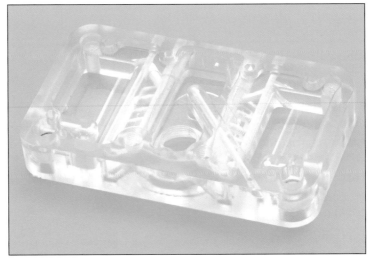

Fig. 2.40. This is a clear plexiglass metering block machined by BLP. It gives an idea of how the fuel circuits are routed within the block. (This photo has a green tint to better illustrate the features of this metering block.)

CALIBRATION REQUIREMENTS

This chapter is all about calibration of a Holley-style carb. It is not so much how to do it but more about what is required in order to do it. Without this knowledge you absolutely cannot "super tune" a carb. As simple as it may initially sound, only two factors need to be right for perfect carburetion: the mixture ratio and the mixture quality (how evenly the fuel is mixed with the air that contains it and how well it is atomized). Each must be exactly what the engine requires for the particular circumstances.

Fig. 3.1. This 870 vacuum secondary Street Avenger did a stellar job right out of the box. Although Holley sells carbs with really close calibrations, you have to accept the fact that unless you are lucky, arriving at totally optimal calibrations is going to require some effort on your part.

Max-Power Mixture Ratio

Before continuing, it is a good idea if you reacquaint yourself with Figure 2.13 on page 17. You can see that dyno tests have shown that there needs to be more fuel than with the chemically correct, or stoichiometric, ratio. For a typical non-oxygenated gasoline that ratio is about 14.6 to 14.8:1. (It is somewhat different for alcohols and alcohol blends, covered in Chapter 13.)

This ratio is the amount of air (in pounds) required to completely burn 1 pound of fuel and, at the end of the combustion event, leave no unused fuel or oxygen in the spent charge. In the process, all the available oxygen in the charge combines with all the available fuel. At first this seems to be an ideal situation for maximum output but the dyno tests in Figure 2.13 on page 17 indicate otherwise.

Variations

There are a number of reasons why a stoichiometric mixture ratio is not where things need to be for maximum power. Some are big, some are small, and some almost indeterminate. There are lots of theories flying around about the electrical or magnetic charge of the fuel. Several would-be inventors have tried to convince me that there is something significant in terms of power and economy that is brought about by the charge characteristics of the fuel. As of 2013, I have yet to see any real proof of this on the dyno, on the road, or on the track.

Although there may be fringe factors that have a small influence on output, there are three principal factors that affect exactly how much richer than stoichiometric the maximum power mixture can be.

First, there is oxygen-to-fuel proximity at the point/time of ignition. If the atomization of the fuel is less than optimal, the larger droplets do not have sufficient oxygen immediately adjacent to them to ignite as quickly or as completely as smaller droplets. The way to fix that is to put in a little more fuel than required for complete usage of the oxygen available.

The second reason for a slight excess of fuel is related to charge temperature. The extra fuel cools the charge more and thus allows a greater amount of air to be drawn in. It's a small effect but still significant in terms of output.

The third factor is fuel distribution within the intake manifold. If a manifold has poor fuel distribution between the cylinders, the best power is made on an overall richer mixture than would otherwise be the case.

The fuel's component blend can be considered the major influence on just how rich the mixture needs to be for maximum output. Remember, we are not dealing with a single chemical entity in a typical gasoline. (See Chapter 13 for more on the subject of fuels and their specific calibration needs.)

For now, let us consider the consequences of those three factors and their effect on the optimum air-to-fuel ratio. The easiest way to do that is to consider typical "best-case" and typical "worst-case" scenarios.

Positive Consequences: For naturally aspirated engines, I have seen air/fuel ratios for maximum output range from 13.4 to 12.5:1. The most recent engine that impressed me in this department was a Steve Schmidt big-block Chevy drag race unit of about 612 ci. It produced BSFC figures of 0.32 lb/hp/hr at the lower end of the race RPM range (about 4,000) and a shade under 0.40 at peak power (about 7,000 rpm). These are excellent figures, as was the overall 1,245 hp produced on the single 4-barrel Holley-style BLP carb.

The factors that produced the excellent results on a mixture ratio less rich than usual were:

- Good fuel atomization; not too coarse and not too fine
- Good wet flow characteristics from the manifold plenum right through to the combustion chamber
- Good combustion characteristics from the combustion chamber itself

Negative Consequences: Engines have come into my shop that needed sorting out because they were not making competitive power. (Engines like this are far more numerous than the "good" engines, such as the Steve Schmidt big-block discussed above.) An initial setup for such an engine typically yields the best results when the air/fuel ratio is in the 12.5:1 range. Even after diligent jetting for maximum output, power is still off

the mark and the BSFC figures are poor. They are typically in the high 0.4s to low 0.5s at the beginning RPM of the dyno pull to about 0.55 at peak power.

Making several dyno pulls typically causes the engine to develop a very black exhaust and plugs that are black and sooty. In that situation, the engine is down on power and also consumes much more fuel, fouls plugs easier, and wears out bores significantly faster.

If you are testing an engine that looks as if it falls into this category (in terms of air/fuel ratio and mixture quality), the fixes are to investigate the atomization at the carb's venturi. It could be that the venturi is just too big for the application and fuel atomization is suffering as a result. It could also be a case of having a booster that is just not boosting the main venturi signal enough, resulting in insufficient signal to atomize the fuel. Yet another problem could be that the particular combination of the booster and the air correction jets are not getting the job done.

If the mixture quality coming out of the carb is poor, the trend most likely continues downward. In most cases, the mixture quality becomes worse as the air and fuel travel through the induction tract. If the mixture quality coming from the carb is questionable, things such as the shiny ports with lazy flow areas compound the problems. (Refer to my book *David Vizard's How to Port & Flow Test Cylinder Heads*, which details this and the fixes, as well as those for a host of wet flow problems.) Adding a combustion chamber that is a little off the pace in terms of its ability to deal with excess wet flow can cause the engine to fail to live up to expectations.

As unexpected as it may seem, many Holley-equipped engines, as they came from the factory, have (due to less-than-stellar carb spec'ing) poor mixture atomization and consequently poor mixture quality from the carb. But, back in the day, factories used a couple fixes that you should never use if you are seeking engine performance: manifold heat and high vacuum, which are easy to achieve with a short street cam but not with a big-performance cam. This should tell you that, to an extent, the odds start stacking against you as soon as you step outside the "stock" arena.

Idle Mixture

Now let's take a serious look at idle mixtures with a view toward using the least amount of fuel to get the job done.

At idle, several significant factors come into play. Some are a great help and some are a hindrance. What we have going for us, in terms of aiding an effective combustion process, is the fact that at idle a typical short-cammed street engine has quite a lot of manifold vacuum. When the intake pressure drops significantly below typical atmospheric pressure, the fuel has a far greater propensity to vaporize. This, and the temperature of the induction system as a whole, means that most, if not all, of the fuel is vaporized and transformed into a gaseous state. As such, it is in the most ignitable form for the engine to deal with. Not only is it easy to light off, but any cylinder-to-cylinder mixture variations are minimized.

All the foregoing favors an idle mixture that could theoretically run very lean. What prevents this from happening is the dilution of the incoming charge by exhaust residue left in the combustion chamber at the end of the exhaust stroke. In addition, you can also have exhaust dilution due to exhaust-flow reversion at the end of the exhaust stroke. This is where the overlap generated by the cam comes into play.

Also, exhaust pollution of the intake charge within the intake manifold can occur if the manifold is a single-plane type where all the cylinders are connected to a common plenum. A dual-plane intake with induction pulses separated by 180 degrees instead of 90 does not have this inter-cylinder pollution. (The effects of different manifold styles on intake vacuum are covered in Chapter 6.)

The charge remains in the combustion chamber at TDC on the overlap, which is the end of the exhaust cycle and the beginning of intake. The cam overlap itself and manifold configurations play a great part in diluting the charge emanating from the carb with exhaust. This makes it more difficult to ignite, and the fix is more fuel for any given amount of air. In the case of a big cam and single-plane intake, this setup requires more idle air with a lot more fuel.

If not for exhaust dilution/pollution you might be able to run an idle mixture as lean as 18:1 or more, given a stout ignition system.

For a street engine, an important part of getting a good idle is having the highest compression ratio (CR) possible, which achieves two things. First, it reduces the residual exhaust because the chamber volume is smaller. Second, the higher the CR, the less overlap the engine needs to achieve a target top end. The reduced overlap is typically seen as a wider camshaft lobe centerline angle (LCA).

Any effort put into reducing exhaust contamination of the intake charge can pay worthwhile dividends. Unfortunately, no matter what the effort may be to counteract this contamination of the idle mixture, it is always going to occur. The final result is that it is necessary to run a richer mixture than would otherwise be the case. Also, the greater the contamination, the richer the mixture needed to get a decent idle.

As if all that were not enough, there is yet another factor coming into play: the bigger the cam, the lower the manifold vacuum. This means the fuel is less likely to vaporize. Additionally, with a high-performance engine, which typically has a much cooler intake manifold, one major asset (fuel vaporization) for a smooth, low-RPM idle is being seriously eroded.

All the idle mixture issues discussed so far add up to the fact that as the manifold vacuum decreases, the mixture ratio needed gets richer and the total amount of air required for best idle increases. Work at it and you can get a street engine equipped with a short-cammed 180-degree intake manifold to idle at 500 to 600 rpm on a 14.5 to 15:1 air/fuel ratio. At the other end of the scale a typical race engine needs 12.5 to 13:1 for its best chance at a steady idle. Even so, that idle can well be in the 1,000- to 1,100-rpm range.

Emissions

Before concluding this discussion on idle mixtures, I have a few words on emissions. If you have a street machine you should make every effort to have it run as clean as possible. At idle, the ignition timing is crucial if the minimum amount of fuel is to be consumed. Unfortunately, at minimum fuel consumption, the parts/million of unburned hydrocarbons and the carbon monoxide emissions are highest. Minimum fuel consumption at idle usually entails manifold vacuum pulling in about 25 degrees or more of additional timing. The optimum idle advance is typically about 35 to 40 degrees for a short-cammed street engine and (though not commonly realized) as much as 50 degrees for a street/strip engine.

For OE situations with strict emission standards, the targeting of minimum idle fuel consumption was, for emissions reasons, unacceptable. This led to the introduction of "ported vacuum." Here is how it works.

First, the vacuum port connecting the carb to the distributor is above the butterfly. This means no vacuum signal is seen by the distributor until the throttle is opened just enough for a low-speed cruise. Idle ignition timing is whatever the initial timing is set at. That's typically 8 to 12 degrees BTDC.

To get the engine to idle with less timing than it actually wants,

the throttle must be opened quite a bit more. This reduces the amount of idle vacuum so less exhaust is pulled back into the intake during the overlap period. This, in turn, reduces the exhaust dilution. The extra air pulled in for the idle requirement is now potentially better for combustibility so it can run with a leaner mixture.

The result is less idle emissions but a higher idle fuel consumption because the throttle is open significantly wider. As soon as the butterfly passes the vacuum port the timing is pulled in to whatever is appropriate for the current part-throttle conditions.

Cruise Mixture

When it comes to fuel economy, getting the cruise mixture to the optimal setting is where the most mileage is found. Two words are crucial here: lean burn.

Chapter 1 discusses the mythical 100-mpg carb, but that does not mean that your carburetor choice and its calibration are not significant. To effectively burn a super-lean ratio (less than about 15:1), focus on the engine spec. If the engine is built with power output as the

main priority, a typical Holley-style carb spec'd more toward power output can still deliver a burnable 15:1 ratio. This gets reasonable economy and is easy to achieve.

Things get more demanding when greater emphasis is put on fuel economy and power takes a back seat. This does not mean losing power of any real consequence. Calculations based on fuel economy results indicate that it is entirely possible to build a 300-hp, 375-ft-lbs 302 in a 5-speed 5.0 Mustang returning somewhere close to 30 mpg on the freeway at 65 mph. A car with that output and weighing 3,200 pounds would run the quarter-mile in about 13.35 seconds with a trap speed of around 102 mph. Increase the power by 30 to 40 horses and the mileage may only drop about 2 mpg while performance increases to a high-12-second ET and a trap speed of about 104 to 105 mph.

When performance was a substantial priority but the engine had to remain totally streetable, I have built 420-hp, 390 ft-lbs 302s that returned better than 25 mpg on the freeway and ran 11.85 and 115 in the quarter. Such an engine still has a fully functional cold-start system and a vacuum advance distributor. With that much power, though, slicks are a vital part of the equation.

These mileage figures rely on the ability of the carb tuner to select an appropriate

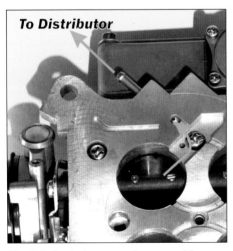

Fig. 3.2. Ported vacuum is sourced from above the butterfly while manifold vacuum (shown) is sourced from below the butterfly.

Fig. 3.3. Just how lean an engine can run for maximum economy depends not only on the choice of carb but also on the spec of the rest of the engine. Modern dual-plane intakes do a good job of getting economy while still delivering impressive horsepower.

carb spec and also to tune it to deliver as lean a mixture as the engine can tolerate. Assuming the ignition system is really hot, a cam that has appropriate timing for economy, a good exhaust, and a decent compression ratio (10:1 plus), air/fuel ratios of more than 17:1 are realistic. Given development time, the engine spec could handle mixtures as lean as 19:1.

When an engine gets to this stage, the calibration of a Holley-style carb becomes hypercritical. The biggest obstacle is the transition from a steady-state lean burn at one RPM to another as the throttle is opened wider. The amount of manifold vacuum is generally much higher than average (on this mileage-spec engine), and even a small change in throttle position causes fuel to momentarily drop out of the air/fuel mixture. Because the mixture is already near the lean limit, any further leaning out, even a very small amount, runs the engine into a momentarily lean misfire. This, as you may imagine, causes drivability problems.

These are the biggest obstacles to overcome for fuel economy.

Brake Specific Fuel Consumption

An engine's BSFC is almost certainly one of the most misunderstood numbers, even by professionals, in the engine performance field.

In my experience, novice enthusiasts most commonly confuse and misinterpret two numbers that are virtually joined at the hip: torque and horsepower. And it is surprising that even big-time race engine builders with big-time race wins still fail to fully understand what I perceive as the third most important number: brake specific fuel consumption.

Let's start with what it is not. BSFC is not a measure of the mixture ratio. I sometimes hear engine builders say they like to see the BSFC in the high 0.3s to low 0.4s, inferring that this is better than, say, 0.28.

While lecturing at UNC Charlotte some years ago, I asked a highly successful NASCAR Cup Car engine

This Chevy 350 small-block was built for the magazine story "Son of Sledgehammer," which appeared in the September 2007 issue of Popular Hot Rodding. *Brake specific fuel consumption was good because the numbers were low. However, if the low numbers had been interpreted as a lean mixture (about 15 hp of the 470 hp), the engine produced would have been jetted out!*

builder what he thought were optimum BSFC figures. He was under the impression there was an optimum somewhere in the 0.3 to 0.45 range, so I posed the question to the entire audience.

Of the 115 attendees (standing room only in a 100-seat auditorium), about 100 were engine builders, one was a member of the press, and the rest were students. Of all the answers given only the press guy, Johnny Hunkins, editor of *Popular Hot Rodding*, got the answer right.

The optimum BSFC is zero. This means you have an engine that is producing power and using no fuel to do it. Let's be honest here, you can't get more efficient than that.

Let's consider the individual words. First it is called "brake" because it is measured on the brake. This is an old term for a piece of hardware now more commonly called a dyno. It is "specific" in as much as it applies specifically to the weight in pounds (lb) of fuel needed to generate one horsepower (hp) for one hour (hr). This is commonly written as lb/hp/hr and is a direct measure of the amount of fuel, in pounds per hour, consumed by each individual horsepower of the engine being tested. That makes the number useful across the board as a means of comparing the fuel efficiency of engines regardless of their displacement and specifications.

The truth is that the BSFC figure can change while the mixture is unchanged. If that is the case, the BSFC figure is hardly applicable or reliable as a gauge of the mixture ratio.

Let's look at an example:

Assume we have a test engine that makes 500 hp at 6,000 rpm, and it loses 100 hp (in pumping losses and

Brake Specific Fuel Consumption *continued*

internal friction). Attached to this engine is also a means to simulate added internal friction, achieved by means of a disk brake on the front of the engine. This simulates the loss of another 100 hp in internal friction.

The engine is dyno'd and, with a 13:1 air/fuel ratio, it uses 200 pounds of fuel per hour. This means the BSFC is 200 pounds per hour of fuel divided by 500 hp, which equals 0.40 lb/hp/hour. So for every 1 horsepower generated, the engine uses (in one hour) 0.4 pound of fuel.

If the brake at the front of the engine is applied to simulate a 100-hp loss then, at the same 6,000 rpm, we see only 400 hp, as measured at the flywheel by the dyno. The induction system has no idea that power is being absorbed by something other than the absorber on the end of the flywheel so it continues to feed an *identical* amount of fuel (200 pounds per hour) and mix it with an *identical* amount of air. Since neither the flow of fuel nor air has changed, the air/fuel ratio is still exactly 13:1.

The same cannot be said for the BSFC, however. It is 200 pounds of fuel per hour divided by 400 hp. That comes out to 0.50 lbs/hp/hour. We have made no change in the mixture but the BSFC has changed by 20 percent. So we can, with total certainty, say that the BSFC is *not* a measure of the mixture ratio!

Now some old-timers who have been looking at BSFC to determine if the engine is rich might be pleased to know that one of the symptoms of poor (i.e., big number) BSFC is an overly rich mixture. However, poor BSFC could also be the result of incorrect ignition timing or a number of other reasons.

A really good spark-ignition piston engine can get down to the low 0.3s. An example is the 18-cylinder Wright Cyclone compound turbo engines used in the last derivatives of the Lockheed Constellation airliners of the late 1950s. They had a BSFC of 0.32. Getting much below that seems hard to do, but there are developments in the pipeline that could crank the barrier down to an estimated 0.28.

Today, the best way to measure mixture with the minimum of unaccountable error is by a wide-band oxygen system. I have extensively used the system by Innovate Motorsports on the dyno.

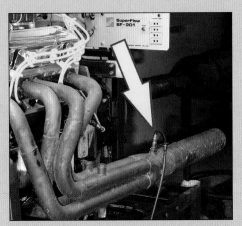

I built this hydraulic-roller valvetrain, Chevy 383 small-block test engine in 2007. The way to get the mixture right was to use a wide-band oxygen unit. The best option was to have one in each header pipe, but failing that an excellent job can still be done with one in each collector (as shown here). This 10:1 engine made more than 530 hp and easily eclipsed the 500 ft-lbs mark on a hydraulic roller and out-of-the-box AFR 200-cc port heads. Additionally, the engine turned flawlessly to 6,700 rpm.

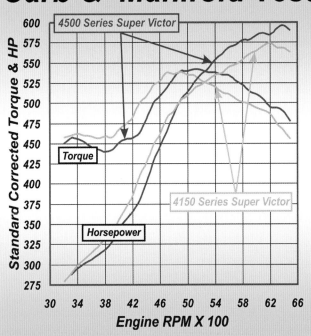

This chart illustrates the torque and horsepower curves of an engine equipped with a 4500 Series Super Victor and a 4150 Series Super Victor manifold.

SIMPLE MIXTURE MEASUREMENT

Early in my career, people asked me, "How come your car goes so quickly with so little done to it?" The fact of the matter was that I was only one step short of TV and radio broadcasting my "secret" to the world. For some reason, however, it was really hard to convince the mainstream enthusiast that my secret was dyno tuning. No one wanted to believe it was a legitimate reason. For the typical enthusiast, this is where the chassis dyno really stands out as a tool for winning. And clearly, it is not a tool to tell you how many horses your vehicle has but one to allow you to find horsepower that until then has been eluding you.

Here's an example. In the late 1960s and early 1970s I did quite well selling what I called my dyno pack for the twin-cam Lotus Ford Cortina. These cars had a quoted 105 flywheel horsepower figure from the 1.5-liter engine. This typically translated into about 75 or so at the wheels, which in my mind left the claimed flywheel horsepower somewhat in question. With a few lengthy chassis dyno sessions, I got to know the idiosyncrasies of this engine quite well, and so I was in a position to sell my expertise for top dollar.

I investigated and found the best air filter of the day. I optimized carb calibrations, and that meant more than just a jet change or two for the Weber carbs concerned. I had found the best spark plugs and plug cables for the ignition. For the distributor, I set up the advance curve and equipped it with a contact breaker set that worked better and to higher RPM than the stock equipment. I even swapped out the fan belt for one that showed the least amount of loss and set it to the most mechanically efficient tension.

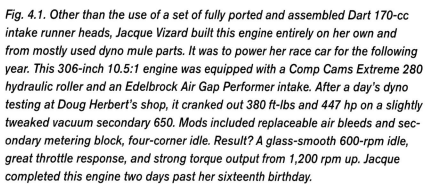

Fig. 4.1. Other than the use of a set of fully ported and assembled Dart 170-cc intake runner heads, Jacque Vizard built this engine entirely on her own and from mostly used dyno mule parts. It was to power her race car for the following year. This 306-inch 10.5:1 engine was equipped with a Comp Cams Extreme 280 hydraulic roller and an Edelbrock Air Gap Performer intake. After a day's dyno testing at Doug Herbert's shop, it cranked out 380 ft-lbs and 447 hp on a slightly tweaked vacuum secondary 650. Mods included replaceable air bleeds and secondary metering block, four-corner idle. Result? A glass-smooth 600-rpm idle, great throttle response, and strong torque output from 1,200 rpm up. Jacque completed this engine two days past her sixteenth birthday.

Fig. 4.2. This 1990 5.0 Mustang with a 5-speed was inexpensive to build. The 220,000-mile bottom end was freshened up with new rings and bearings. A 274-degree Comp Cams hydraulic flat-tappet cam took care of the valve motions in a set of ported, iron factory heads. We installed a 750 vacuum secondary Holley on a dual-plane intake and spent four hours dialing in on the chassis dyno. The result was 302 rear wheel horsepower. As seen here that was enough to easily burn those drag radials.

All this resulted in an increase in rear wheel horsepower to about 95. That's 20 percent more power, and this increase was mostly in the form of additional torque. Did my customers notice this increase? You bet. They were over the moon with their car's performance; but when looking at the engine, they saw nothing different from stock.

So hopefully I have made my point here. If you want to get the best from your efforts, a chassis dyno is the way to go. That said, though, it is a good idea to get the engine tuned in as close as possible beforehand so as to minimize what could be expensive dyno time.

There are, however, instances where a chassis dyno session to sort out your engine is simply impractical. From either cost or location difficulties, it may be necessary to adopt the next most viable means of determining a gain or loss from a change. Here is where knowledgeable use of a drag strip can be a huge benefit.

Because the subject of this book is carburetors, let's focus on the two most important aspects of an engine setup: mixture and ignition timing. Getting the best from your engine means understanding how the carb settings affect what the engine needs in the way of ignition timing, so at some stage of the procedure, you have to look at both factors.

Having established the importance of calibrations, let's discuss the simplest means of analyzing the mixture being delivered by the carb.

The First Circuits to Calibrate

To make your first mixture ratio assessments, get your Holley-equipped engine running. Although it is a little out of sequence, I detail initial idle setup here, so you can make your first mixture assessments.

The starting point is to establish whether the mixture is in the ballpark. When tackling carb calibrations, the very first move is always to set up the idle and transition circuits so the engine runs without stalling every time you attempt to make an adjustment. The idle setup then needs to be followed by the accelerator pump system, putting you in a position to blip the throttle and get instant response. Only after this is done should you start to look at any WOT calibrations.

Even before contemplating a dyno run or a pass down the strip get the idle, transition, and accelerator pump system functioning reasonably well. You cannot make the assumption that these factors are going to be close enough. In most instances they may be, but the calibration could be off by a significant amount

If you buy new, the initial setting of the idle and transition could as often as not, be close to optimum The bottom line here is that you do not know how close the idle and transition settings are until you star the engine. This means making some basic determination of the mixture ratios that are being delivered by the carb's initial calibrations. Achieving good ballpark settings for the circuits is actually simply recognizing visual cues.

First-Time Startup

First, be sure the carb has been installed correctly, it is mechanically functional, and its operation isn't hampered. Check that the throttle pedal fully opens the butterflies, the return spring fully closes them, all vacuum hoses are attached, etc. After checking all this, the next step is to start the engine.

If you want to avoid an induction/carb fire, your very first move is to make sure that the timing is not too far retarded. By whatever means make sure that the initial timing is at least 8-degrees advance; it doesn't hurt to have as much as 20 degrees of initial advance so long as you promptly reset it with a timing light to about 10 to 12 degrees.

Idle Mixture

Here I cover the basics of getting the engine started for the first time. See Chapter 8 for a more in-depth breakdown of what you need to know about the idle circuits.

Before starting the engine, get the idle mixture in the ballpark by turning all the idle mixture screws fully in, then back them out two turns.

First-Time Start with a Choke-Equipped Carb

If it's the first time starting a newly installed engine either in the vehicle or on the engine dyno, I go in there with it. This allows me to get the enrichment required to start a cold and totally dry engine by operating the throttle to activate the accelerator pump system. At this stage, getting the engine to idle is a bigger priority than getting the choke to function.

If the carb has a mechanical choke, the driver directs its operation on an as-needed basis. This in effect means there is no real setup involved. If we are talking about electric chokes, the situation is a little different.

Most of the electric chokes on Holley-style carbs come with the preset that takes into account the average temperature conditions seen during the year in the United States. You only make adjustments when the weather conditions show that it is required.

For the very cold weather in northern states, it is often necessary to adjust the bi-metal spring housing so the choke stays on longer. In the hotter climes of southern states it can save a little fuel by having the choke come off a little sooner.

If it is necessary, adjustment of the electric choke is simple. To hold the choke on longer, rotate the housing.

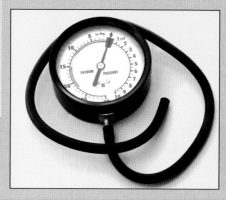

Any good parts store sells inexpensive large-dial vacuum gauges, such as this one.

Note that some carbs, usually street applications with short-cam engines, have an idle system on the primaries only. However, when a hot cam and less intake manifold vacuum is involved, you should use a carb with a four-corner idle system. Although fuel calibration is present, a four-corner idle setup may not have a regular idle-speed adjustment screw on it.

If this is the case there is an idle-speed stop adjustment screw accessible from the underside of the base plate. Not having a secondary idle adjustment screw is usually limited to carbs for no more than a hot street application. If you buy a carb for use on a big-cam engine, you should get one with an idle-speed adjustment screw in the secondaries. Keep in mind, there is no downside other than initial cost to having a full four-corner idle system.

The next step is to open the idle-speed adjustment screw sufficiently to produce a fast idle. Remember, some Holleys have idle speed adjustment on the primary barrels only; some for racier applications also have it on the secondary barrels.

For a street engine, you are looking for an initial idle speed of about 1,000 rpm and about 1,200 for a race engine. Just how far open you turn the idle adjustment screw depends on several factors. If the engine is a short-cammed unit and the butterflies have no additional air holes, open the butterflies until about 0.050 inch of the transition slot is uncovered. You can see this from the manifold side of the base plate. (See Chapter 8, page 79 for a good shot of the extent of the opening; the function/need for idle air holes in the butterfly is discussed in Chapter 8.) Uncovering the transition slot by the requisite amount usually entails about two turns of the idle-speed adjustment screw. If the engine has

Fig. 4.3. For those carbs not equipped with a secondary idle-speed adjustment screw on the linkage, the idle-speed stop, situated on the underside of the base plate, adjusts idle speed.

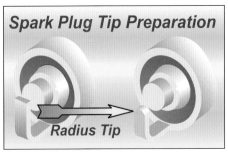

Fig. 4.4. A serious high-performance engine should use this form of plug tip. It reduces the heat in the electrode and provides a better spark path for cleaner ignition.

Fig. 4.5. I use this type of plug for my race engines. It doesn't last as long, but it usually contributes to a better charge light-off.

a big street cam, open the secondary butterflies a like amount.

If the engine has a race cam that generates minimal idle vacuum, you should have a carb with holes for additional air drilled into at least the primary butterfly, if not both primary and secondary butterflies.

Further, note that many of the latest Holly performance/race carbs (from about 2010 on) have an idle air bypass adjusting screw under the centrally located air filter stud hole. This does away with the need to drill holes in the butterflies.

Assuming the float level is correct, you are ready to fire up the engine. If the float bowl level is not correct, set it as explained in Chapter 12. If it is a "dry" engine, switch on the fuel pump for about three seconds then switch it off, wait a few seconds, and hit it again for about three seconds then back off. Switch it on again and check for fuel leaks.

If you have a fuel-pressure gauge in the system (highly recommended) verify that the fuel pressure is stable at around 6 psi. If it exceeds 9 psi, take steps to reduce it.

If you are starting an engine with a new flat-tappet cam, be sure you perform the correct break in for the cam, as that takes priority over all else at this stage.

If it is a newly installed engine, be sure you have filled the cooling system. If everything checks out okay, give the throttle three good stabs to the wide-open point. This puts fuel from the pump jets into the still dry intake manifold.

If you have everything just as I have detailed, the engine should fire right up. If it does not, check for a good spark.

Assuming the engine does as it should and starts the first time around, to keep it going in the absence of a cold-start system, you may have to put in some fuel from the pump jet system by giving the throttle some short stabs. After about a minute or so, the engine should idle on its own. If it does not, adjust the idle-speed screw for faster idle. If that does not fix the idle, more fuel is needed, so adjust the idle-mixture screws to a richer setting.

If the engine still doesn't run, the idle system may be delivering an idle mixture that's too lean. This can be established by actuating the accelerator pump lever arm to see if the fuel injected from the accelerator

pump temporarily fixes the situation. If it does, it's a fair bet that a bigger idle jet is needed. (See Chapter 8 for changing the idle jet). At this point you should have the engine running.

As soon as it is hot enough to run without your attention on the throttle, take a look at the exhaust. If there is any trace of black smoke, the mixture is too rich. If this is the case you need to make an idle mixture screw adjustment. Turn in each idle screw progressively until the exhaust is free of black smoke. As the mixture is leaned out, it becomes progressively

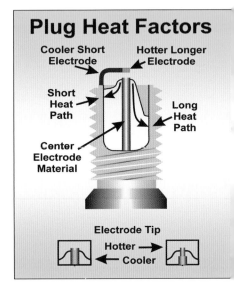

Fig. 4.6. The spark plug should run at a temperature to ensure deposit burn-off and no hotter. Here are the factors that affect it.

harder to see any black smoke. Under artificial lighting, it's particularly difficult to see black smoke. (If you are indoors, make sure there is *plenty* of ventilation because a rich mixture produces a lot of potentially fatal carbon monoxide.) To help see the last remnants of black smoke, hold a sheet of white paper in close proximity of the exhaust pipe for about a minute.

This gives you a guide to the mixture status from two aspects. If there is still black smoke, it shows much more against a white background. And if the mixture is still too rich, it discolors the white paper and the paper has a smell tinged with a gasoline aroma. Be aware that excessively rich mixtures considerably accelerate bore wear, so avoid running at an overly rich mixture as much as possible.

At this point, you have now carried out the simplest means of analyzing the mixture. And all it has cost is the price of a piece of white paper!

The engine should be warmed up sufficiently to transmit heat to the intake so that the intake is hot to touch but not so hot that you cannot hold your hand on it. Typical operating temperature is about 120 degrees F for a race engine and about 140 to 150 degrees F for a street engine, as measured about an inch below the carb mounting pad just below the base of the carb. Reset the idle to about 100 rpm more than the likely stall RPM of the engine. For instance, if you wind down the idle speed, and it gets to 800 rpm and sounds ready to stall, you then wind it back up to 900 rpm.

After you have established a steady idle speed you can start to calibrate idle parameters a little closer. Your first step is to turn in the idle mixture screws. Do this progressively for each one. If the idle jet is about

right, you should find the idle mixture adjustment that gives the maximum RPM or vacuum measured on a vacuum gauge, which occurs at 1½ to 2 turns out. Reset the idle speed to about 100 rpm more than the perceived or determined stall speed. Now reset the ignition timing with a timing light to whatever is appropriate for the application in hand. (See sidebar "Idle Speed Ignition Advance" on page 38 as a guide as to what the ignition timing is likely to be.)

Now the mixture should be close but one more reset doesn't hurt. Again use the tach for RPM or a vacuum gauge (or both) to adjust the idle screws in or out until the best RPM/vacuum is achieved.

Reset the idle RPM to a little more than the lowest speed that won't stall when, if applicable, the vehicle is put into gear (automatic transmission) and/or the A/C is turned on.

Accelerator Pump

To see where you are, initially blip the throttle and have someone check the exhaust to see if any black smoke came out. If some was seen, the pump system is adding too much fuel. The best pump shot is one that supplies just enough fuel to cover the effect of fuel dropout with rapidly diminishing intake manifold vacuum. Two things determine what is needed: the pump squirter nozzle size and the stroke of the pump as delivered by the cam on the throttle spindle.

If the throttle opening causes the engine to produce black exhaust smoke, you need to reduce the squirter size. If dropping the squirter size a few numbers does not fix the problem, go to a slower-acting accelerator pump cam. Keep making adjustments between the squirter

size and the cam until (no matter how quickly it is opened) a clean RPM pickup is achieved.

Plug Reading

Many experienced carb tuners may be asking why it took so long to get to the subject of plug reading. It has its place in the grand scheme of carb tuning, but it is all too often assumed to be far more accurate and easy to do than is actually the case. Although plugs can be read to good effect and provide a reasonable picture of carb calibration, doing so takes a lot of experience. Any time plug reading can be replaced with something a little more precise (such as an oxygen sensor mixture analyzer), you should do so if your budget allows.

Here's a comment I have heard many times: "If plug reading is good enough for Smokey, it's good enough for me." Smokey Yunick once told me that, even after 30 years of regularly reading plugs, he was still refining the art. As I write this, my experience doing so exceeds 50 years. I am well aware of its potential limitations and pitfalls. The guys who are really good at plug reading are also packing better than a quarter century of experience. If you are new to the sport of motor racing, ask yourself if you can afford to spend 25 years acquiring a skill that can be done faster, more accurately, and *right now* with some appropriate equipment, such as an oxygen mixture analyzer. Your answer should be "No, I can't." But plug reading will always have a place in the carb tuner's tool box.

Coloration Factors
Before going any further, let's look at some factors that can throw

Fig. 4.7. I pulled this plug from one of my Chevy big-block 496-ci engines while dyno testing. The jetting had just made the best power curve and the oxygen mixture readouts showed 13 to 13.2:1 throughout the pull. Get the mixture right on, and this is about what you can expect to see on 93-octane pump fuel.

Fig. 4.8. You can learn a lot from a close inspection of the plug. This Moroso illuminated magnifier allows a far better inspection to be made.

Fig. 4.9. Even though Terry Walters Precision Engines' (TWPE) Jack Sein has all the high-tech equipment you need to test engines, he still relies on an experienced eye. At the end of the day, understanding what is being shown can reveal or confirm anomalies that even a sophisticated oxygen system or in-cylinder pressure measurement may only allude to.

off a mixture interpretation. First, changing the plug heat range can change the plug color for a given mixture ratio. The location of the plug in the chamber and the style of combustion chamber can also affect how the plug looks. Though rarely the case, this factor can dramatically throw off plug reading accuracy.

One race engine I built for Chrysler many years ago showed a plug that indicated a lean mixture (about 14:1 or 15:1) when all the mixture measuring equipment showed it was actually right on 13:1, and one jet size larger in each carb barrel would reduce output.

Unless this discrepancy was a known factor, using plug reading to calibrate the engine's carburetion would have been nothing short of a disaster. It would not have shown a commonly acceptable plug coloration until the mixture was in the 11:1 range. At this point the engine was over 5 percent down on its best output. This demonstrates that what you think you see in terms of plug-indicated mixture ratio is not always what your carburetion is delivering.

Another factor that affects plug coloration is the type of fuel. Alcohol and alcohol-based fuels color

Idle Speed Ignition Advance

The more vacuum an engine pulls at idle, the more rarefied the charge is as the piston approaches TDC on the firing stroke. The lower the cylinder compression pressure at the time of ignition, the slower the charge burns. This calls for more advance, so that the cylinder pressure still peaks around 15 degrees after TDC. Advance becomes less sensitive after about 35 degrees. To get an optimum idle for the least amount of fuel consumption, timing often needs to be as much as 45 to 50 degrees before TDC.

As soon as the engine RPM comes off idle and even a small load is put on the engine the timing needs to drop back considerably. Building a conventional mechanical distributor to give the right advance characteristics is difficult, but if the budget covers it, many programmable electronic ignition systems can accommodate an engine's true requirements at idle and in the low-load, low-RPM mode. Once above about 1,500 rpm, giving the engine what it wants in the way of timing is a straightforward job, whether it's a mechanical or electronic programmable system.

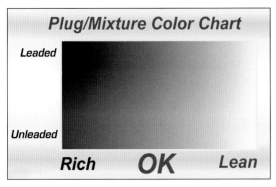

Plug/Mixture Color Chart

Leaded

Unleaded

Rich OK Lean

Fig. 4.10. This chart is for a gasoline-fueled engine. Left to right is rich to lean with the middle third of the chart being your target color. Top to bottom is the change in color that's seen between leaded and unleaded fuels.

Fig. 4.11. I have run high-performance street engines with the street Avengers from 570 to 870 and a dual-plane intake on an appropriately spec'd small-block. They have all delivered stellar results. WOT jetting was within two or three sizes of optimal while pump and idle circuits were close enough to need no further jetting.

differently than gasoline and leaded colors differently than unleaded fuel.

Also consider that a plug reading only gives an average indication of the mixture ratio over the time span and RPM range involved. If you are looking at plugs that experience slightly rich to slightly lean and back to slightly rich over the test RPM range, the plug coloration only reveals the average mixture ratio. You do not get the best unless an instrument such as an oxygen mixture analyzer is used on the engine to read the instantaneous mixture ratio, which can see these mixture fluctuations. The lesson here is: Don't assume that plug reading is absolutely accurate.

Determine the Mixture

So, with the carb's limitations in mind let's look at what can be done in the way of optimizing power from its main-circuit WOT calibrations. In essence almost all plug reading is based on the presence (or lack) of soot from the combustion process. If there is insufficient oxygen for the fuel present (the mixture is too rich), an appreciable amount of soot forms. The soot, incidentally, is nothing

more than the carbon left from the heat that the unburned fuel has experienced. It has decomposed from a hydrocarbon to a nearly pure carbon.

Remember, maximum power typically occurs at 13:1 and the chemically correct mixture (stoichiometric ratio) is right around 14.7:1 for a typical gasoline. This being the case, the presence of a little soot on the plug is typically just what you want to see. The question is just how much soot you should expect if the mixture is right. To answer that question, see the coloration chart in Figure 4.10.

You can determine more than just the overall mixture with a reasonable degree of functionality and accuracy. Here is how to make the most of plug reading to set the mixture.

Set the idle mixture so that it is about as lean as it can be while still having a decent idle. If the engine is on the dyno, this is not so important because you can do a "plug cut" at the end of the test. (A plug cut, or chop, is closing the throttle quickly and killing ignition at the end of a test, so you have colored the plugs at that particular RPM.) You can also do this at the track at the end of a pass. The usual practice is to close the throttle, kill ignition, and hit neutral.

Next you have two options. After cutting the engine at the end of the

pass, you can coast to somewhere convenient to do the plug check. Or, you can tow the car back to the paddock. Both of these options are a little inconvenient, but there is a little-appreciated but easily accomplished alternative.

You set the idle mixture right around the stoichiometric ratio, and set the idle speed at just enough for the car to return to the pits under its own power. It takes a long time for such running conditions to recolor the plugs. This is because there is neither free oxygen nor fuel present under these conditions, so unless you lean on the gas pedal and blow/burn off whatever evidence of mixture the plugs might reveal, the plug coloration doesn't change fast enough to be significant.

And this is as good a time as any to make sure the accelerator pump action produced no black smoke; if it does, it skews the results. By adopting this technique plug reading is only very minimally affected by your return drive from the end of the strip to your spot in the paddock.

Track Practice

Should you use a 1/8- or 1/4-mile drag strip? I have successfully used both, but a 1/4-mile track has the advantage of coloring the plugs to a greater extent. It's harder to read a plug after only a 1/8-mile run, and on occasion you may have to run two or three passes to get any sort of worthwhile indication of the mixture. If it proves necessary to make additional passes to color the plugs sufficiently make subsequent passes as close to the first as possible. Also do not do a burnout for the subsequent passes. Drive around the wet burnout box and go directly to the start line.

Set up your launch parameters so as to make the most consistent starts possible. This means making the most consistent but not the fastest 60-foot times. Now take note here: You must judge the results based on the trap speed, not the ET. If the start is consistent, your average power over the RPM used is completely represented by the trap speed. With this in mind, don't try fine tuning on a day with wind gusts; a 5-mph head wind on one run versus a 5-mph tail wind on another affects your assessment of the carb's maximum power calibration.

Before actually starting any power calibration tests, set the total advance ignition timing to about 2 to 3 degrees *less* than you expect it to be in its optimal position. It is relatively important that you do not overestimate the amount of total advance needed. Start with a slightly retarded ignition timing, set up the carb for the fastest trap speed, and then do the timing. In most cases, this procedure is quicker, easier, and safer to get optimum results.

If the timing is just a few degrees too far advanced and the initial mixture from the carb is too lean, the engine can run into detonation and, on an open exhaust, you don't hear it. Persist in traveling this road and the first indication that something is

wrong could come in the form of a melted piston or two!

The next step is to install new plugs after the engine is near or at operating temperature and right before you start testing. If you want to make the most of plug reading, you can perform a couple preliminary steps that help determine factors other than just the air/fuel ratio.

The first is to prep the spark plugs as shown in Figures 4.4 and 4.5 on page 36. This gap spec ensures the best spark possible. (Autolite race plugs come with an electrode length that requires minimal reworking to get what you are looking for. I like using Autolites because the dyno tells me they work because torque and horsepower are higher, and the cost is low for a quality plug.)

Use as much spark plug gap as possible for strong running but not to the point of a misfire. With most race ignition systems the plug gap tends to be in the 0.050- to 0.060-inch range. Once gapped install all the plugs.

The next move is to get a rough idea of the extent and the pattern (in relation to the plug) of any wet flow that may exist during full-throttle operation. To do this, you put a dab of paint on the side of the plug adjacent to the intake valve. (For a small-block Ford, that means all the paint marks are on the front of the plug on one bank and on the rear on the other bank. On a Chevy, the marks face each other in pairs down each bank.) Marking the plugs this way allows a quick reference as to which side of the plug is wettest/coolest and this is largely affected by which side of the plug the intake valve is on.

Now you are ready to make a pass or two down the drag strip. After that, it's time to inspect and assess what is going on in the cylinders.

Analyzing Run Results

Assuming the fuel is unleaded or low-lead (an important factor to remember) let us consider mixture ratio extremes.

If the plugs are well blackened and sooty after just one or two passes down the strip, the average mixture is way too rich, so lean it out. The simplest solution is to use smaller main jets all around. However, there is more to fixing an overly rich mixture than just putting in smaller main jets, but for now, this is the easy option. (See page 82 where I detail the correct procedure to get the main circuit doing just what it is supposed to: deliver a maximum power mixture only while the throttle is near or at wide open.)

If the plugs show little discoloration and they look tinged gray or nearly white, the mixture average is too lean. If this is the case, install larger main jets.

If all the plugs look okay when compared to the coloration chart in Figure 4.10, you are in good shape. But chances are that (due to uneven mixture distribution) only some of the plugs look like they should. So now you need to check for uniformity, one plug to another.

Now I think it's worth discussing air and fuel distribution issues within an intake manifold because it greatly influences subsequent jetting decisions.

First (and this may come as a surprise too many), mass flow of air between the cylinders and the mass flow of fuel can be and usually is different. On a V-8 with perfect induction, you expect 12.5 percent of the fuel as well as the air to go to each cylinder. In practice a poorer flowing manifold runner may only deliver 11.5 percent of the air to the cylinder it's feeding, and that's less than it should. However, it may also deliver 13.5 percent of the fuel (more than its share).

That initially looks as if there is a 2-percent difference from what it should be, but it's actually a lot more as you have to look at the ratio between 13.5 and 11.5 percent. To do that you divide the smaller number into the larger, which reveals a whopping 17.4-percent increase in air/fuel ratio to that cylinder. That is significant power detraction and warrants a real effort to bring about a correction.

The air and fuel flow idiosyncrasies of each manifold runner cause variations in the air/fuel ratio arriving at each cylinder. Usually the worst offenders here are dual-plane intake manifolds. Some dual-plane intakes deliver a very consistent cylinder-to-cylinder ratio; these are usually stock replacement emissions-legal manifolds. Of the performance air-gap-style manifolds, even the best of them can suffer a significant cylinder-to-cylinder variation.

Stagger Jetting

Power is lost when some cylinders are too rich and others are too lean. So how do you fix this? The first step is to jet each corner of the carb in an attempt to compensate.

I once drag raced a car where the rules called for an out-of-the-box dual-plane intake where port matching only 1 inch from the manifold face was allowed. This meant the only recourse to evening out the mixture between cylinders was to "stagger jet" the carb. Differences for a good race spec single-plane intake, such as an Edelbrock Super Victor (and others from Professional Products, Dart, and Weiand) usually require minimal stagger jetting.

Single-Plane Intake

Do not let the simple-looking runner design of a single 4-barrel, single-plane intake lull you into believing jetting anomalies are minimal or unlikely. Assuming that could cost a sizable chunk of power. Let me give you an example.

It was about 1984 and I had one of my 355 small-block Chevy mule engines on my Super Flow dyno. This 530-hp unit was essentially a race intake test engine. It was equipped with an Edelbrock Victor Jr. which, at the time, was one of the best intakes available. I had this mule on the dyno a while and was confident I had the jetting just about optimum. The dyno printout showed a 13:1 air/fuel ratio from the start of a pull to the end.

Then a friend of mine brought in the prototype oxygen mixture sensor setup he was building for me. This was intended to look at the mixture delivered to each cylinder individually. Up to this point, we had been identifying the mixture ratio by means of the measured air mass going into the engine along with the fuel mass. One divided into the other gives the overall air/fuel ratio. But note that it is "overall," not the mixture delivered to each cylinder. After installing the new oxygen setup we found that at the back of the engine, cylinders 5 and 7 (90-degrees phase separation) as a pair pulled less air than the other back pair of cylinders, 6 and 8 (270 degrees phase separation). With a stock firing order there is an interaction between cylinders 5 and 7.

Cylinder 5 gets the air going, and as 7 starts to draw air in 90 degrees later it takes advantage of the fact the air in the plenum is already moving in nearly the right direction. Also, and this is the real influence, during the overlap, a good exhaust system produces an exhaust-driven induction pulse from cylinder 7 that is far stronger than the piston induction pulse from cylinder 5. This results in cylinder 7 robbing 5 of some of its charge.

Fig. 4.12. With any single-carb setup on even the best single-plane intakes, an uneven venturi draw is seen due to a pair of adjacent cylinders having an intake event within 90 degrees. On Chevy engines with a 1-8-4-3-6-5-7-2 firing order, cylinders 5 and 7 draw 90 degrees apart so cylinder 5 is only halfway through its intake event when cylinder 7 starts its intake event.

The beginning of an intake event is the most severe because the exhaust produces a substantial scavenge effect to drive the intake event. The result is that the venturi directly over runners is slightly overloaded, and consequently runners 5 and 7 rob the two adjacent venturis of some of the fuel. To compensate the 2-barrels indicated are richened. (This effect moves around the jetting pattern when alternate firing orders are used.)

This is not the only jetting scenario you may find with a Chevy firing order, but it is a good one to start with. With a dual-plane intake, stagger jetting is more about compensating for the uneven flow of the runners and is far more difficult to sort out. Good plug reading skills are key here.

In terms of overall airflow, cylinder 7's greed does not fully compensate for 5's loss. However, the longer pull from that corner of the intake affects how the two adjacent barrels deliver. To compensate jetting has to be increased as shown in Figure 4.12.

Now that you understand what is going on within the intake, let's get back to the 355 test engine. By dropping two jet sizes in the number-5 and number-7 corner and increasing the jet two sizes in the number-6 and number-8 corner, horsepower increased to 546. That's a 16-hp gain just by putting fuel into the intake to compensate for a distribution problem.

Granted, for a single-plane intake, that was an extreme example. But conscientious stagger jetting can produce 6- to 10-hp increases.

Dual-Plane Intake

With a dual-plane intake and the bigger runner-to-runner flow differences, stagger jetting can pay off. In a race engine, this jetting produces an 8- to 10-hp increase almost every time. However, getting the distribution to the best possible state is far more complex than it is with a single-plane intake.

You have to take into account that one corner of the carb feeds one cylinder on each bank. You almost certainly find instances in which one cylinder sharing a carb corner has a distinctly different jetting requirement from the other.

As an example, consider the cylinders fed by the front right-hand barrel of the carb. On a small-block Chevy this feeds cylinders 1 (right-hand bank) and 4 (left-hand bank). If jetted to get cylinder 1 correct, then cylinder 4 runs lean. If you correctly jet cylinder 4, then 1 runs rich.

In practice, I have been able to get at least six of the cylinders to run right with the other two averaged at the best possible mixture. With some intakes, this has called for jetting, ranging from smallest to largest, having a span of about eight numbers. Was the effort worth it? Judge for yourself: On an 1/8-mile track, with the particular race car in question, I went from a 6.49 to a 6.43 ET with about a 1-mph increase in speed.

Fuel Wash

A fuel wash signature is not hard to spot because it directly affects plug coloration. Most obvious is that the plug is wet. It is a relatively consistent pattern from cylinder to cylinder; so to spot it, lay out all the plugs and make sure you have correctly identified each particular plug with its respective cylinder. Use the paint dots I mentioned earlier. If the black, sooty part and the wet part of the plug are in a similar position relative to the paint dot, there is, for some reason, excessive wet flow entering the cylinder.

As for the uniformity of this test, take into account the effect manifold runners have on the flow pattern arriving at the intake valve. With a single-plane, single 4-barrel intake, the runners on one end of the engine can and usually do enhance mixture swirl and suppress it at the other end. This factor can change the wet-flow wash pattern on the plug. With a dual-plane intake any uniformity you might see is very much modified from cylinder to cylinder by an intake manifold that can have major effects on the wet-flow pattern arriving at the cylinders.

If the engine is equipped with a tunnel ram intake where the carb barrels are situated almost exactly over the runners, the fuel distribution is usually good. However, and this depends on the manifold design, there is still an influence between any adjacent cylinders that draw only 90 degrees apart. For example, cylinders that draw 90 degrees apart on small- and big-block Chevys are 1 and 2, and 5 and 7. And any of the influences I discussed here need to be taken into account.

Wet Source

A wet look can come from one or more of three sources. One, water is getting into the cylinder, and that means a head gasket problem or worse yet, a cracked head. The fix for that is obvious. Two, oil is getting into the combustion chamber. This indicates the intake oil stem seals are not doing their job properly or the piston rings are not working as they should. Three, you have a new engine; it could be that the rings have not yet seated in. No matter the reason, the problem has to be fixed.

When an oil film is deposited on the plug body, it takes quite a lot of running with no further oil deposited to burn off the oil that is already there. If the plug shows any sign of oil deposit, wash the plug in a strong

Fig. 4.13. This is a head chamber from a Ford 289 Falcon vintage racer. You can see the chamber wash from wet flow. Fixes lie in many areas including booster selection, manifold finish, and general port shaping.

solvent. My number-one preference is lacquer thinner but spray-can brake cleaners also work. Be sure to blow the plugs off afterward. Also, just to be sure, I also heat the plugs with a propane torch until they are good and hot. Before installing the plugs (you should have all of them out), crank the engine to blow out any residual fuel in the cylinders that might re-wet the plugs. At this point make some passes down the strip to reestablish the cylinder's burn properties.

Fuel Wash Fixes

If the plugs indicate fuel wash, it could stem from two issues working together. It could be that the cylinder heads have poor wet-flow characteristics. Although it may fundamentally be a cylinder head and intake manifold problem, carb calibrations can minimize any negative impact. You must not lose site of the fact that the better the fuel is atomized at the carb, the better the mixture quality upon its arrival at the cylinder.

Be aware that an overly rich mixture has more wet-flow problems than a correct mixture. This makes your first step in fixing a fuel wash problem one of leaning out the mixture until the plugs indicate a slightly lean condition and then going back up a jet size or two. The principal challenge in fixing the fuel wash almost always means fixing a lack of fuel atomization.

Here is a list of possible issues that can lead to wet flow problems:

- Carb is too big for the engine and has insufficient venturi air speed in conjunction with limited booster signal.
- With a mechanical secondary throttle system, too much venturi area is presented to the engine too soon. In such a case, a vacuum secondary would have probably been better.
- Booster style and venturi size are not generating enough signal.
- Booster design has insufficient fuel-shearing properties.
- Fuel temperature and vaporizing characteristics are not right for the engine. More intake temperature or more light-front-end hydrocarbons helps fix the problem (see Chapter 12 and Chapter 13 for more details on fuel).

As you can see, all of these problems are beyond the scope of fixes at the race track. However, if the budget allows for a dyno session, a possible fix with the right parts and tools is more likely and convenient. As for the fixes themselves, acquaint yourself with the ins and outs of booster design and how they interact with the air correction jets and the emulsion well (see Chapter 9).

Ignition Timing

When you have arrived at a point where plug checks and time slips or dyno readouts show no useful gains then, and only then, can you turn your attention to optimizing ignition timing. The reason for doing this last is that the speed of the flame travel is affected by the mixture ratio. For instance, best output with an overly rich 11:1 air/fuel ratio might be as much as 42 degrees. With the same fuel but a 13.2:1 air/fuel ratio, 36 degrees could well be best. Usually a mixture slightly richer than stoichiometric needs the least timing for most power while both richer and leaner mixtures require progressively more timing.

Back when every experienced guy I worked with was older and usually more experienced than I was, I often heard it said that more or less ignition timing can also affect the mixture. While this has some truth, the degree to which it takes place is very minimal, particularly if the engine is already in the ballpark. The lesson here is: If you are working with a somewhat older generation of racers, and they make this point, nod politely and ignore them.

The procedure for putting the final touches on the timing requirements is best done in small increments. Usually from an assumed retarded setting, I advance the timing

Fig. 4.14. This set of plugs was used in a stagger-jetting exercise that produced the best performance. The engine is a Chevy big-block (the front is to the right). Only plug 6 is showing different by a readable amount. The arrow points to a slight amount of soot that cylinder was producing and it was slightly richer than the other seven plugs.

by 2 degrees and make a pass. If the car goes a lot faster (in my judgment), I move it 2 more degrees for the next run. If the gain is small I only move it 1 degree at a time. The idea is to establish where the gains level out as further advance is dialed in. You need the least amount of advance that gets the job done.

Also be aware that highly leaded fuels have a longer ignition delay time than unleaded fuels. The igni- tion timing you come up with o■ the test day suits what you have i■ the tank on that day. Changing fuels however, means a reevaluation of th■ timing required.

High-Tech Mixture Check

So now that you know where things stand without any mixture measuring equipment, it's time to eliminate the need for an experienced eye and employ technology to get the job done.

If your budget only allows for one of the cheaper narrow-band oxygen sensor mixture analyzers, go for it. This type of unit from a reputable supplier is about 85 to 90 percent as good as a significantly more costly wide-band unit.

Although a little more costly than a budget narrow-band unit, the wide-band version I have been using on the McCoig/Vizard race car for some years is from AEM Electronics and has served me well.

For our setup we use a unit for each bank. These AEM units have proved to be valuable as an aid to wring out the last ounce of power from an engine that was about the cheapest in the class and about 40 ci smaller than our principle competition.

At times, in spite of our cube deficit, we ran as close as 0.1 second and 0.07 mph of the record with an engine costing close to a third of that of our top competition.

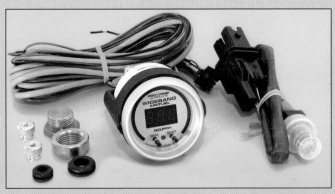

I have used several Autometer oxygen mixture analyzers to good effect. The fact that they match the style of all my other Autometer instrumentation is a plus.

Be sure that there is adequate clearance around the oxygen sensor so that the collector reinstalls without any interference from surrounding body/chassis parts.

The K&N oxygen unit is one of the less-expensive brands available. It comes in two style as seen here.

MILEAGE CALIBRATION

So far I have discussed power-related calibrations of a Holley-style carb almost to the exclusion of all else. But in this day and age, I feel that we should only burn the minimum amount of fuel possible while achieving our goals in other quarters. Sure, I like a street performer that can make a 12-second pass, but I like it a lot better if it also does 25 mpg instead of the usual 15 to 18 mpg.

Good, even very good, mileage figures are possible with a Holley carb. However, it's not all about the carb's basic design, but the selection of a suitable spec in the first place. It's also about calibrations and how the carb is used. In this chapter I discuss what you need to know to get good mileage from a Holley-equipped engine.

Mileage Makers and Breakers

At this point, I need to address a number of things pertaining to good mileage so you don't end up going in the wrong direction.

Lean Mixture

The first thing on the list is to set up the engine so it burns as lean a mixture as possible. Follow this by calibrating the carb to deliver that "lean as possible" mixture.

As counterintuitive as it may seem, the leanest mixture before misfire occurs is not the best for mileage. One that has just a trace of a miss every once in a while is better, but it is too lean from the emissions standpoint. There's a fine dividing line between the two.

During my in-depth efficiency tests for mixture versus fuel usage, I went to that minor miss point and came back to where a miss was extremely rare. This gave the cleanest exhaust while giving away only a fraction of a percent of fuel economy.

Venturi Size

Along with the leanest of mixture ratios, the mixture arriving at the cylinders, ideally, needs to be completely vaporized. If the rest of the engine is mileage oriented to at least a reasonable degree, a suitable mixture quality is not hard to achieve.

The first step is to make sure that the fuel is well atomized as it leaves the booster. Achieving this entails having primary venturis that are definitely not oversized.

Fig. 5.1. Every Holley has the potential to be a fuel miser, but achieving ultimate success means making a wise initial choice. A 600 vacuum secondary, such as this unit (PN 0-80457SA), was used on one of my Chevy 383 small-block budget builds with the intent of making torque and mileage the prime requirements. The result was 365 hp, 488 ft-lbs, and almost 22 mpg in a 1990 Sierra truck with a 5-speed transmission. All this came with a 13.9-second ET and 97-mph trap speed at the drag strip.

Fig. 5.2. This Ford 302 with Scat stroker crank for 347 inches was a dyno mule for three months of testing carbs and manifolds. I ran about every brand of carb I could find, including Barry Grant (shown), Edelbrock, and Holley. It pumped out about 562 hp on a single-plane intake. However, the best drivability and fuel efficiency at part throttle were seen on a dual-plane intake and a vacuum secondary carb. With perfect street manners and a smooth 620-rpm idle, this 347 made 472 ft-lbs and 532 hp.

Booster Signal

The venturis need to be paired with a booster that has a high gain and good fuel-shearing properties. An example here is a main venturi in a 4150-style carb that is no bigger than, say, 1.4 inches paired with one of Holley's high-gain annular discharge boosters.

By creating a large signal, there is a need to increase the size of the air corrector in relation to the main jet size. When this is the case, the fuel emulsion in the emulsion well has a higher percentage of air in it by volume. This produces a more finely atomized fuel discharge from the booster. The smaller the mixture droplets, the greater the area they have in relation to their volume. This causes them to evaporate quicker.

However, there is a point at which the fuel is so finely atomized that it turns into a vapor and delivers no measurable advantage. This point is reached when the fuel droplets are 5 microns or smaller. Getting droplets down to this size is not easy so, in conjunction with efforts toward fine atomization, you need to employ other tactics as well.

Secondary

Under normal driving conditions, a typical V-8 has way more power than is ever needed with just the primary barrels in operation. This fact implies that a vacuum secondary is a far better choice for a street-driven machine than a mechanical secondary. Just in case you feel there may be a loss of performance from a vacuum secondary, let me assure you a correctly set up 650 vacuum secondary carb can make exactly the same top-end power as a 650 mechanical carb.

But that's not the end of the story. At low RPM (from about 1,000 to about 2,500 to 3,000 rpm), the vacuum secondary more often than not shows better torque figures than a mechanical secondary carb, unless the mechanical throttle is driver modulated to limit the amount of venturi area presented to the engine.

The lesson to learn here is that although racers don't use vacuum secondaries they are often best when it comes to area under the power curve, drivability, and street fuel efficiency. (See Chapter 9 for more about the advantages of vacuum secondaries.)

Vaporizing Factors

After atomized fuel is discharged from the booster, it is subjected to manifold vacuum and heat. These play an important role in effective ignition and combustibility.

Intake Manifold Vacuum

You should have a decent amount of intake vacuum, which is at least 10 inches Hg under the cycle parameters expected during economy driving. This means that almost all, if not all, the fuel is vaporized by the time it gets to the intake valve. Effectively vaporizing the fuel also means that inter-cylinder mixture distribution tends to fall directly in line with the air distribution. This results in virtually the same mixture being delivered to each cylinder.

Intake Manifold Heat

Intake manifold heat also evens out mixture distribution and improves combustibility. By adding heat, you increase the volume of the intake charge and make a small reduction in the amount of residual exhaust that remains in the combustion chamber during the overlap period. This means slightly less mixture dilution and results in a charge that is marginally easier to ignite.

Just how much heat is required can vary from engine to engine. Comprehensive tests on just one engine showed that some heat is good, but more can be too much. One scenario included ambient heat and whatever heat-soak was received rom the rest of the engine. The next cenario utilized a coolant-heated ntake that held the manifold temperature to between 180 and 190 egrees F. The last scenario was with n exhaust-heated intake.

The worst fuel efficiency came n the first scenario in which only mbient heat and heat-soak were nvolved. The middle efficiency was chieved with the exhaust-heated cenario. The best was from the scenario with a coolant-heated intake. or a performance-minded engine uilder the middle scenario was a ood compromise as it costs, on a ypical 350-inch V-8, only about 5 hp ver an unheated intake, as opposed o about 10 to 12 hp from an exhaust-eated intake.

Enhancing Combustion Conditions

The next thing to consider is hat the engine needs to turn your arburetion efforts into the best mileage results. In Chapter 1, I pointed ut that most mileage gains come om the engine and not the carb self, other than having it suitably alibrated. So let's look at what the ngine has to offer regarding potental mileage gains.

Compression Ratio

An engine's compression ratio CR) is the number-one mileage naker, or fuel-efficiency factor. To see ow this is so we actually consider ne expansion ratio (ER), which is ne other side of the CR coin. When ne CR is higher, the expansion atio is higher. When the CR (and onsequently the ER) increases, the mount of energy extracted from the ylinder pressure generated increases. n effect, fuel is utilized more effec-

tively. (For a full explanation read my best-selling CarTech book *David Vizard's How to Build Horsepower*.)

Ultimately, fuel octane limits the amount of compression that can be used, but there are other things that can help enhance the CR situation a little beyond what the engine can stand at WOT.

Ignition Timing

You really need to understand the importance of having the optimum ignition timing for the mixture ratio and all its attributes, such as temperature, pressure, etc., that exist at the time combustion is initiated. If that timing is not set optimally your quest for mileage is compromised.

Let's consider the detonation-limited CR at WOT. If the engine took, say, 32 degrees of total timing advance to make the most horsepower, but the fuel put it into obvious detonation, you can save the day by backing out some timing.

Usually, in a situation where the fuel is a 3- or 4-octane number less than wanted, or the CR is 1 to 2 ratios more than the fuel can stand, retarding the WOT ignition advance by 2 to 4 degrees is the answer. How-

ever, the lower the cylinder pressure, the lower the octane value needed to stave off detonation. So, at part throttle, an engine with a little more CR than the fuel tolerates at WOT benefits from the extra CR at part throttle, where it is still a ways off from the WOT detonation limit.

With some lean-burn tests, the timing for a 60-mph cruise is as far advanced as 55 degrees. Don't be surprised by the amount of advance. The fastest burn is achieved when the mixture is a little on the rich side. Going richer or leaner slows the burn. The target is to have the cylinder develop peak pressure about 15 to 20 degrees after TDC on the power stroke. To make that happen, a very lean, slow-burning mixture needs a lot of advance.

Cylinder Fill

A certain amount of horsepower is needed to push a vehicle along at a given speed. Either a lesser amount of torque and a higher RPM or a greater amount of torque and a lower RPM can develop that power. For example, let's say you want 60 hp from a typical small-block V-8 to

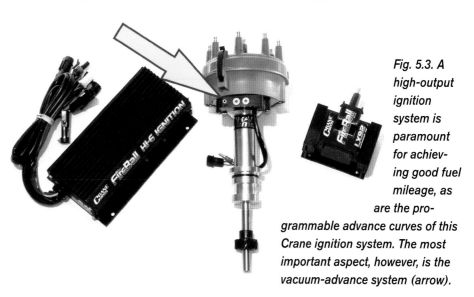

Fig. 5.3. A high-output ignition system is paramount for achieving good fuel mileage, as are the programmable advance curves of this Crane ignition system. The most important aspect, however, is the vacuum-advance system (arrow).

push the vehicle along the freeway at, say, 70 mph. This could be done by making 60 hp at 2,000 rpm with the throttle open far enough to make 157 ft-lbs. Or it could be done by letting the engine turn 3,000 rpm at 60 mph, which at that RPM, means it develops 105 ft-lbs.

The higher the RPM, the less efficient the development of that power becomes. This is because the cycle efficiency drops due to a less-efficient expansion cycle, and the fact that more of the power generated within the cylinder is being used to overcome internal engine friction.

Let's assume your vehicle can reach its true maximum speed for the power it has while in a 1:1 high gear. If you add an overdrive gear, which in effect over-gears the vehicle so it is actually faster in a lower gear, the mileage can improve dramatically. My tests in this area demonstrate the value of a high final drive. When the final-drive ratio of a mileage test vehicle was increased by 20 percent, the mileage at a 60-mph cruise improved by 19 percent.

The idea here is to pick an overall cruise-gear ratio that is sufficiently high so that you have to open the throttle quite a ways to make sufficient engine torque to push the vehicle to the desired cruise speed.

Diesels are well known for their high fuel efficiency capabilities. This is partly due to the fact that they have very high compression ratios (20:1 is typical). They also do not have a throttling system on the intake. In effect, the throttle is wide open all the time. Power demand is controlled solely by the amount of fuel injected into the cylinder at the top of the compression stroke. What you are trying to do is emulate a Diesel's power stroke. To do that, you add as much throttle (and

consequently air) in the cylinder with the least amount of fuel.

With a higher gearing, the amount of power developed within the cylinder suffers less frictional loss because the RPM is lower. The greatest frictional loss within an engine is due to the piston and ring friction on the cylinder bores. For this reason, if you are building an engine from scratch, it's necessary to research rings and select a ring pack that is likely to have the minimum friction.

The narrower the rings, the less friction they have. The ring-to-bore preload is also a factor, and many specialty ring companies offer low-tension rings. The "low tension" part of the ring pack is usually the oil-control ring. Be aware that to make significantly less oil ring preloads work it is necessary to pull some vacuum on the crankcase. Aside from a correctly prepared bore finish, lower pre-load rings may require a vacuum of at least a couple inches of mercury to be pulled on the crankcase.

The Spark

Another critical factor for good fuel economy is the spark. The leaner the mixture becomes, the harder it is to effectively light it off. The difference between the spark required to fire a full-power rich mixture and a 20:1 economy mixture is like night and day.

Throttle Adjustment

On one occasion, my high-tech engineering friend David Ray and I managed to successfully light off a 22:1 mixture ratio and transition from that to a full-power mixture ratio with no misfire. I mention this because there is a transitional issue

to address here. Under steady-state conditions on the dyno, it is possible to slowly lean out the mixture while equally slowly adjusting the throttle to maintain a given power output and achieve very lean burn without a misfire.

However, the moment the throttle is opened at any sort of typical rate the engine simply signs off. The reduction in manifold vacuum due to an increased throttle opening causes some of the fuel to drop out of its vaporized state and form as a liquid on the manifold walls. This leans out the air/fuel ratio of the mixture flowing in the port itself and results in an unburnable charge. In effect the leaner the mixture you can run at steady state, the more critical the accelerator pump function becomes.

Spark Energy

The spark must be big, intense and hot to successfully fire a super lean mixture. With an optimally prepared charge in the combustion chamber, near fully effective ignition can be achieved with as little as 0. millijoules of energy at stoichiometric mixture ratios. When a richer full power mixture is used, this energy requirement can increase by a factor of 10. The same goes for moderately lean mixtures. If you are dealing with mixture ratios leaner than about 16:1, the spark energy required can go even higher.

What we are considering here is spark energy values for a well-prepared mixture in an effective combustion chamber. The question to ask is, How closely does a particular application emulate a laboratory test engine? In reality you can only guess. What this means is that your ignition system needs to have plenty of overkill capability. This is certainly one of the few

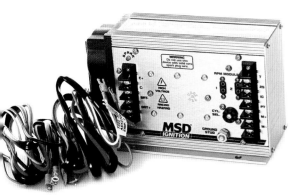

Fig. 5.4. When it comes to ignition systems, there is almost no such thing as "overkill." I use MSD systems on most of my race engines and my mileage-oriented street engines.

Fig. 5.5. There is a lot more science in coils than you might think. Though the design of the coil is important, one of the most influential factors for generating an effective spark is how fast the current to the primary winding is cut. That is a function of the ignition box.

Fig. 5.6. This MSD distributor is a great unit to use on a race engine, but not on a street engine where mileage is required. Why? Because it does not have a vacuum advance. Don't listen to anyone who tells you vacuum advance is not really necessary, even for a street machine.

...reas where the Stroker McGurk Syndrome actually pays off. According to Stroker, "If some is good, more must be better, and too much must be just right." When it comes to effectively igniting lean mixtures, the amount of energy required can escalate to typically unprecedented values. So, when selecting an ignition system, overkill is more than just okay.

Duration

If everything is good in terms of mixture quality, mixture motion, etc., what happens spark-wise in the first few hundred nanoseconds to a micro second pretty much dictates what happens from there on out. There are 1,000 nanoseconds in a micro second, 1,000 micro seconds in a millisecond, and 1,000 milliseconds in one second.) A nanosecond is a very short time. Because of the energy distribution pattern during the entire spark, it is only the first part of the spark that does any real mixture ignition. You need the energy in the initial part of the spark to be as high as possible. Also, because you do not know exactly how ignitable the charge is in your hot rod engine, you often find that firing the spark multiple times or having a long-duration spark is also a benefit, especially at low speed.

Spark Plug Gap

The energy in the initial spark phase is more or less directly related to the spark plug gap. The bigger the gap, the more energy the first and most critical few nanoseconds of the spark has. Countering the ability to fire the gap in the first place, the bigger the gap, the higher the ionization voltage. That's the voltage required from the coil to break down the resistance of the air/fuel mixture between the plug electrodes.

To run the leanest air/fuel ratio possible, use an ignition system capable of the greatest voltage possible without outpacing the insulation of the plug insulator, the plug cables, and other ignition components. Remember, you are looking for a spark at the plug gap, not between the exterior of a plug cable and some random location on the block.

Fig. 5.7. If a plug cable shows a resistance in the thousands of Ohms range, it is for one of two reasons. It could be because of a broken down core, or it could be a carbon string cable. Although carbon string is okay when new, it does not last. It's best to use spiral-wound core cables.

Fig. 5.8. Multi-electrode plugs (such as the one seen here or similar to the Split-Fire plug) are mostly a sales gimmick. The only advantage of multiple-side electrodes is extended life, as spark erosion is shared among four electrodes instead of one.

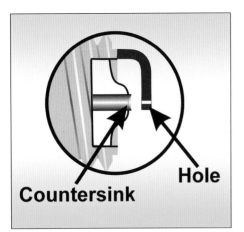

Fig. 5.11. Here is a plug electrode design I developed in the early 1990s. Its main asset was that it produced a very high energy spark while requiring a considerably lower ionization voltage.

Fig. 5.13. All other things being equal, a prepped wider-gap plug (right) gives a spark of as much as 20 percent more energy in the initial light-off phase than a conventional plug (left).

Fig. 5.9. The electrode on this plug has been converted to the lower voltage/ higher energy design in Figure 5.11.

Fig. 5.10. Plugs with the pin-style platinum center electrode can last up to 60,000 miles and work well with a high-output ignition system.

Fig. 5.12. If you are going to get the timing right, you need to find TDC and make sure it is established accurately.

Temperature

Another factor of importance is the temperature of the spark. A typical spark from an inductive ignition system is about 3,300 to 3,800 degrees F. My own dyno tests have strongly indicated that even a full-power rich mixture benefits from a higher spark temperature than that. A capacitive system typically develops a spark that is hotter but also shorter in duration than an inductive system. However, there are systems (other than the extremely high dollar laser ignition systems) that can bring about much higher plug energy levels and do so with significantly higher temperature.

System Sources

To get the job done for a typical cruise RPM (about 3,000), a good place to start is by looking through MSD's catalog. The basic MSD 6 gives a strong spark and multi fires up to about 3,000 rpm on a V-8 and to higher RPM on engines with fewer cylinders. Do the multiple sparks pay off? For a typical, hopped-up production V-8 the answer is yes in nine out of ten cases.

If the ignition system delivers only one spark per firing cycle, spark duration can also play a part in dictating the lean-limit misfire point. In many ways, a longer-burning spark can replicate what a multi-spark

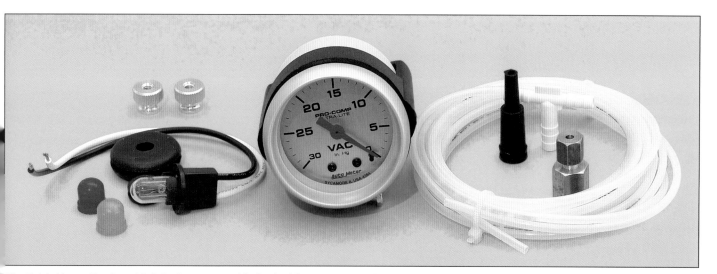

Fig. 5.14. No matter how high-tech you get with the ignition system and any data acquisition system, remember that one of the best tune-up devices is a simple vacuum gauge such as this Autometer unit.

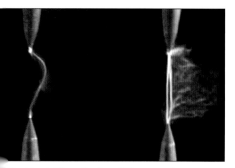

Fig. 5.15. Here is the difference between a single GM HEI spark (left) and a Plasma boosted one (right).

system does in the way of lighting off a very lean mixture.

Crane's system (directly competing with the MSD range of ignitions) does a very good job. I used one of them for a research project; it was a multi-spark system in which each spark had a longer than average burn time. The results were top line, but whether that was due to spark duration or spark intensity is hard to say.

Some Unconventional Systems

Still on the subject of spark, and justifiably so because of its strong influence on the leanest burn practical, let's consider some unconventional systems for super-spark generation.

David Ray Experiment

My first involvement with a "way out in left field" ignition system was in the mid 1970s. I received a call from my friend David Ray, with whom I had been working and dyno testing on my Round America Economy Drive project. He had heard, through some mutual Cosworth engineer friends, of a system that had been presented to Cosworth for evaluation. It was

Fig. 5.16. My Canadian friend Bill Ball is on the crew of this Merkur XR4. On two separate occasions Bill tested the Okada plasma system. The first time, it produced 9 additional horsepower on the Merkur's Ford 302 small-block. The second time, it produced 5 hp more than a conventional ignition system.

apparently the brain child of a guy who would fit a Disney movie representation of a totally brilliant scientist, but one who was not quite in the same world as the rest of us. This guy had come up with a system that initially fired the plug with a super-high voltage and immediately the gap ionized it; it put a very high-amp DC voltage across the gap. This turned the spark plug into something akin to an arc welder. Needless to say the plugs did not last long. But for an F1 race, if they were good for 300 miles, it was fine.

When David and I tested this, we rigged it up to see what the spark looked like in open air. We were amazed because the system was able to put a small bolt of lightning across a gap about a foot or so in size. When activated, the noise it made sounded like a pistol shot. On the Cosworth DFV F1 engine it was reputed to add 11 hp over the ignition of the day.

The big problem was not with the system's capability in terms of delivering performance, but in terms of safety. One shock from it, and you really were 100-percent dead! But the lessons learned were not lost on me. Testing this system demonstrated that sustained high energy and temperature can, in a less-than-perfect combustion situation, be key factors in firing mixtures as lean as 22:1; and that was in 1975 before the term "lean burn" was in vogue.

You're probably asking yourself, Are there any systems that go at least part way to emulating this deadly system? The answer is yes. I am sure there are more than the ones I discuss next, but to save you the effort of hunting down such systems, let me run through the ones I have had experience testing.

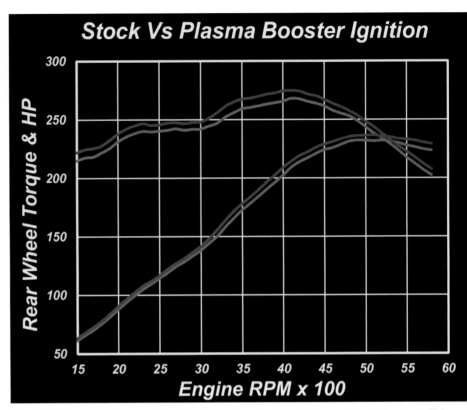

Fig. 5.17. These are the results of just one chassis dyno test on a Ford Mustang. This test was on a 5.0 pushrod engine. Tests on the 4.6 Modular engines consistently delivered greater increases.

Nology Engineering, Inc.

Other than the potentially deadly system that I tested with David Ray my first test of a "different" ignition was that of the Nology plug cables. They not only have a connection directly to the plug but an outer stainless-steel sheath around the plug cable connects to the block at some convenient point.

Nology cables function like this: When the coil voltage to the plug builds up instead of firing the plug it charges the plug cable, which is acting as a capacitor. When the voltage reaches a very high value it fires across the plug in an extremely short time. Because the available energy is dumped into the plug gap in such a short time, the wattage increases dramatically by a factor of about one million. This extremely powerful spark is also at a very high temperature that is typically close to 50,000 degrees F.

When I first tested these plug leads, I felt it was a question of determining if the increase in spark size, intensity, and temperature offset the dramatically reduced duration of the spark. After much testing, the results showed that the vastly more aggressive spark, even though it was of an extremely short duration, paid off in increased power and lean-burn capability.

Okada Projects

The next system on my short list is the Ignition Solutions Plasma multi-fire system from Okada Projects. This system piggybacks onto whatever ignition system is already in use. Its capacitive/inductive mod

ig. 5.18. A Blue Phoenix system is shown in a high-speed video sequence of the developing plasma. It is far more energetic than the ?park from even GM's High Energy Ignition (HEI) system.

f operation means it is extremely ?liable; in the unlikely event of fail- re, it automatically reverts to the :ock ignition. This unit not only roduces a very hot, intense spark ut multi fires the spark or sparks of ?e original system. So if you have, ay, an MSD 6 system delivering four parks, the Plasma Booster multi parks each of the MSD's four sparks.

I tested this system on two-, ?ree- and four-valve engines and ?ot positive power results every time. ll the vehicles were Ford Mustangs. saw the least gain on a 1990 Mus- ?ng 5.0.

The 1990 Mustang 5.0's baseline ?nition system was already mildly ?worked with a higher output ?il and top-notch plug cables and ?worked electrode plugs. There were ?nly minimal gains up to the mid- ?nge RPM and an increase in output ?pped out at 5 hp on peak.

At the other end of the scale I saw ?e most gains on the four-valve-per- ?ylinder Mustangs.

Because the system only took a ?w minutes to install it was good in ?rms of cost versus install time. As ?r as typical results from an ignition ?op-up are concerned, it also scored ?ell. Gains of this magnitude are ?sually only seen when the original

system is mediocre.

The results of my first tests on the 5.0 Mustang prompted me to test on some of Ford's newer pony cars. The idea was to see if the Plasma Booster was capable of increasing output for an engine with an ignition designed to be a high-performance system. Ford's Modular engines (4.6- and 5.4- liter V-8s) have a coil-over plug sys- tem, which was used with the intent of maximizing ignition capability for the best power and economy possible. After three tests on different Modular designs (two-, three-, and four-valve variants), I found the Plasma Booster to be an effective hop-up tool.

Blue Phoenix Ignition Systems

In many respects, the Blue Phoe- nix system is similar to the super- high-output system that David Ray and I tested in the mid 1970s. Remember, the goal is to ionize the plug gap with a conventional high- energy spark and then, when the resistance drops due to the plug gap ionization, a DC voltage is superim- posed on the gap. This produces a long-burn plasma arc that persists for 20 degrees or more of crank rotation.

Sure this sounds exotic, but does it work? From the 1975 tests with the "deadly" system I knew that, at

least in principle, the system works. Though hardly "tame," this system was in effect a tamer version of the one from which Cosworth reput- edly saw 11 hp more during F1 engine tests.

I tested the Blue Phoenix sys- tem on one of my big-block Chevy builds. The test engine was a really well developed street engine of about 525 ci. The wet flow, swirl, and port velocity of the heads was ideally suited to the MSD multi-fire ignition system and its plugs and cables.

The combustion properties of this project engine were such that I could run 87-octane fuel (R+M over 2) with mean best torque timing without any sign of detonation. This indicated an efficient combustion process was being achieved. The Blue Phoenix system would have to prove the value of its long-burn plasma arc so it needed to show well.

Rather than show you yet one more dyno curve I thought it bet- ter that you see the actual tests I ran with the guys at Terry Walters Preci- sion Engines. As of the writing of this book, a video of the dyno test was posted on Youtube.

When you watch this video, note the very slow idle speed on the test engine. This is a true street engine in all respects, including the fact that it was being run on 87-octane fuel. The final output was just shy of 800 hp.

Economy Tuning

The Round America Economy Drive project had some heavyweight backers and was highly promoted by *Popular Mechanics* in the UK. This project was centered around the original A-series British Leyland (now defunct) Mini.

To measure fuel consumption as accurately as possible, we made up a system that employed solenoids, timers, and a very tall, skinny burette. Here is how it worked.

Typically, the engine ran on fuel directly from the dyno cell's fuel tank. After the engine had been stabilized at a particular road load and engine speed, a start button actu-

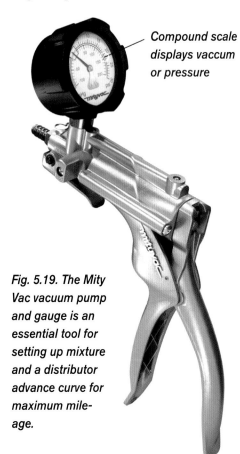

Compound scale displays vaccum or pressure

Fig. 5.19. The Mity Vac vacuum pump and gauge is an essential tool for setting up mixture and a distributor advance curve for maximum mileage.

ated the solenoid that swapped the fuel supply from the cell tank to the burette. At the same time, this started an electronic timer. The engine continued to draw fuel from the burette until it had run long enough to accurately establish how much fuel it had drawn out of the burette in, say, 60 seconds. At that point, I hit the stop button.

I was left with a very accurate measurement of the amount of fuel used in that amount of time. With diligence we were able to measure BSFC to a significant third decimal place. To test and make fine-tuning adjustments to this degree takes a really good dyno, a lot of time, and some very accurate fuel-flow measuring gear.

As you can imagine that test procedure is not exactly a user-friendly way to go about tuning a Holley-equipped engine for economy. Fortunately there is an easier way.

First, find a long stretch of flat highway; it needs to be truly flat for at least 2 miles and preferably 4 to 5 miles.

Next, get a Mity Vac vacuum pump/tester as shown in Figure 5.19. Install a vacuum gauge to read intake manifold vacuum. You can use a typical Autometer (or similar) vacuum gauge, but a commercial/industrial big-dial gauge is better because it can be read more accurately.

Economy tuning can be done without a wide-band, oxygen-mixture measuring system, but I highly recommend using one.

A good cruise control unit is also an asset.

You also need an assistant with a pen and notebook to record the data you are about to measure.

To get the best results, it is important to understand what you

want in the way of vacuum gaug readings. As far as spark timing goe the higher the vacuum, the mor efficiently your engine is burr ing fuel at the test speed. As far a mixture is concerned the opposit applies. As the mixture is leane out, it becomes necessary to ope the throttle more. This reduces th vacuum in the manifold. This ma not be intuitive, but keep in min that you want to get as close to Diesel cycle as possible with you spark-ignition engine.

Before getting into tuning detail let me remind you that getting an real economy figures means hav ing vacuum advance on the engine Without that, you can be sure tha at least 30 percent of your engine cruise speed economy potential ha been sacrificed.

Also, before starting the actua tuning, be sure to record the distribu tor or ignition system's RPM-relate (usually referred to as mechanica advance. Plot this in increments c about 100 rpm from just over idl to about 3,000 rpm (or whateve the maximum cruise RPM is likel to be). This needs to be plotted ou in large scale on a sheet of grap paper. Your tune-up assistant need this during the tune-up procedure so make it easy to read while ridin in the vehicle.

Tuning Steps

After you have the required gea follow this tuning procedure:

First, install the vacuum gaug and the oxygen system.

Next, disconnect the vacuur advance from the intake manifolc plug the port, and then connect th manifold end of the distributor vac uum advance tube to the Mity Va vacuum pump. You can now advanc the ignition, at will, from within the driver's compartment.

On the test stretch of highway, bring the vehicle up to the test speed. For a truck, such as our race car tow vehicle, I typically choose test speeds of 35, 50, and 65 mph. For a car, I use 35, 55, and 70 or 75 mph.

Once you're consistently traveling at the test speed, slowly actuate the Mity Vac pump to bring in vacuum advance. As the advance nears optimal, the vehicle tries to speed up, but the cruise control reacts by slowly closing the throttle to maintain the preset speed. (This needs to be done by manual throttle modulatiosn if your vehicle is not equipped with cruise control.) This causes the vacuum, at that preset speed, to increase. The ignition timing for the current speed and jetting is optimal when the manifold vacuum is highest.

Record the oxygen sensor output, manifold vacuum, RPM, and Mity Vac vacuum at the current test speed.

Repeat the procedure for each of the test speeds.

Ignition Advance

You are developing a part-throttle ignition curve for the engine. So, back at the shop, open the hood and use the data you have just recorded to determine the advance at each RPM/Mity Vac vacuum reading.

To do this, rev the engine to the test RPM, apply the recorded Mity Vac vacuum setting, and check the ignition timing.

The number of degrees you see is the timing required for the manifold vacuum. The Mity Vac does not provide the vacuum, rather it is just a means of adjusting the timing. Subtract the mechanical advance from the total advance. The result

is the vacuum advance required at that engine speed and load/manifold vacuum.

At this stage, let us assume that the WOT mechanical/RPM advance curve is correct for the engine spec. You have just determined how much vacuum advance is needed on top of the WOT RPM advance. If the mixture was optimum, this is the advance characteristic you seek to get from either programming a computer-controlled ignition system or a regular distributor's vacuum-advance canister.

Cruise Calibration

It is very unlikely that you hit the lean burn limit on your first test but you should have recorded the air/fuel ratio at each of your cruise RPM speeds. With most out-of-the-box Holley carbs, the oxygen reading indicates a mixture around 14:1 to 15:1.

Your next job is to lean out the carb's calibrations, and that is done mostly on the idle fuel and air jets, with the main jet and air corrector coming in only at the higher speeds.

After your initial test, lean out the circuits that control the mixture. You should be able to approach 17:1 relatively easily, but be aware that at these leaner ratios, the action of the accelerator pump and its tuning to meet the transitional needs becomes a lot more fussy.

Retest at the leaner carb settings according to the initial test. Again, you are using optimal timing to maximize engine vacuum.

If the trend is toward the successful use of a leaner mixture, after optimal timing has been achieved with the leaner mixture, the amount of vacuum is a little less than with the previous test.

Basically it is a process of progressively leaning out the mixture and reestablishing the optimum vacuum advance curve at each step. As soon as the engine runs into lean misfire, take a small step back and go richer with the mixture. When the engine is running into a lean misfire, it starts to show readings leaner than expected. Remember, the oxygen sensor is looking at the oxygen in the exhaust. A misfire puts a lot of unused oxygen into the exhaust.

A tune up like this means your engine is delivering close to the best economy it is likely to get with its current spec. Now you must tailor the ignition to deliver the vacuum advance curve required to make the most of the lean mixture being delivered.

Vacuum Can Range

Be sure that you're not out of range of the vacuum advance system's capability. If your system is not in that range, you may have to swap out distributor vacuum cans or even temporarily put more initial advance into the distributor.

You now can determine the exact total advance required at the test speeds. When using a computer-controlled ignition system, in most cases, you are able to meet the engine's advance needs. Be aware that at low-speed cruise and high-manifold vacuum and/or lean burn, the advance required for optimum fuel efficiency can be as much as 52 to 55 degrees. The reason for this is that less-dense charges (high-manifold vacuum) and leaner mixtures burn much more slowly. ∎

CARBURETOR SELECTION

Let me make one thing clear: If you make a poor initial carb selection for your application, it will certainly impede and perhaps prevent you from achieving top results. In this chapter I discuss a rarely covered subject, namely brake specific air consumption (BSAC), and how it directly affects just how much horsepower a given carb's CFM supports. In simple terms, the subject here is how to get a smaller carb than you think the engine needs to support more horsepower than you thought it would allow. From that you should

be able to see that it is an important part of the quest for more from less!

In Chapter 2, I mentioned the advantages of going to Holley's website to use the on-line carb selector. This is a really good way to start your carb selection.

Before you begin the selection process, you need to know two things: The first is the total CFM the engine is likely to require and the second is whether you should use a vacuum secondary.

I start with a process for determining the best CFM for maximum output. Next I deal with all the possible advantages of a vacuum secondary. Finally I delve into the ways and means of utilizing every possible CFM that passes through the carb and into the engine in the fullest manner possible.

How Much Carb CFM is Needed?

The first step in installing the best carb for the job is to make a preliminary selection based on the engine's displacement. Next, modify this result by factoring in relevant engine spec details such as the head

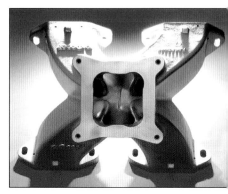

Fig. 6.2. This is the intake from my 2002 Chrysler Cup Car engine. The points to note are the generously rounded leading edges of the runners and the as-cast runner floors. Polishing the floor of an intake is a no-no!

Fig. 6.1. Shown here with a Dominator, this Chevy big-block 572-ci engine proved to be capable of more than 750 hp in street trim with a 4150 carb (850 cfm, PN 0-80531). This was a case of knowing how to utilize the CFM capacity of the carb to the fullest extent.

Fig. 6.3. This is a NASCAR Cup Car intake for a pair of Chevy small-block 18-degree heads. Nothing aids flow into the head like a straight shot to the port. The more efficient the intake, the more carburetion capacity the engine can use.

and cam used. For the initial calculation step, determine the amount of CFM the engine is likely to inhale if it were able to breath at 100-percent efficiency.

To do this, multiply the cubic inches (ci) of displacement by the anticipated RPM the engine is likely to turn to. Let me stress that it is very important to be realistic and therefore as accurate as possible when making the RPM estimation.

Estimate where peak power is likely to occur and then add 200 rpm to allow for over-speed. At this juncture, you may feel your application needs more over-speed that just 200 rpm. Even if that is the case, the ability to effectively run past peak power is a function of the cylinder heads and cam rather than choosing a larger carb. Producing a good over-speed capability for, say, a short track engine that runs in one gear only can make a winning difference.

Equally important is how the engine responds coming off the turns. This is an important factor not just to a circle track racer but also to the performance street enthusiast.

To find the amount of air a 100-percent-efficient engine inhales per minute (CFM), you multiply the displacement (cubic inches) by the engine speed (RPM). And because this is a four-cycle engine, which has an induction stroke every other revolution, you divide by 2. Then, to convert to cubic feet, you divide by 1,728. Here's the formula:

$$CFM = \frac{ci \times RPM}{2 \times 1,728}$$

Volumetric Efficiency

The calculation above assumes the engine has a 100-percent breathing efficiency. For a race engine, where the exhaust scavenging is a factor, the volumetric efficiency can exceed 100 percent by quite a big margin. For instance, a well-built race 350, with no regulatory race restrictions placed on it, can reach about 115-percent volumetric efficiency. This means that such an engine, as far as the carb is concerned, seems to displace 400 ci, not the 350 it actually displaces.

At the other end of the range an absolutely stock street engine may have a volumetric efficiency of only about 75 percent. This means that an engine of the same 350-ci displacement appears, from the carb's point of reference, to be displacing only about 290 ci. Carburetor selection needs to take this into account.

An engine's required airflow depends primarily on the cam and the breathing capability of the heads. Assuming that the compression ratio and exhaust system are appropriate for the engine, the heads and cam are the most influential components in carb size selection. As cams get longer, the engine's volumetric efficiency improves. The volumetric efficiency also improves as the cylinder head's flow capability improves.

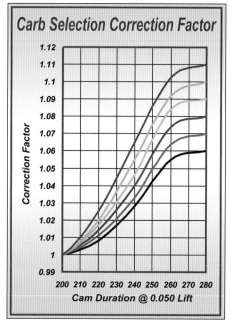

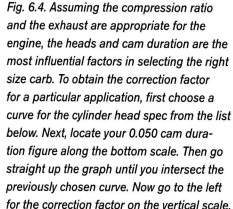

Fig. 6.4. Assuming the compression ratio and the exhaust are appropriate for the engine, the heads and cam duration are the most influential factors in selecting the right size carb. To obtain the correction factor for a particular application, first choose a curve for the cylinder head spec from the list below. Next, locate your 0.050 cam duration figure along the bottom scale. Then go straight up the graph until you intersect the previously chosen curve. Now go to the left for the correction factor on the vertical scale.

Red = super race heads such as ProStock and NASAR Cup Car heads
Orange = top-of-the-line race-ported heads such as used by pro racers
Green = race-ported conventional heads
Blue = street-ported heads
Magenta = pocket-ported pre-1990 heads or stock Vortec or aftermarket heads
Black = stock OE heads of pre-1990 design

Figure 6.4 gives a correction factor (CF), which takes into account cam duration and cylinder head flow capability. Using this correction factor, here is the formula for predicting the required carb CFM:

$$CFM = \frac{ci \times RPM \times CF}{2 \times 1,728}$$

As an example, let's use one of my 482-ci Chevy big-block engines. This street/strip build, which was mostly in the low-buck category, targeted peak power at 6,800 rpm so the maximum RPM figure (at 200 over that) would be 7,000. The CF for a Comp Cams street roller (248 degrees at 0.050) with the basic race-ported Dart Iron Eagle heads (using the green curve in Figure 6.4) came out to 1.065. Putting this data into the equation, you get:

$$CFM = \frac{482 \times 7,000 \times 1.065}{2 \times 1,728} = 1,039.7$$

The answer rounds up to 1,040. The carb selected was a 1050 Holley Dominator, which worked out very well.

Here's another example: a Ford small-block 5.0 built for my road race Mustang. This 306-ci engine featured race-ported Dart heads, a Comp Cams solid street roller cam with 258 degrees duration at 0.050, and peak power at 7,600 rpm. The correction factor (using the green curve in Figure 6.4) came out to 1.07. Putting the numbers into the equation you get:

$$CFM = \frac{306 \times 7,800 \times 1.07}{2 \times 1,728} = 738.96875$$

The answer rounds up to 740 cfm. The carb used was a 750 Street HP and this pump-gas 306 turned out 525 hp and 396 ft-lbs of torque.

This example targets just about the biggest carb you should use. However, it makes no allowance for the fact that a tricked-out carb with high-gain boosters can successfully use greater CFM.

Let's say you took a stock 750 and spent time streamlining the throttle shafts and butterflies. This can increase the airflow by about 35 cfm if you do a halfway respectable job. This allows a little more power to be developed without sacrifice in the lower RPM range. Going this route means you have to know your carbs or work with a carb specialist.

Factoring in Dual-Plane Intakes

So, you should be able to calculate, to within relatively precise limits, what is needed in the way of carb CFM for any given application. But the previous examples assume the engine is equipped with an effectively flowing single-plane intake. When a true dual-plane is used, in which one plenum is completely separated from the other, the carb CFM seen by any one cylinder is almost halved. Unless this is allowed for, the engine could be very short of its true potential.

However, dual-plane intake design must, in many cases, take into account issues that are relatively unimportant for a high-performance single-plane. Such things as exhaust gas recirculation (EGR), hood clearance, installation compatibility with A/C, etc. need to be factored in. All these and many more issues influence, to a greater or lesser degree, just how flow efficient the intake can be.

To demonstrate let's consider the dyno figures from a couple different intake manifolds. The first is a Weiand dual-plane used on a Ford 351

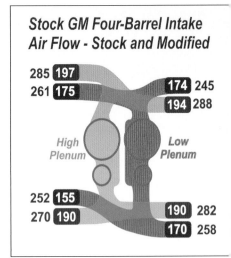

Fig. 6.6. This is a port runner schematic for a production Chevy small-block with dual-plane intake. As you can see, there is no such thing as a "straight shot" route for port runners from the carb to the head's intake ports. The stock flow numbers are the ones posted in the port openings and then modified on the outside of the runners.

Fig. 6.5. A well-designed single-plane manifold, such as this Parker Funnel Web for the Ford small-block, can have great airflow capability compared to a dual-plane intake.

Fig. 6.7. I used this stock-port factory intake on my dirt race car. Although rules mandated no porting, I found an extra 20 ft-lbs and 20 hp. (See Chapter 12 for more details.)

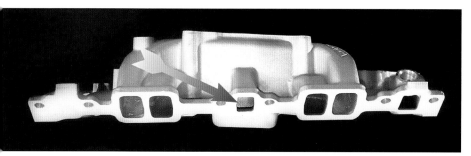

Fig. 6.8. There are two things to note on this intake manifold. First, it is a stock-height, or "low-rise," manifold. Second, it has an exhaust heat crossover (arrow). Neither factor is good for output.

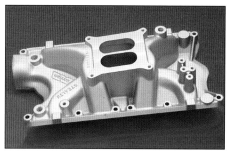

Fig. 6.9. Many manifolds, such as this Weiand Street Warrior for a Ford 351 Windsor V-8, are compatible with all stock factory equipment so they are a direct replacement. The downside is that they give up flow potential over a high-rise intake design.

Fig. 6.10. If your intended carb is too small for the engine (as this 950 is for the 572-inch big-block), a street single-plane makes better results than a dual-plane intake.

High-Performance Dual-Planes

By the time the new millennia started some serious steps had been taken among intake manifold manufacturers to design and produce a new class of high-performance dual-plane intake manifold. This was a category that bridged the gap between the typical dual-plane and the one that retained a dual-plane layout but featured a raised carb pad and runner shapes that maximized airflow to the cylinders.

In effect these types of dual-plane intakes bridged the gap between the conventional "stock replacement" intakes and high-performance single-plane intakes. They were also

Windsor equipped with a Scat Enterprises 1/2-inch stroker crank, which produces 408 ci. I tested this engine with a 750 HP Street carb and a black 950 Ultra Race carb.

The Weiand intake was designed to be compatible with all OE installations. The manifold carb pad was virtually at stock height so making the manifold taller to get a more favorable runner shape was not incorporated in this design. This manifold's strong point is that its design produced very good cylinder-to-cylinder mixture ratios to the extent that no stagger jetting was needed. Its airflow, though, compared to some of the taller, raised-pad manifolds, was down by a measurable margin.

The result was that the 408 cubes this engine had could be satisfied in the low and mid ranges but not at the top end. Because the manifold became the prime restriction, the 750 HP Street carb produced as good an output as a 950 all the way to about 4,800 rpm. It was only between 4,800 and 6,000 that the 950 showed any benefit. Even then it only improved by about 5 hp! The point to note here is that if the manifold is not really strong on flow the need for a higher flowing carb is largely negated.

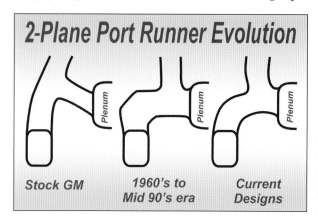

2-Plane Port Runner Evolution

Plenum

Plenum

Plenum

Stock GM

1960's to Mid 90's era

Current Designs

Fig. 6.11. This illustration shows how dual-plane intake runners evolved from a very inefficient shape to the current high-efficiency designs.

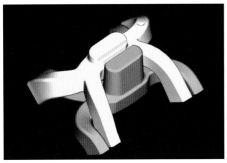

Fig. 6.12. Forms, such as these, are typically used to manufacture modern high-rise dual-plane intakes. Given the right carburetion, this type of intake can show extremely good performance increases throughout the entire RPM range. The performance potential and effectiveness of this style of intake is proven by the Chevy 383/408 small-block build that produced streetable outputs between 530 and 560 hp (featured in my book How to Build Max-Performance Chevy Small-Blocks on a Budget).

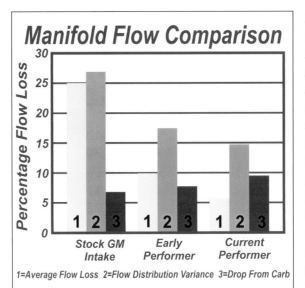

Fig. 6.13. This graph shows why a modern, high-tech, high-flow, dual-plane needs much more carb CFM than an older and significantly less efficient design. Look at the average flow loss (Columns 1 in yellow) of the three sample intakes. You see that the current Performer-style intake is far more efficient, so it reduces head flow by much less than the stock intake. Shown in Columns 3 (red) is what happens to the flow when a 750 carb is installed on the intake: The intake flow is reduced by a smaller amount on the inefficient stock intake.

However, because the more efficient Performer intake can convey a greater demand to the carb via a more efficient manifold, the 750 carb itself becomes the "cork" in the system. This is why current high-efficiency dual-plane intakes run best with more carburetion than might be expected.

probably the first volume-production manifolds to be designed using computational fluid dynamics (CFD).

In terms of carb CFM, these intakes require a serious amount of consideration when it comes to choosing a carb. Because the runners are far more efficient than a typical dual-plane intake, they are able to communicate the engine's air demand to the carburetor far more effectively. In turn, this means that an engine so equipped is far more sensitive to carb capacity.

On a single-plane intake, all cylinders see all four barrels of the carb to draw on. But consider this: Given a dual-plane intake with efficiently flowing runners, the carb flow seen by any one cylinder of the engine is half of what it is on a single-plane intake. This means the 750-cfm carb that worked so well with a good single-plane manifold looks more like a 375- to 400-cfm carb. With such intake manifolds the required carb capacity can go way over what you might ordinarily expect (see Figure 6.15). A good dual-plane, air-gap-style intake for a small-block Chevy or Ford that is physically capable of about 550 hp given all the induction it wants, stops showing output increase at about 1,100 cfm of carb capacity because the limit is now the manifold's runner flow capacity.

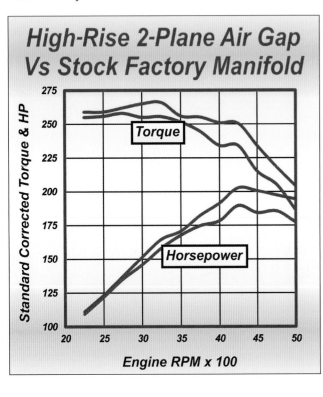

Fig. 6.14. A high-performance, dual-plane intake cannot deliver much increase on an otherwise stock smog-gear-laden engine such as this 1980 Chevy 350. The red lines represent the hampered Chevy 350, and it doesn't produce much power unless the highly restrictive exhaust is uncorked first. When that's done, installing a good intake results in an entirely different story. The blue lines represent the stock factory manifold.

Dual-Plane Cutout

Some high-performance dual-plane intakes have the divider between the plenums cut away to form a communicating passage between them (see Figures 6.16, 6.17, 6.18). The purpose of the cutout is to allow any one cylinder to see more than just the two barrels of the carb immediately over the plenum. This has the effect of improving output at the top end. The drawback is usually reduced low-speed torque and idle to low-speed cruise vacuum.

This cutout brings about various consequences. In effect, it turns a dual-plane manifold into a single-plane manifold with much longer but more tortuous ports. In other words, the cutout turns a potentially good dual-plane into a substandard

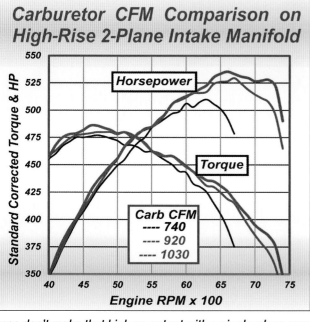

Fig. 6.15. Dyno tests support my "think bigger" philosophy when using a flow-efficient, dual–plane intake. The relatively basic 383 test engine has a set of Gil Mink–ported World Products Sportsman iron heads with a 10.5:1 CR. The cam is one of my hot street-spec hydraulic flat-tappet grinds. As you can see, it produces 536 hp and that's pretty respectable output for an engine like this. Most engines with this sort of spec don't make that high an output with a single-plane race-style intake.

The point, however, is that if the typically recommended 750 carb had been used, the output peaks would have been 476 ft-lbs of torque and 511 hp. Although that's hardly an output that anyone would complain about, it is not the 487 ft-lbs and 536 hp seen with the big carb. A couple of points to note to validate the results here are that the intake had no plenum cutout and the torque curves of all three carbs were virtually identical up to 4,000 rpm.

Fig. 6.16. This Weiand high-rise air-gap-style intake does not utilize a plenum cutout, which is commonly at the point indicated by the upper arrow. The bulge indicated by the lower arrow is an attempt to equalize the plenum volume seen by each pair of carb barrels. With no cutout, this manifold is far more sensitive to carb CFM. Given sufficient CFM this style of manifold can produce excellent results at both ends of the RPM range.

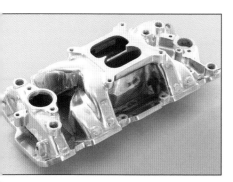

Fig. 6.17. This particular high-performance intake features an inter-plenum cutout. This slightly compromises idle quality and reduces torque at the bottom of the RPM range. However, it does make the intake a little less sensitive to carb CFM.

Fig. 6.18. If you need to keep overall costs down without compromising quality, a high-flow dual-plane intake with a plenum cutout (shown) used with a 750 vacuum secondary Holley works well. In such instances, a bigger carb on, say, a 383 shows less of a gain over the 750.

Fig. 6.19. Dual-plane, air-gap intakes, such as this one for the Ford 302 small-block, really work well. They ramp up the low-speed torque of these engines, which provides an important performance improvement because low-speed output is not a 302's strong point.

Fig. 6.20. I had a Holley 950 body, a big-butterfly base plate, and the goal to build as high an airflow carb as possible without getting into anything too drastic. I dressed up the boosters and venturis and then reworked the butterflies and shafts. These modifications delivered 990 cfm. This worked well on one of my 468-inch, dual-plane intake, big-block Chevys.

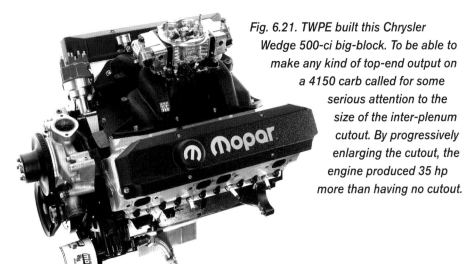

Fig. 6.21. TWPE built this Chrysler Wedge 500-ci big-block. To be able to make any kind of top-end output on a 4150 carb called for some serious attention to the size of the inter-plenum cutout. By progressively enlarging the cutout, the engine produced 35 hp more than having no cutout.

single-plane. That factor may not be good as, in part, it indicates that if the cutout were necessary then maybe you should have chosen a streetable single-plane intake. Also, if the cutout helped top-end output, it is a sure sign that the carb is too small for the application.

There is most certainly a delicate balance here. My thoughts are that it is better to use a slightly bigger CFM carb without a cutout in the intake than a slightly smaller carb with a plenum cutout in the manifold.

There are times when a cutout for carb barrel sharing between the cylinders becomes essential, but again, it is because the carb for the application is just too small. A good example is the use of a 4150 carb on a dual-plane intake that has to feed a 500-inch (or more) engine. Some excellent big-block (Chevy, Chrysler, Ford) dual-plane intakes have good runner design, and that's despite a runner design requirement that impedes flow. However, at the end of the day, the 4150 carb so often used

is woefully short of adequate CFM capacity. For these intakes to make a decent top-end output, their plenum cutouts extend to the very limits of what the wall between the two plenums allow.

Let me remind you that if the plenum is cut out, it is progressively turning a dual-plane intake into a single-plane intake, but without the flow advantages of a single-plane. If you are in a position to perform tests, my advice concerning dual-plane intakes is to use as large a carb as possible first. If that does not satisfy the top-end output needs, start slotting the divider. It helps if you have access to a dyno.

Multiple Carbs

Much of the popularity of the single-plane, single 4-barrel carb is the fact that it works well for the money spent. However, it might just leave you to wonder if and by how much a pair of Holleys on a tunnel ram would better a single 4-barrel setup.

It is very often claimed by many who should know better that a tunnel-ram-style intake is for the race track only. If you consider nothing other than installation hassles and the inevitably large hood scope, that viewpoint is largely correct. However, if you are attempting to make

Fig. 6.22. If your intent is to use a 4150 carb big-block, consider the use of a single-plane street intake as this makes more use of the carb's full airflow potential. (This Chevy big-block intake manifold is PN 88961161.)

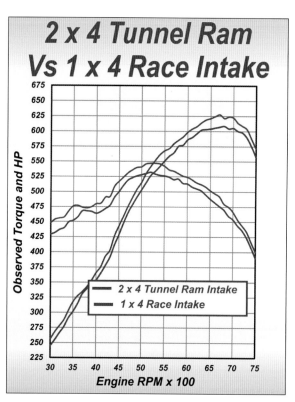

Fig. 6.24. This graph shows what you can expect in the way of additional output by utilizing a pair of mildly modified 600-cfm 4-barrel Holleys versus a single 1,020-cfm unit. Note that in spite of often being labeled as "race-only," a tunnel ram setup can produce a more streetable output curve than even the best single-plane 1x4 installations.

Fig. 6.23. This Chevy 505-ci big-block sported two tricked-out 750 Holley carbs. It had extremely good manners for an engine with 300/320-degree (at lash) nitrous-oriented cam and made, in its final form, about 835 hp on the engine and 1,540 on a relatively conservative amount of nitrous. Idle was a smooth 780 rpm.

the best torque over the widest RPM range possible, the "race only" label is totally wrong.

I have built a few street/tunnel-ram setups and they have delivered great drivability and output. Also, mileage was better than might have been expected considering the strong bias toward performance. A typical power advantage by using "two fours" is shown in Figure 6.24. For this test, the carbs used a four-corner idle setup. This proved to be an asset because the amount of power that can be developed while still in the idle/transition mode is considerably higher, as the engine has eight barrels to draw on. This also means that if you have a street cruiser, a meticulous setup of the idle/transition circuits can bring about some respectable fuel mileage.

Another fuel mileage move is to use vacuum secondary carbs. As far as carb capacity goes, if you purchase

Fig. 6.25. There seems to be a renewed interest in the three 2-barrel performance street intakes that were popular during the 1960s and 1970s. This is Holley's latest for small-block Chevys.

a set of carbs specifically calibrated for 2 x 4 use with a CFM as indicated by the calculations given on page 58 you will be in good shape. Going this route on the carb CFM selection may cause you to wonder where the extra power is going to come from if the CFM is about the same as with a 1 x 4 single-plane manifold setup. The

tunnel ram has several assets that allow it to produce a better output.

First, the port runners are a straight shot to the cylinder head ports, so the manifold is more flow efficient. Second, the carb barrels are directly over the manifold's port runners so fuel distribution problems are minimized. Third, most wet flow problems arise due to a runner's change of direction but because a tunnel ram's runners are almost straight it has fewer issues with wet fuel flow. Finally, the pressure-wave tuning brought about by the interaction of the plenum and the port runners is far better than with any single-carb intake. All this adds up to a better result for a given amount of carb CFM.

Let's look at the possible hitches you may run into and how to avoid them. The first and largest pitfall is buying a pair of carbs not explicitly calibrated and otherwise set up for running in a 2 x 4 configuration. Sure, given time you can get any pair of similar Holley carbs calibrated to produce positive results, but it's very time consuming and complex. If you feel you can afford a 2 x 4 setup your absolute best plan is to call Holley and buy what they recommend. This is the shortest and easiest way to achieve some really worthwhile results.

Once you have a set of carbs with the correct general calibration, it generally becomes a straightforward procedure to fine tune the calibration.

Three Twos

From the 1950s into the 1970s, three 2-barrel carbs were offered by several Detroit manufacturers as a V-8 street-performance package. The idea was that for sedate street driving, the engine ran on the center carb, which had calibrations biased toward fuel economy. When power was called for, the throttle linkage or vacuum actuation opened the other two carbs and fed the system, with the front and back carb feeding a full-power mixture charge.

Be aware that designing an intake manifold to satisfy this carburetion

configuration is not without its flow-efficiency problems. However, even with the greater difficulty of designing high-flow runners this concept can actually work well. As for carb capacity, the sum total of the three carbs should be about 10 percent more than if it were a single-plane intake. However, the 3 x 2 configuration has a far more limited selection of carb sizes.

On a typical small-block the usual configuration seems to favor 325 cfm for the center carb and 350 cfm for the outer carbs. Those carbs are rated at 3 inches of depression, so you have to divide by 1.4 to get the equivalent 4-barrel rating.

The potential for better fuel economy, with careful calibrations, is available. As for outright power, a good air-gap dual-plane with the right carb still beats a 3 x 2. That said, a well set up 3 x 2 can have great drivability on the street while turning in excellent drag strip times on an otherwise street-orientated carb setup.

Last point: They also look pretty cool on the engine.

Spacers

Spacers are seen as anything from the expert carb tuner's black magic to a simple parts change on the dyno to explore what the engine might need. As simple as a spacer is, its mode of operation is often not understood. The reality is that spacers work because they have increased something that the engine likes. That increase may take the form of extra flow, more velocity, greater anti-reversion properties, or additional plenum volume.

It takes little more than lifting the carb and installing the spacer and longer studs to find out what the engine likes. This means it is a good idea to test a spacer any time the opportunity presents itself. But be aware that installing a spacer always increases the plenum volume, often making a small but relevant reduction in the sharpness of the signal at the booster. Consequently, if the jetting was on the money before the spacer was installed, the carb may need to have a size or two larger main jet to compensate.

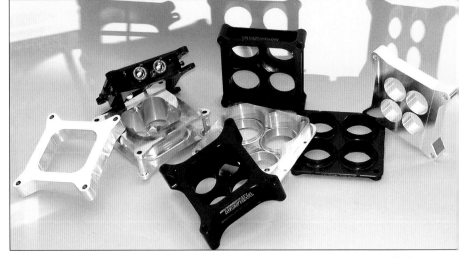

Fig. 6.26. This variety of spacers should just about cover the ones you are likely to come across. Each has its virtues. The dyno and the drag strip are likely to establish which one performs best for your application.

Fig. 6.27. A spacer has the ability to make the plenum volume larger and, usually, helps the air flow through the carb by up to 20 cfm. Because a stretched big-block is always hurting for air it is worthwhile finding out whether or not a spacer helps. In most cases they do.

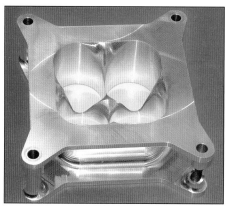

Fig. 6.29. This type of exit-blended spacer not only increases plenum volume but also aerodynamically tidies up the air/fuel charge's exit from the carb barrels. The result is that the engine sees greater flow from the carb. If the carb is a little on the small side, this type of spacer almost always pays dividends in output.

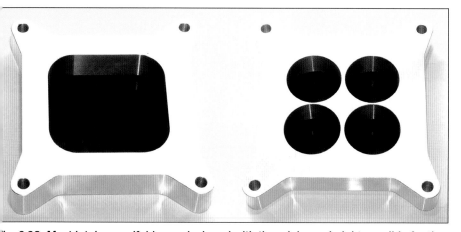

Fig. 6.28. Most intake manifolds are designed with the minimum height possible for the application. This means that the plenum is often too small, so the use of an open spacer is an easy fix and it reaps the benefits of additional output.

Vacuum Secondaries

Because successful racers use mechanical secondaries many street performance enthusiasts tend to regard vacuum secondaries as something of a necessary performance downgrade dictated solely by the need to have a streetable induction system. In reality nothing could be further from the truth!

The correct way to view a vacuum secondary carb is as a high-flow performance carb fitted with a device that allows you to use that carb in a far more effective manner on the street. In fact, a well set up vacuum secondary carb can provide better performance and faster times on the track than a mechanical secondary carb. The reason is that, in effect, a vacuum secondary carb is like two carbs rolled into one.

A small-CFM 2-barrel (due to a sufficiently active venturi and booster combination) can supply a well-atomized mixture to the engine at part throttle and low-speed WOT.

When the engine's demand for air outpaces the primary barrels, the secondaries open up and provide the mid- and top-end airflow and fuel requirements. In practice, this means that the user of a vacuum secondary carb can ultimately select a slightly bigger carb CFM without any penalty at the low end.

A vacuum secondary is of little or no advantage when the stall speed of the converter is above the RPM at which a vacuum secondary comes in. The vehicle's gearing and its weight are contributing factors as well. If the car transitions through the first gear to RPM somewhere at or above peak torque RPM very quickly then, once again, a vacuum secondary might not be of any advantage.

So here is my advice on the subject of vacuum secondaries: If the torque output of the engine (below 4,000 rpm for smaller engines around 300 inches or 3,000 rpm for larger engines of more than 380 inches) constitutes part of the engine's operating range, you should be looking

Fig. 6.30. This spacer is a four-hole/open-hybrid type. On about 1 in 10 engines, they seem to deliver what is called for. This spacer provides the same effect as using both the four-hole and open spacers.

Fig. 6.31. This spacer has tubular, sharp-edge extensions, which protrude into the plenum of the intake manifold. This provides a measure of anti-reversion properties to the flow exiting the carb.

Fig. 6.32. This spacer not only has anti-reversion lips on the four exits but also fuel-shear ridges on the wall of the open part of the spacer.

Fuel Re-distributing Anti-Reversion Spacer

Fuel Distribution Cutout

Fig. 6.33. This type of spacer acts as a means of altering fuel distribution to a more favorable pattern and as an anti-reversion devise. The slot allows the fuel to enrich a weak area within the plenum. This spacer seems to work best when used in conjunction with a 1- to 2-inch open spacer.

at a vacuum secondary carb. If you select a vacuum secondary carb for an engine that does not really need one, there is no real downside. If you select a mechanical secondary for an engine that could really use a vacuum secondary the downside is a possible reduction in output everywhere.

Sizing with Alcohol-Based Fuels or Nitrous

So far the subject of sizing the carb CFM to the engine has been discussed assuming that gasoline was the fuel being used. Let's consider the changes that may be needed with methanol and ethanol-based E85 fuels and nitrous oxide.

Alcohols

With methanol and ethanol-based E85 fuels the vaporization curve is far less favorable for good combustion initiation than with a good gasoline blend. On top of that, the amount of fuel for an optimal-output air/fuel ratio is far greater. This means that any potential mixture quality or wet flow problems that might be imminent with gasoline can be greatly magnified to the point that any power gains that may have been possible with the alcohol fuels are nullified. To combat this, make sure that the fuel is well atomized.

Rule number one here is: Do no use a carb with venturis too big fo the application. Rule number tw is: Make sure that the booster is c high enough gain to generate goo atomization. Rule number three is: is often better to err on the smalle side for an alky carb.

Because these fuels cool the car so much more than gasoline doe the mass flow (lbs-min) can increase However, countering this is that th fuel takes up a lot more room in th intake so carb CFM is reduced. Th bottom line here is that you want a high a speed in the venturi as po: sible along with the strongest booste signal possible. For example, if th carb is a 4150-style unit, conside a main venturi minor diameter c 1.45 inches maximum but prefe ably about 1.4. This, along with a bi throttle bore, seems to work well.

Nitrous

If you're using nitrous oxid there are two avenues to conside The first is a street/strip situatio where having good manners an decent fuel mileage are prime consic erations. Under such circumstance choose a carb that errs on the smaller side by about 50 cfm. The rationale here is that the nitrous produces all the extra power required within the realm of streetable mechanical reliability. This being the case you may as well have the benefits of good street manners from your engine; selecting a carb a little smaller favors that aspect.

For a race-only situation, things change a little. Here you have three goals. First is to go as fast as possible, second is to use as little nitrous as possible, and third is to have your engine survive the rigors of a very substantial power output.

When the nitrous comes into action the temperature of the charge in the intake drops considerably. This causes the air that passes through the carb and into the manifold to shrink. At first, this looks as if it should increase the airflow into the engine, but the reality is actually the reverse. A portion of the liquid nitrous entering the induction system turns to a gas, and consequently it takes up room that would have otherwise been occupied by the air from the carb. This usually more than counters the potential increase in flow from the charge's temperature reduction.

All this might be leading you to think that using a smaller carb as for the street is the best route, but in many cases, the reverse applies. The use of a slightly larger carb usually pays off, especially if the nitrous is port injected.

Brake Specific Air Consumption

Some advocate rating a carburetor by the horsepower it can readily support. In my opinion, it's far better to obtain ultimate performance by matching the carb's CFM to the engine volumetric capacity. At first sizing a carb according to the horsepower it can support seems like a better method, but it makes an assumption that can throw a wrench into the works. For example, a NASCAR Cup Car engine makes the point. Before NASCAR's top series made the change to fuel injection (2012) the carb called for was a version of the 830 that Holley originally brought out for such use. This carb, when fully prepped, was good for about 960 cfm (although some teams were running radically modified carbs with well over 1,000 cfm) and, for a Cup Car application, supported the needs of a 900-hp 355-ci engine.

Another example is the use of a 4150-platform carb on a modified 572-ci big-block Chevy. Although way too small according to the CFM calculations presented earlier, a 950 Ultra HP can pass enough air to support more than 800 hp from a street/strip 572.

If you do the math in terms of the required CFM, these carbs look far too small to be able to allow the production of such big horsepower numbers. But there is one factor that you should be aware of: An engine may well draw in a certain amount of air, but it is very important how efficiently it uses that air.

To demonstrate, let's use two big-block Chevys as examples. Each engine made virtually the same 1,100 hp. The first had very well sorted combustion characteristics. In fact, the induction system produced a well-prepared charge and delivered a BSFC of 0.39 pound of fuel per horsepower per hour at peak power. This engine also ran at leaner-than-normal air/fuel ratio because manifold distribution was nearly perfect. As a result it produced 1,100 hp for the 96 pounds of air it consumed each minute. This works out to be a BSAC of 5.2 lbs/hp/hr. This translates into a carb flow demand of 1,260 cfm.

The other big-block ingested 110 pounds of air for 1,100 hp. That was good but not as good as the first example. The same output was delivered with a BSFC of 0.46 lb/hp/hr while the best air/fuel ratio was 13:1. These figures indicated a more than reasonably well sorted induction system. However, this engine had a BSAC figure of 6 lb/hp/hr and, therefore, it had an air demand of 1,450 cfm.

So at the same pressure drop across the carb, the second engine needed a carb of about 200 cfm more.

Say you are installing a carb that passes a certain amount of air at a certain pressure drop into the engine. Whatever volume of air the carb flows, it is now up to you, as the engine builder, to utilize that air as efficiently as possible. My engines make a lot of power on a relatively small carb because I have 50 years of experience and sufficient proficiency for spec'ing engines to make the most of the air passing through the carb.

As an example, a 750-cfm carb on one of my street/strip Chevy 383 small-blocks can make more than 600 streetable hp, whereas an engine less well spec'd may only make 540 to 550. For what it is worth, it is possible to get the BSAC figure below 5 lbs/hp/hr. Couple this with good head and induction system flow and you can expect output numbers that trailer your competition (see my best-selling CarTech book *How to Build Horsepower*).

BOOSTER SCIENCE

The design of the booster can have dramatic effects on the engine's output and fuel consumption. Having an understanding of boosters can put you in the position of being able to enhance high-RPM output without sacrificing low-speed output.

Never one to avoid controversy, I have stated on many occasions that there is almost no such thing as a carb that is too big. Although a slight exaggeration, it's not as far off reality as you might think. As an example, the constant vacuum of an SU pulls the air valve open just far enough to satisfy the engine's air demand. Therefore, at low speed, it is a small carb; at high speed, it is a large carb. This in turn means that you can put a giant SU on a small engine with little fear of having a carb that is too big.

With a fixed-jet carb the situation changes. A big Holley on a small engine means that at low RPM, WOT produces a venturi speed that is too slow to meter or atomize the fuel sufficiently well. This, in turn, compromises combustion efficiency. But just how much "too big" is depends greatly on how effective the boosters are.

If the boosters have a really high gain (i.e., step up) over the main venturi depression by 300 to 400 percent, a big carb is far less of a low-speed liability. A couple examples illustrate this: A small-block Chevy 350 with a Holley flowing 985 cfm (which produces big torque numbers from idle up) and a similar 350 with a 1,020 cfm Holley for a Trans-Am.

I realize much of this flies counter to conventional wisdom. But the reality is that carb manufacturers (in this case Holley) make that statement to simplify carb calibration for the typical consumer. But it doesn't tell the entire story.

You may want to install a highly functioning carb right out of the box, but to get the most out of it, you need to properly set it up. It takes some time and inclination to learn about and properly set up a carb. Don't use a carb that is too big unless you know how to select or design a booster that still gives an appropriate signal at low speed.

Again, if you have a working understanding of boosters, it can put you several steps ahead of your competition at the race track. Knowing what works and how to get there allows the use of greater carb CFM before you experience any negative impact on

Fig. 7.1. A 406 (6.65 L) Chevy small-block powers my 1980 Pontiac Trans-Am. The 550-hp engine utilizes a highly modified Holley flowing about 1,020 cfm. The editor of **Motor** *magazine tested the car and as seen here it delivered 0-120 mph in 12.5 seconds along with perfect street manners.*

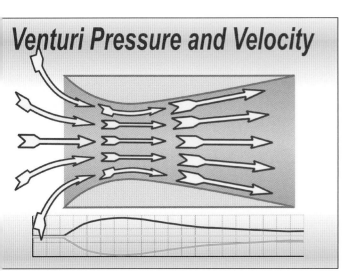

Venturi Pressure and Velocity

Fig. 7.2. Suction by the cylinder pulls air through the venturi. In so doing, it speeds up as it reaches the minor diameter (as depicted by the red curve on the graph). As this happens, the pressure drops (blue line). Tapping into the minor diameter of the venturi and connecting it to a fuel supply results in a simple carburetor.

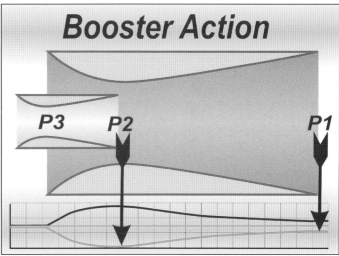

Booster Action

Fig. 7.3. The engine's suction at P1 dictates the air flowing through the main venturi. The much greater pressure drop occurring at the minor diameter (P2) of the main venturi dictates the air flowing through the booster. This brings about a much higher pressure drop and velocity at P3.

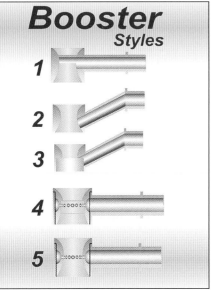

Booster Styles

Fig. 7.4. Booster 1 is commonly used on many street replacement Holleys. Booster 2 is often used in performance-oriented carbs. Booster 3 is a dog-leg booster as per 2 with a step machined into the underside. This is a popular hop-up move used by carb specialists to assist fuel atomization. Booster 4 is a stepped annular discharge design while 5 is a similar annular discharge style but without the step. Booster 4 and booster 5 are the high-gain types most often used in big-CFM carbs.

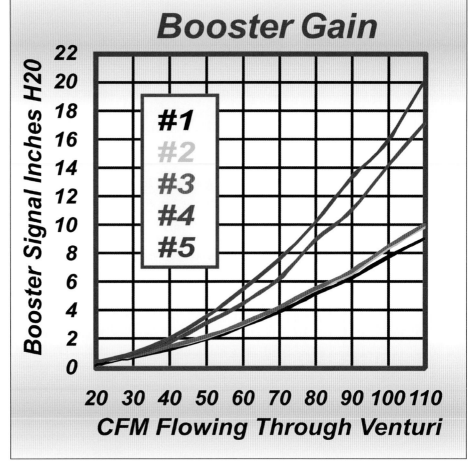

Booster Gain

Fig. 7.5. This graph shows the signal strength for each of the booster styles depicted in Figure 7.4. Note the big difference between the lowest and highest.

Boosters and Venturis for Economy

Want to build the ultimate fuel-economy/performance carb? You can either build it yourself (if you have the machining capability) or have a carb specialist build it for you. Here is the formula to work toward:

- It really should be a vacuum secondary carb.
- Select a main body that has venturis a little smaller than you think might be needed for the overall flow rating of the carb.
- Clean up the primaries and enlarge the secondaries to about 0.100 inch larger.

- Adapt the main body to a base plate that is consistent with the larger secondary venturi. For example, if you selected a body with 1.4 venturis and enlarged the secondary to about 1.5 as with an 850, use the big-butterfly 850 base plate.
- Install an annular discharge booster in the primary and a dog-leg booster (preferably a stepped one) in the secondary.
- As for the base plate, be sure to do a good airflow job on the butterflies and shafts because this not only helps overall airflow for maximum output but also improves booster signal.

low-speed drivability and torque. Also there is no universally "best" booster. It is always a case of selecting whatever is best for the job at hand.

When Holley seriously committed to racing in the 1960s, it became apparent that making bigger, high-flow carbs also meant increasing booster design research. Even to this day, much of that knowledge remains in the possession of only a few professionals within the industry. To many performance enthusiasts, booster science looks more like booster black art. But in this book, I hope to dissipate the fog of confusion. Chapter 2 introduced a brief description of booster function; this chapter goes into more detail on the booster's workings and interaction with the rest of the carb's functions.

Venturi Action

A booster's function hinges on the events that take place as air is drawn through a venturi. Take a look at Figure 7.2. The suction (partial vacuum) of the engine draws air through the venturi. As the air passes through the

venturi's minor diameter it speeds up. The red curve on the graph below the venturi illustration depicts the increased air speed. When this happens, the air pressure drops (blue line). As the air expands in the exit area of the venturi, it slows and a pressure recovery takes place. The greater the airflow through the venturi, the greater the pressure drop at the minor venturi.

On a running engine, the volume of air flowing through the venturi depends on the amount of suction, which is created by the pressure drop at its exit end (i.e., the intake manifold end). By installing a smaller (booster) venturi into the main venturi as shown in Figure 7.2 you get a certain effect. If the smaller venturi has its exit end precisely at the smallest diameter of the larger venturi, it experiences a pressure drop greater than that seen by the main venturi. This comes about because the main venturi is subjected to the suction produced by the engine while the greater depression that occurs at the main venturi's minor diameter dictates the booster venturi flow.

As a result the airflow through the booster (P3) is faster and the resultant pressure drop at its minor diameter is greater.

Because air is being sucked in not by the smaller pressure drop at P1, but by the much larger pressure drop at P2, the signal at the main venturi is amplified (or "boosted") at P3 by the booster venturi. Hence the name "booster."

The importance of the booster-amplified pressure drop is that it is the signal used by the carb's fuel system to not only meter the amount of fuel for a given amount of air, but is also a key factor in producing sufficient fuel atomization for effective combustion. If either metering accuracy or fuel atomization are off by too much, power output suffers.

Booster Gain

To achieve optimum top-end horsepower, use a carb with sufficient airflow to fully meet the engine's needs at peak RPM. This inevitably calls for a bigger carb than required i power at low and mid speed was the

Booster Hop Up

Except for converting a regular booster to a stepped booster, there is not much you can do to alter the basic design of a booster. You can improve the signal gain. If you take a close look at a Holley booster, you see that it has either a flat face top and bottom (about 0.025 inch wide) or a rough-cast, rounded edge. This is because the casting process typically used to make boosters cannot produce a sharp edge. Removing a little metal from the booster's inner form produces an increase in signal far beyond what you may expect from such a minor mod. It does so because the sharp edge causes more air to go through the booster rather than be deflected around the outer diameter. This mod also produces a couple of extra CFM per barrel so it is definitely a win-win move.

Another popular move is to convert the often-used dog-leg booster to a stepped-style design. Holley and most custom prep shops make this move. The step does little to increase the booster signal, but it does bring about better fuel shearing at the discharge point, thus bringing about better fuel atomization.

At this point, you may be wondering what performance you are giving up by having a less-than-optimal booster design and venturi sizing. That's a difficult question to answer. If you select the wrong carb size along with the wrong booster, output can be decreased by as much as 30 to 40 ft-lbs even on an average high-performance 500-hp small-block. My best advice here is to heed what I said about sizing, so you don't have an overly large main venturi and then go for a reasonably high gain booster. The most versatile booster for general, all-around, good results is the stepped dogleg.

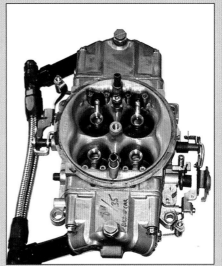

This $1,500 Holley for a NASCAR Cup Car is a very refined carburetor. Note the detail work to remove all casting imperfections around and into the main venturi. In addition the dog-leg boosters have had the legs streamlined and the booster's venturi edges sharpened.

Booster Mods

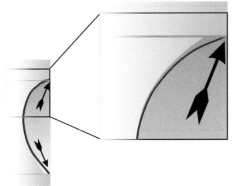

Arrows indicate booster edge sharpening

A little detailing can result in a 10- to 20-percent increase in booster signal. Do not remove material from the OD of the booster to produce the sharp edge as this encourages air to pass outside the booster where it does nothing to enhance the signal.

Stepped Booster

By machining a step in the underside of a dog-leg booster the fuel shearing action is increased. This provides for better atomization of the fuel.

main criterion. The bigger the carb, the more critical the booster design becomes if the carb is to operate over an acceptable RPM range.

Before Holley could introduce the Dominator series of carbs with their big barrel/venturi sizes, the company had to come up with booster designs that produced sufficiently high gain. In other words, the needed boosters had to take a relatively small signal as generated at the minor diameter of the main venturi and amplify it into a sufficiently strong signal for the purposes of metering and atomization.

Over the years Holley has broken much new ground in terms of booster design. In Figure 7.4 you see the characteristic form of the main variants. These are shown in

Fig. 7.6. Big-CFM carbs, such as this Dominator, are able to produce workable results over a wide RPM range mainly because of high-gain annular discharge boosters.

Fig. 7.7. A modified Holley 950 HP allowed quick booster changes to be made. The four different designs shown here were the most tested.

approximate order of gain. For instance, at a typical WOT flow and pressure drop, booster 1 amplifies the main venturi signal by about 1.8. However, booster 5 (with all the casting flash removed and a cleanup on the entry and exit) delivers an amplified signal nearly four times that of the main venturi. Figure 7.5 shows how each of these booster designs reacts when tested in the 1.5-inch-diameter venturi barrel of an 850 Holley carb.

Carb Sizing

If you need a carb that delivers good performance over a very wide RPM range, the bigger the carb is for a given engine size, the higher the booster gain needs to be. With a very high gain booster, you can expect a large-CFM carb to produce nearly flawless low-speed performance. If

such a booster is used, it is entirely practical to use a 1,000-cfm carb on an engine that typically required about 650 cfm. The advantage of the bigger carb is that it allows the engine to make more top-end power while the high-gain boosters still produce an adequate signal to meet the metering and atomization requirements for low speed.

So, for typical performance, there is almost no such thing as a carb that is too big; only one with an inadequate booster signal.

Variable CFM Design

Getting an adequate booster signal by utilizing a high-gain design is not the only way to get a 4-barrel engine to perform at the top and bottom ends of the spectrum. All too often, street rodders make the mistake of assuming if the racers use it they should too. In the real world

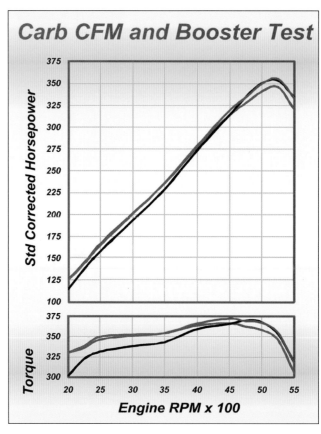

Fig. 7.8. This engine initially made 346 hp on a stock 650-cfm carb (blue lines). Note that low-speed output is more dependent on having sufficient booster signal than it is on outright carb CFM. Also note how well a stock 650 performed compared to a stock 850 (black lines). By installing a high-gain annular discharge booster in the 850 the best of adequate atomization from a high-gain booster and the added airflow was seen (red lines). This resulted in a peak torque increase of 6 ft-lbs and a peak power increase of 10 hp.

that usually means big-CFM carbs with mechanical secondaries.

Such an arrangement just doesn't make it at the low end, but how about a variable-CFM carb? That is small at low RPM and big at high RPM. It is readily available and commonly known as a vacuum secondary carb. Holley offers many smaller carbs, such as the 4150 and the like. But if you are into big-blocks just think what a useful piece a vacuum secondary Dominator would be!

To see by how much it is possible to "cheat," the commonly accepted "too-big carb" philosophy is shown in Figure 7.8. Here a basic stock cam/valvetrain Chevy small-block 350 equipped with pocket-ported production-line 186 head castings and dyno headers was tested with a single-plane race manifold. The carburetion for this test involved the use of a 650 carb and an 850 carb. Typically a conservatively spec'd engine, such as this, is equipped with no more than a 650-cfm carb.

From the graph in Figure 7.8 you can see how an 850, with first a stock booster and then high-gain boosters, stacks up against a stock 650. The first lesson to be learned is to not assume that bigger is better as the stock 650

Fig. 7.9. Boosters work in conjunction with the air-correction jets. The greater the gain, the bigger the air corrector needs to be; otherwise the mixture becomes too rich at the top end. The high-speed (main circuit) air correctors (top arrow) are the most affected. The idle-circuit air correctors (bottom arrow) are virtually unaffected while, on Dominator-style carbs, the intermediate circuits (middle arrow) may need some minor correction.

showed far better results than the stock 850.

Also, when the 850 was equipped with boosters that delivered about the same signal strength per CFM as the 650, a different pattern emerged. With the 850 the low-speed output was almost the same as the 650 but the top end was significantly better.

Atomization Requirements

From what we've learned so far, it seems that the more gain a booster has, the better a carb works. And that's true over a wide operating band. But if it's a race engine that you're optimizing for output over, say, 2,000 rpm, things are a little different, and additional booster gain is not desired because it is possible to have a booster that brings about a too finely atomized charge.

Droplet Size

The smaller the fuel droplets, the more readily they evaporate into a vapor. When a droplet becomes vaporized to a gas, it takes up much more room in the intake manifold and reduces the volumetric efficiency of the induction system. Although a charge of vaporized fuel and air displays about the best combustion characteristics, it doesn't produce the best power because there is less air in the cylinder with the vaporized fuel than with liquid fuel droplets of a suitable size. Although a charge with fully vaporized fuel delivers the best drivability and fuel efficiency, a certain optimum droplet size is required to make maximum power.

Booster Tweaks and Fuel Distribution

The fix for any fuel distribution problem within an intake manifold is usually regarded as a fix to be done on the manifold itself. However, modifications to the exit end of the booster can also be made to correct a fuel distribution problem if it is not too severe. A modified booster can also be used as part of a package to fix a more severe distribution problem.

If a V notch is cut in the bottom of the booster, more fuel exits at that point. If the booster notch is situated over the area that is running lean it puts more fuel into that area. This is the opposite approach to a manifold mod that commonly seeks to lean out a runner that is too rich by diverting fuel on the plenum floor to other cylinders. By combining booster mods, stagger jetting, and manifold mods the cylinder-to-cylinder fuel distribution can be made very even.

Booster Signal and Nitrous

Before Nitrous Oxide Systems (more commonly known as NOS) had its own dyno, I did quite a lot of testing for owner Mike Thermos on my dyno. Much of the testing was focused on overall output versus fuel droplet size. This factor, and not unexpectedly so, proved to be very critical. Since the nitrous exited the nitrous nozzle at about minus 128 degrees F, we concluded that little or no fuel actually vaporized in the intake manifold. So, in the absence of any vapor, initializing effective combustion was significantly more difficult.

We also knew that the smaller the fuel droplets were, the more likely they were to act as a vapor. Most of those tests were aimed at breaking down the fuel stream issuing from the fuel element of the nitrous system into finer droplets. This work paid off big time, as gains on typical street kits targeting the 125- to 150-hp range increased by as much as 40 hp.

Eventually NOS got its own dyno but I continued to look at fuel atomization in relation to output when nitrous oxide was used. Here is what I learned: The better the fuel is atomized at the booster, the better the overall results when a nitrous system is in operation. What this means is that an annular discharge booster that might have provided too much atomization comes into its own on a nitrous engine. When tested on a typical summer day, an engine with fuel fed by an annular discharge booster could be 10 hp less over a stepped dogleg booster, but 10 hp more when the nitrous is in operation.

Another factor I considered was carb sizing with nitrous systems in the 100- to 200-hp range. On several occasions I found that although an 850 carb (1.5-inch main venturi) made the best power without the nitrous, a 750 (1.4 main venturi) produced more overall output when the nitrous was on. Again this looks like a fuel atomization factor at work here. The 750, with its smaller ventures was doing a better job than the 850, so nitrous-augmented output increased.

By selecting a carb a little smaller than indicated for non-nitrous use and pairing it with a set of boosters that can atomize the fuel better than commonly needed, the nitrous engine made more overall power for the same amount of nitrous injected.

Along with this comes some side benefits that are more than welcome for the street performance enthusiast. When nitrous is not being used, a nitrous-oriented carb has the potential to deliver better low-speed output and better overall drivability.

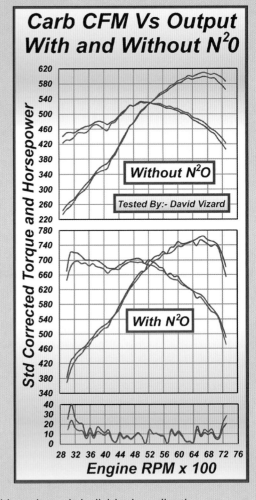

Carb CFM Vs Output With and Without N^2O

Std Corrected Torque and Horsepower — Engine RPM x 100

Without N^2O

Tested By:- David Vizard

With N^2O

Although each individual application can vary somewhat, the graph shows results that are generally in the middle of the road.

To get a better perspective on the gains it's best to consider the average torque and horsepower increase. With a 125-hp nitrous installation the average torque increased by a little more than 15 ft-lbs and the horsepower by a bit more than 10. All this came with much better low-speed torque when the nitrous was not in operation so going this route is not only good for performance at the track but also for street driving.

When big race cams were used, the situation was reversed. Certainly on small-blocks with cams of more than 300 to 305 degrees or so at lash, a slightly bigger carb, still with a high-gain booster, produced slightly better results when the nitrous was in operation.

Induction Temperature

It may seem to be an easy task to develop a booster that delivers the required droplet size and solve the problem. Unfortunately, high-performance engines are rarely that simple. In practice, many factors influence what happens to the fuel after it leaves the booster.

The most important of these is how well the fuel stays in suspension in the air and the temperature of the induction system. Ports with a high and uniform velocity and good wet flow characteristics are a good start, but unless you are in the cylinder head business, you don't have much influence over that factor other than to choose your cylinder head supplier wisely. You also don't have control of wet flow other than making a knowledgeable purchase.

However, as an engine builder, you *can* have a significant influence on the induction temperature. What arrives at the cylinder is an air/fuel mixture with a range of droplet sizes from very small to overly large. Fuel separation also leads to a certain amount of fuel-forming rivulets and that is really bad for the engine's output.

Fuel entering the cylinder in rivulets (and the larger droplets) produce a poor charge quality. This charge does not ignite very easily and does not become part of the combustion process until the ignitable fuel has created enough heat to vaporize the wet fuel. Indeed, some of the fuel fails to burn at all.

In practice, the presence of liquid fuel means that a certain proportion of the air/fuel mixture entering the cylinder needs to be in an easily ignitable vapor form. Without some vapor, the ignitability and subsequent burn is not very effective. In other words, because finer droplets evaporate easier, the cooler the intake charge becomes, the more finely atomized the fuel delivery needs to be. (If you are building a nitrous engine, see sidebar "Booster Signal and Nitrous" on page 74).

Where power is the sole concern, the basic rule is to have low-gain boosters for heated intake manifolds and high-gain boosters for cool manifolds. If you are experimenting with thermal-barrier induction systems and/or artificially cooled intakes, be aware that without reevaluating the booster design you may not see the gains in output you hoped for.

What's It Worth?

David Braswell and I ran some tests in the 1970s, which illustrate just how much an engine can gain or lose by failing to get the right booster for the job. For this test David built two carbs, one with high-gain boosters and one with low-gain boosters. Each was run on an engine that was

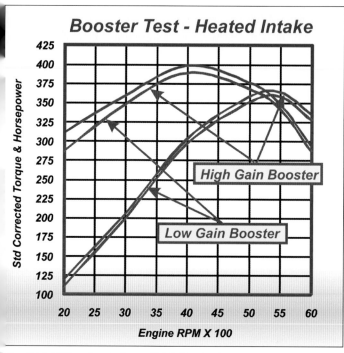

Fig. 7.10. With a heated manifold, fine fuel droplets from a more active booster/air corrector system causes a larger portion of the fuel to vaporize. This reduces volumetric efficiency and output.

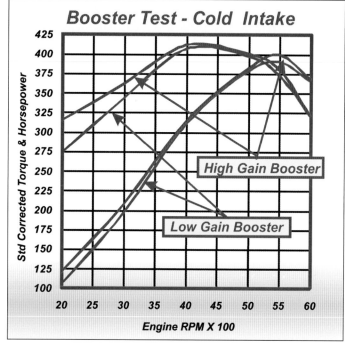

Fig. 7.11. When used with a cool-running, single-plane race manifold, the high-gain boosters not only produced about 9 hp more at peak but also an impressive 42 ft-lbs increase at 2,000 rpm.

first equipped with a hot manifold, then with a cold manifold.

The first was an aftermarket manifold that had crossover heat applied. The second was a single-plane race manifold with no crossover heat and was air cooled. Figure 7.10 shows a comparison between low-gain boosters delivering relatively large droplets and high-gain ones delivering considerably finer fuel atomization. With low-gain boosters delivering larger droplets, the heat applied to the manifold plenum vaporizes a nearly optimal percentage of the fuel. Tests with the heated manifold resulted in the low-gain boosters outperforming the high-gain boosters. This was because the high-gain booster's smaller droplets resulted in too much vaporization.

Figure 7.11 shows the same two booster styles, but this time the engine is equipped with a cool-running, single-plane race manifold. Bearing in mind that this is the same engine as in Figure 7.10 you see that the carb/booster combination that worked best on the heated intake manifold did not work so well on the significantly cooler race manifold. Note how the low-gain booster-equipped carb dropped a huge amount of low-

end torque. In many instances, this is accepted as a shortcoming of the race manifold's design. After all these are back-to-back tests of the hot manifold low-gain booster.

In reality, many race intakes, such as the Holley/Weiand Strip Dominator, have much more low-speed potential than they are often credited with. The low-speed potential is just a case of having the appropriate degree of fuel atomization. The golden rule here is: Reduce temperature, increase atomization. If you fail to do that, your cool-intake system can't meet its full potential. Reduce that intake temperature enough with an indifferent booster design and you may find your efforts are rewarded with reduced power rather than the increase you expected.

Annular Discharge Booster Myth

I have heard it said that annular boosters are not good for a high-performance engine because they block the main venturi, but this is not so. They only appear to block the main venturi because of their bulk when viewed from above. In reality, if it is sharp, the end of the booster has no

Fig. 7.12. Although the stepped dog-leg booster (arrow) has only marginally more gain than the regular dog-leg booster, the step brings about better fuel atomization. This style of booster is about the most versatile currently in use and is a good choice if fuel atomization appears to be inadequate.

area at its installed height in the main venturi. In other words, the booster's knife edge takes zero area away from the minor diameter of the carb's main venturi. The test for this is on the flow bench. A well-prepped annular discharge booster costs little, if anything significant, in the way of airflow.

The moral here? Don't dismiss the annular discharge booster as a non-entity for your performance Holley. There are plenty of real-world performance situations where the annular discharge booster is the best choice.

Booster Buffeting

A carb's performance is greatly related to booster capability. There is an irony here, however; almost all booster testing is done on a flow bench while all driving is done in a car. When a carb is used for an application that puts it in a high-speed airstream, such as seen on so many drag race cars, the highly turbulent flow over the carb greatly affects the booster's performance. This turbulent flow leads to what I call "booster buffeting."

Tests with sensitive electronic pressure measuring gear on a 350-ci 9.5-second drag race car were revealing. As speed built, the booster signal fluctuated at a variable frequency, but on average about 6 to 10 cycles per second with amplitude spikes of as much as 60 percent of the steady-state booster signal were seen on the flow bench.

Also as speed increased, the average booster signal dropped, thus leaning out the mixture to the detriment of the vehicle's performance. The fix resulted in more speed and is simple: install a large K&N filter.

IDLE AND TRANSITION CALIBRATION

At the risk of sounding repetitive, let me say once again, that if you bought an application-specific carb, you probably are only going to need to do minimal adjustments to mixture calibration. You are only likely to run into a problem with the idle and transition calibrations if the carb you have is way off spec for the application.

As an example, I had a 10.5:1 350-ci race engine that was a stout runner but the class it was running in changed engine rules. I felt this engine would make a great street engine. The 830-cfm carb (modified 750) was a heavily reworked piece and was top-notch for the race application. This engine's transformation to a street engine took little more than a change of cam from a big race grind to a moderate street grind. The difference was an idle vacuum of about 4 to 5 inches for the race cam and 11 to 12 inches for the street cam.

Among other things, the successful conversion involved resizing the idle jet and replacing butterflies, which had excessively large idle-bypass holes in them. In addition, smaller accelerator pump squirters and a pump cam were installed; a mechanical secondary linkage that delayed secondary opening as long as possible was used. The result was about 490 ft-lbs of torque and horsepower just shy of 515.

This chapter provides what you need to know to make good on the idle and transition circuit to allow almost any carb to work for your application or simply to fine tune one that is just short of perfect.

Idle Mixture Calibration

At this point, you should have a running engine (see section "Idle Mixture" on page 29 in Chapter 3). With the engine at operating temperature, you can begin.

Assuming that an oxygen sensor is not part of the tune-up equipment everything needs to be done

Fig. 8.1. These are the idle mixture adjustment screws (yellow circles). Although they have the biggest influence on final setting of the idle mixture, they are by no means the only factor.

visually by reading the tailpipe smoke or a vacuum gauge, or simply by listening. Your first move is to attach a good vacuum gauge to a manifold vacuum source (that is, one originating from beneath the throttle butterflies).

Check the fuel levels in the fuel bowls and adjust as necessary (see Chapter 12 for details).

If the original settings are still in place, the idle mixture screws should be two turns out from the seated position. If the idle jetting is about

right this setting should be deliver ing a mixture that tends toward th rich side (see Figure 2.21 on pag 21). If you are serious about tunin the idle and transition circuits fo best results, especially maximun fuel efficiency usage, you start t

Fig. 8.2. Virtually all cast base-plate carbs have a vacuum port (arrows) connected to the underside area of the butterfly to read manifold vacuum. Billet base plates most often do not, so you need to drill the intake manifold and install a fitting. Note the size of the vacuum gauge used here. This is about the minimum size you should use.

Fig. 8.3. Idle feed restriction (idle jets) can be located in different positions for different metering blocks. On the left (red arrow) is the fixed type most commonly seen in regular metering blocks. On the right (yellow arrow) is the replaceable style for the Ultra range of Holley carbs.

Fig. 8.4. Replaceable idle air bleeds (yellow arrows) are used in the top-of-the-line street and race Holley carbs, making a change easy. If you have a regular carb, the air bleeds are press-in (red arrows) items, so changing them is limited to drill ing larger or pulling them out and installing smaller ones.

Manifold Vacuum

Why is a vacuum gauge such a good idle setup tool? The answer is that it's a prime indicator of the amount of air needed to idle the engine. If the mixture is about right, the fuel is burned in a more effective manner and that means less air consumption. Less air consumption is the result of the throttle plates being closed that much farther and this means that the manifold vacuum is higher.

Also tied in with this is the fact that the best idle manifold vacuum also coincides with close to the best fuel efficiency. It varies from engine to engine, depending on the compatibility of the parts specifications that it was built from. Generally the best idle vacuum happens at an air/fuel ratio of 13.0 to 14.5:1.

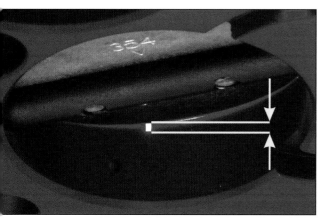

Fig. 8.5. Here the base plate is backlit to show how much slot the butterfly should uncover at idle. The maximum is 0.04 to 0.06 inch, with closer to the lower limit being preferable.

appreciate a carb with replaceable air bleeds in the carb's main body.

Here are the steps for calibrating the idle mixture:

Progressively turn the idle-mixture screws in. Start with a quarter turn on each one and readjust the idle speed to an appropriate RPM. A big-cam engine needs a higher idle speed, which is usually about 1,000 rpm; a regular street cam needs about 600 rpm.

Here, some idle-speed experimentation is worthwhile. Try adjusting the RPM to the point the engine is just short of stalling. When you have established this RPM, set the idle speed to about 100 rpm higher. Continue progressively adjusting the

mixture screws in until you achieve the lowest manifold vacuum short of a misfire. As the mixture nears optimal, you may need to readjust the idle speed again, as something a little rich of a misfire also allows a lower, stable idle RPM.

If the idle mixture screws make little difference to the idle from the full-in to the full-out position, it's a fair bet that the butterflies are too far into the transition slot. If the idle jetting is okay, the idle mixture screws should ideally be about one turn out, although 1/2 to 1½ turns is acceptable.

Next, check the position of the idle speed adjustment screws. As per

Fig. 8.6. Holley's Ultra models have an adjustable idle air bypass screw (yellow arrow). Air for the bypass goes through the holes indicated by the blue arrows.

Chapter 4 you started with these at two turns into opening the butterflies of the primary (or primary and secondary). If a satisfactory idle speed is achieved with the idle speed screws less than two turns in you are looking good.

If it takes more than two turns you may be on the verge of, or even into, using up too much of the transition slot. If this is the case the engine probably exhibits a stumble just prior

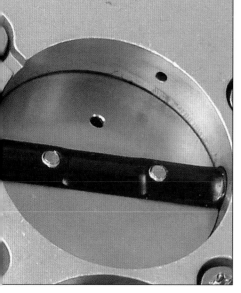

Fig. 8.7. To supply the required amount of idle air without using up all the transition slot, it may be necessary to drill holes into the butterflies.

Fig. 8.8. The primary idle speed adjustment screw is common to virtually all carb models.

Four-Corner Idle

If your engine has a respectably big cam (usually 280 degrees or more duration at lash), a four-corner idle carb is what your engine needs. Do not think you can buy a cheaper carb with primary-only idle circuits and expect to upgrade to a four-corner idle just by adding an idle circuit metering block. A four-corner idle system typically has differences not only in the metering block but also in the throttle plate and the carb body itself.

The best thing to do is get it right the first time or you'll have to pay a carb specialist to modify the body and supply the appropriate metering block. Going that route costs you a lot more than buying the right carb in the first place. If you have a pristine carb you might be able to have it modified by a carb specialist but be aware the cost for doing so varies greatly among shops.

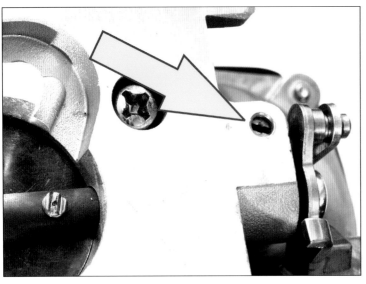

Fig. 8.9. The secondary idle speed adjustment (arrow) is done from the underside of the regular cast base-plate models.

to coming on to the booster-driven main jet circuit.

You can perform a cursory check to determine the existence of two potential issues: idle jetting size and the transition slot usage.

Idle Jetting Size

One way to check on jet size is to use the 3,000-rpm test. You slowly open the throttle so the accelerator pump is not brought into action. This establishes whether the engine runs cleanly to 3,000 rpm without a hesitation or misfire. If it does, the setup is at least close to the requirement. If the engine stumbles and the

mixture screws are more than 1½ turns out, it is a sign that the mixture is going lean. If this is the case, the idle jet needs to be larger or the air corrector smaller.

A good test is to stick a wooden toothpick into one of the idle air corrector jets to see if it helps with the 3,000-rpm test. Although rarely the case, be aware that this may richen the circuit too much and the engine now stumbles because it is too rich.

Because the air corrector jet is more accessible and quick to change, I usually rejet here rather than at the idle jet. With either jet, resizing

should be done at about two thou sandths at a time. If the carb is no equipped with replaceable jets, inser a fine piece of fuse wire (with a ben in it so it does not go all the way int the idle well) to block off some of th air going into the air corrector jet.

If you have a fixed-idle jet, resiz ing is best done with a pin chuck an a jet drill set.

Transition Slot Usage

Before you attempt any idle je resizing, be sure to look into the pos sible alternate issue that can lea to an off-idle stumble. It could b that too much of the transition slo is used up to get an acceptable idl although this problem tends to shov up more often when putting th engine under a load commensurat with a low-speed cruise.

If too much of the slot is uncov ered at the idle position there i insufficient slot length to effectivel carry through from the transition t the main circuits. About 0.060 incl from the carb's underside should b regarded as an absolute limit.

Excess transition slot usag also causes the idle mixture screv adjustments to be insensitive. Thi is only possible if the cam is bigge than a typical stock one. So, because of the reduced vacuum, you need to increase the flow area available through the carb while at idle. Drilling a small hole in the primary butterflies takes care of it.

Start with a 1/16-inch hole and work your way to about 1/8 inch. If the problem has improved but not completely cured, start drilling the secondary butterflies. Be aware that only a big-cammed all-out race engine requires as many as four 1/8-inch holes.

If the carb has an adjustable idle air bypass located under the air filter stud, this hole drilling exercise is redundant. If too much transition slot is uncovered, open the idle air bypass more so the throttle butterflies can be more nearly closed.

Oxygen Sensors

If you have oxygen sensor mixture measurement, the idle calibration is a whole lot easier. To do the idle/transition calibration, you go through the same process as described above, but you have the benefit of knowing what the air/fuel ratio is at any given moment.

The question most often asked here is, What ratio should be used for idle? Which ratio gives the best results tends to vary from one engine to another. You should tune for the leanest air/fuel ratio that provides the desired idle results. For the most part, you find that high-compression short-cammed engines with efficient exhaust systems run the leanest while still producing good idle characteristics. Engines with big cams tend to want more fuel so you should run a richer mixture for a good idle. Most engines fall into the spectrum of 13.0 to 14.0:1 although an engine target-

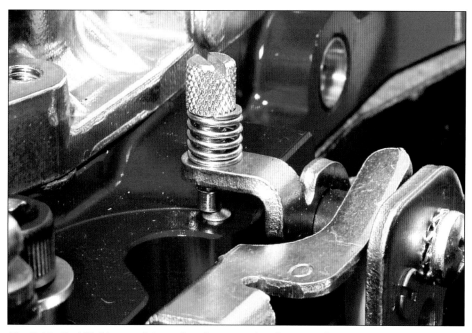

Fig. 8.10. On billet base-plate carbs, the secondary has an adjustment screw on the top as well as underneath.

ing economy may well, in my experience, be able to run as lean as 15:1.

Road Test

Now is time to put your tuning skills to the test. You may not want to go to the extremes detailed in Chapter 5 in an effort to get maximum fuel economy. But you should verify that your calibrations are doing a respectable job.

Take the vehicle onto a flat road and test the calibrations from idle through transition to the main jet system and make sure the carb is functioning as required. To do so, very slowly depress the throttle so as to avoid any pump jet action. The engine should drive smoothly throughout the speed range from zero to 60 or 70 mph without hesitation. Note the oxygen sensor readings as the throttle opens and speed builds. The mixture should not be any richer than 14:1 but if everything is good in terms of the engine

spec and condition, you should see air/fuel ratios in the 15 to 16:1 range.

The tests should be conducted in high gear and up to about 45 mph. Anything over 17:1 produces a lean miss; that is, unless the engine is specifically built with the intent to fire super-lean ratios. If the engine develops a lean miss, your first move is to reduce the size of the idle air corrector by two or three numbers. If that does not fix the drivability issue, increase the idle jets by a number or two until it is resolved.

If the engine is for a race-only machine, maximizing fuel economy is not an issue. All you need to do is make sure that the idle quality is acceptable and that the low-speed drivability is all it can be.

A point worth mentioning is that if the idle mixture and speed are optimal, the engine has less of a tendency to stall if the clutch is released at too low a speed. A good idle setup makes it much easier to move around the paddock at a race.

FULL-POWER CIRCUIT CALIBRATION

Strange as it may seem, the main jet on a Holley carb is not what you should be using to calibrate the WOT mixture delivered to the engine. That job is the function of the power valve and the PVRC.

The main jet, however, is the most often changed jet; the one changed in an effort to optimize the mixture for maximum power. While a main jet change for a race-only vehicle may be suitable, it isn't necessarily the case for a true street vehicle because in addition to power, both emissions and mileage are concerns. It is time to examine in detail the calibration of the cruise and WOT power mixture.

Main Jet

If you are setting up a Holley-carbureted street-performance vehicle, optimizing the cruise mixture is a major priority.

When calibrating for cruise, only the primary barrels are opening so all cruise jetting is on that end of the carb. A word of caution: Do not shortchange your efforts to optimize cruise calibrations. They directly affect drivability, mileage, and emissions. As a racer of more than 50 years, I appreciate that the real fun is going fast. But you should not have a rough-running fuel-hungry smog-spewing drive when you are not driving flat out.

Remember, a performance street machine does not run flat out all the time, so if your vehicle is smoking, the fun can wear really thin

and do so quickly. If the mixture is too rich during cruise, the engine also experiences much greater bore wear than normal, and this reduces power. Spend the time to get things right here, and you not only reap the obvious fuel saving benefits but also make fine tuning at the track both less fussy and more productive.

Let me be clear about the jets I'm talking about when optimizing the cruise and WOT settings. We are dealing with the main jets, the high-speed air bleeds (air correctors), the PVRC jets, and possibly the emulsion well jets/bleeds.

By now you should be familiar with the main jet; its function and its location. Essentially, the main jet should start to pull into operation when the edges of the butterflies are at, or nearing the end of, the transition slot. If the carb's main venturi is the result of the correct carb selection, the primary barrel's boosters should just start to dribble fuel

Fig. 9.1. A lot of care and attention has gone into the building of this Chevy 505-ci big-block. Now is the time to put an equal amount of care and attention into the calibration of the main jet/power valve circuits, so this monster delivers all the horses it is capable of.

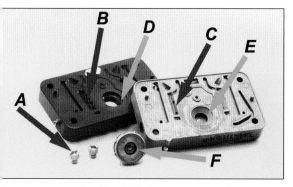

Fig. 9.2. Other than high-speed bleeds, which are in the carb's main body, here are the components for calibrating the cruise and WOT mixture. Arrow A points to the main jets, which screw into the fuel bowl side of the metering block (not shown). B indicates the replaceable emulsion well jets in a race metering block. C (compare it to B) shows the emulsion calibration on a regular metering block. Note that there are only two holes here. D indicates the replaceable PVRC jetting. E shows a secondary metering block with no power valve usage. F is the power valve that locates in position D.

which has been drawn from the fuel bowl via the main jet.

Atomization of the fuel at this point is poor, but there is one saving grace. As the fuel droplets hit the butterfly, they run down the slope of the butterfly and get sheared off by the typically high-speed air passing around the edge of the butterfly and into the manifold.

When the butterflies are about 1/4 inch open and viewed from a point directly above the carb, the booster is reasonably well into its operational mode and is delivering most of the engine's fuel requirement. But, in most cases, this amount of throttle opening is still such that an appreciable amount of manifold vacuum is seen. In other words the

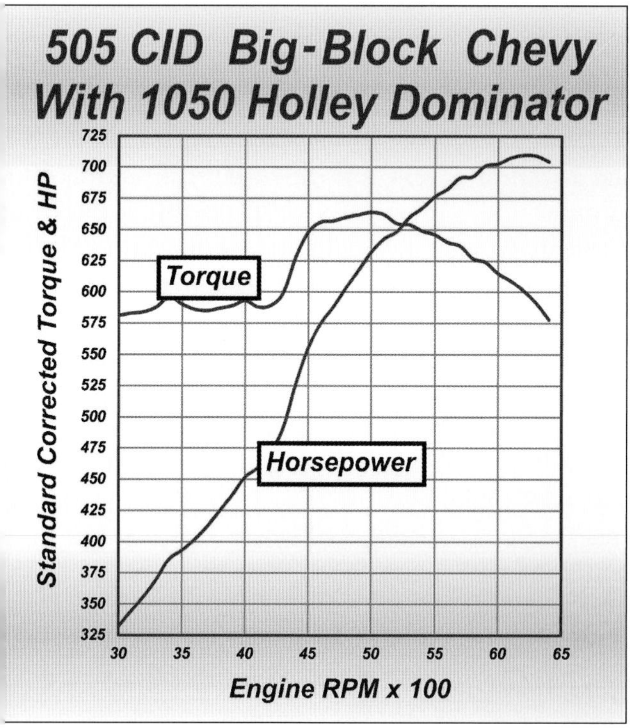

505 CID Big-Block Chevy With 1050 Holley Dominator

(Graph: Standard Corrected Torque & HP vs. Engine RPM x 100, with Torque and Horsepower curves)

Fig. 9.3. This engine produces 710 hp and 665 ft-lbs with drivability right off a 700-rpm idle, and it runs on service-station pump fuel. To get these results, the 1050 Dominator calibrations were given a great deal of attention at WOT and at part throttle/idle. I went down three sizes of main jet and up two sizes of idle circuit air corrector (as it came from Holley). This fine tuning resulted in the 700-hp mark being surpassed.

Fig. 9.5. Until the main jets come into play, the engine relies on the transition slot for calibration. Here, the base plate has been removed from the carb body to better show the butterfly position for the slot's best operation. The amount of slot remaining above the butterfly is shown by the red arrow. The amount of slot as viewed from the underside is shown by the yellow arrow. The slot is open about 1½ turns of the idle speed adjusting screw.

Fig. 9.4. In about 80 percent of cases, a carb calibrated by Holley needs only minor main jet recalibration. To accommodate this rejetting, just purchase jets up to four sizes above and below what is originally installed.

engine is still far from being called upon to deliver its full power.

At this amount of throttle opening, the vehicle would almost certainly be running at mid- to high-speed cruise, which is typically 45 to 75 or 80 mph. The amount of manifold vacuum should not activate the power valve, which brings in the additional fuel that the power valve restriction channel (jet) delivers if the throttle was moved to or near WOT. With the engine running reasonably well, note that manifold vacuum is at about 70-mph cruise. The vacuum switching point of the power valve selected must be at least 2 inches less than the cruise vacuum or the idle vacuum. For a high-performance street machine, that may call for the use of a 4½-inch switching power valve.

Cruise Calibrations

Under typical cruise conditions, you should be targeting calibrations for low emissions and good mileage. If you took my earlier advice, you have at least equipped your vehicle with a good oxygen mixture analyzer. Also (and I consider this a must), you should have a vacuum gauge installed on the manifold to read intake mani-

Fig. 9.6. The fuel is drawn from the bottom of the fuel bowl to a level just above the fuel level in the bowl. The passage goes back down to the idle screw. Somewhere near the top of the passage is a small jet. This is the idle feed restriction (IFR), or idle jet. The idle jet's up-and-down feed path prevents fuel from siphoning off into the engine from the fuel bowl through the idle circuit. The idle jet can be anywhere in this passage.

In the top metering block, the idle jet is at the bottom of the main jet well (red arrow). In the lower plate, it is at the top of the down leg passage (yellow arrow) to the idle mixture adjustment screw. Optimizing the size of this jet is the first step in achieving good cruise fuel economy.

fold vacuum. Remember, it must be *manifold* vacuum not *ported* vacuum.

Once again, you need to know the intake manifold vacuum at idle. To do cruise calibration, the power valve must be closed. Therefore, under both idle and cruise conditions, the vacuum indicated on the vacuum gauge must be higher than the switching vacuum stamped on the power valve. In other words, at idle or cruise no additional fuel is fed via the PVRC to the engine.

When, and only when, you are sure this situation has been met and

no additional fuel is being fed, it's time to size the main jet to give the best mileage while still maintaining drivability. Also do not forget that cruise is almost always done only on the primary barrels. This means that the main jets and, to a slightly lesser extent, the high-speed air bleeds are your concern here.

To accurately size the primary main jets, check the current air/fuel ratio. In the absence of an oxygen mixture analyzer, you need to do a plug check. If your intent is to do

Fig. 9.7. The 1050 Dominator on this low-buck street Chevy big-block 482 was ordered from Holley based on the engine spec. It required minimal jetting to make 650 hp and 636 ft-lbs.

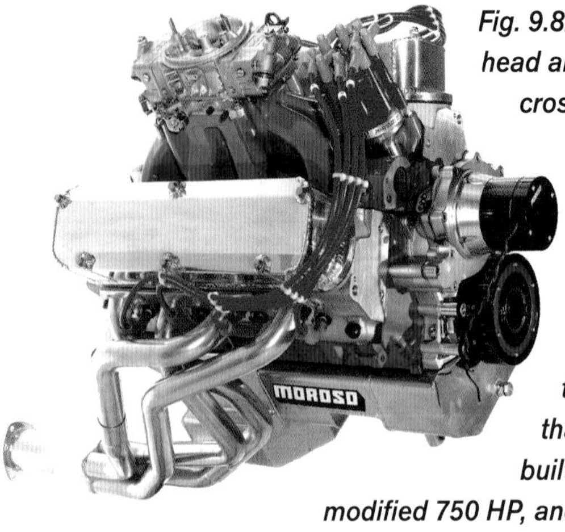

Fig. 9.8. Carefully choose a head and manifold that have cross-sectional areas to deliver the best port velocity over the RPM range applicable. Ideal cross-sectional areas pay dividends, especially when used together with a carb that is sized just right. I built this 347 using a mildly modified 750 HP, and it flowed about 815 cfm but still with near stock size main venturis. On pump fuel, this 347 made 472 ft-lbs and 562 hp. Idle was a smooth 750 rpm.

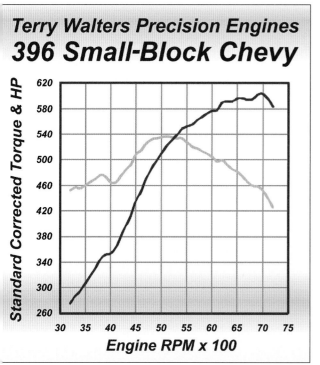

Terry Walters Precision Engines
396 Small-Block Chevy

Fig. 9.9. A street stroker rebuild of a Chevy small-block 350 can produce amazing performance. This is a prime example of a budget-oriented engine built for real street performance. Other than a couple of size changes in the main jets and main circuit air correctors, the 950 Holley was right out of the box. The result was 604 hp and 539 ft-lbs of torque. And all that came with great street drivability.

he job properly, you won't be too far into a plug reading session before you realize that getting a good oxygen mixture analyzer is one heck of a good idea. After all, correctly reading a plug is an art and a science.

But if you choose to read the plugs, here are some tips. Although driving 5 miles along a flat piece of highway colors the plugs somewhat, a 20-mile drive is much better. Read the plugs to see if the mixture needs to go leaner. If it is already lean and the drivability is acceptable, you may want to experiment with an even leaner jet calibration. The best mileage is most likely to happen just shy of any perceptible drivability degradation.

If the plugs indicate that the mixture is rich, lean out the mixture by reducing the main jet until it is as lean as possible, short of producing a drivability issue.

It takes time to drive a while, stop, pull plugs, read them, and jet as required. But if you took my earlier advice, you are using an oxygen mix-

ture analyzer to determine the mixture ratio under these cruise conditions.

In most cases, a good starting ratio is 15:1, as almost every engine runs just fine at that ratio during cruise. If the ratio is richer than 15:1 when making an initial run to test the cruise mixture, take steps to lean it out to about 15:1 by reducing the main jet size. Once you consistently see a 15:1 ratio under cruise conditions, use it as a baseline setting to see if leaner mixtures can be successfully used short of drivability issues.

Keep in mind that almost any Holley-equipped V-8 with a good ignition system can run a 16:1 air/fuel ratio at cruise. If the mixture ratio changes from one cruise speed to a higher speed, you should consider changing the slope by changing air bleeds (see Chapter 2).

The air bleed affects the mixture as the engine RPM increases so the mixture slope becomes progressively richer or leaner due to the air corrector changes. At low speed, when the

transition slot is the primary source of fuel and air, it is the idle air bleeds that need attention. At higher speeds, when the booster has pulled over, the high-speed air bleeds require resizing.

If the mixture is richer at the higher speed than at the lower speed, you need to increase the size of the air bleed. On the other hand, if a leaner mixture is seen at higher speeds, you need to reduce the size of the air bleed. At WOT, the air bleeds tend to be more influential on the mixture for a given size change than the main jets. However, at part-throttle openings, their influence is markedly reduced.

Regardless of the specific situation, make your jetting changes a couple of thousandths at a time. Also, do not lose sight of the fact that what you do here affects any subsequent WOT mixture settings.

Track-Only Settings

We have looked at the cruise calibration and its importance for a vehicle that's primarily driven on the street. But what about cruise calibrations for a race engine? My thoughts are that it is just as important, as the very essence of a race engine is the pursuit of optimal results.

For a circle track application, fuel consumption can be a factor in winning. For a drag racer, having an engine that runs strong at part throttle is an indicator that you have a desire to do things right. I always spend the time on both idle and part-throttle calibrations to get the very best results.

Max-Power Calibrations

Once the cruise mixture has been set, it's time to find the best output calibrations. Again, an oxygen mixture analyzer is the route to quick settings. But here you change the size of the PVRC (not the main jet) to achieve the mixture ratios needed. This is where replaceable PVRC jets are useful.

Fig. 9.10. Be sure to use a power valve that switches at a lower vacuum than the idle or cruise vacuum. A 6.5 (as shown here) is typical for a performance street engine. If it is a really hot street/strip unit, a 4.5 is more appropriate.

Fig. 9.11. Although contrary to what you may have been told about calibrating for max output, you should change the PVRC jet to optimize performance. If the carb does not have a replaceable jet metering block, resize the current PVRC holes. Once close, fine tune using the main jets. This is okay for a race-only engine, but if the mixture had previously been optimized for mileage, any subsequent main jet changes affect the cruise mixture.

If you have a set of metering blocks with fixed PVRC jets, it is a case of replacing the metering blocks or using drills to progressively enlarge the PVRC jets. Without an oxygen sensor to measure the WOT mixture you can be in danger of opening the PVRC jets too far. If that happens you have to install replaceable PVRC jets.

A factor to note here is that most carbs have a power valve installed in the primary metering blocks only. In such cases, you need to calibrate the WOT mixture of the primary barrels by changing the PVRC jets and by changing the main jets in the secondary metering blocks.

At this juncture, we are assuming the mixture curve is actually a straight line. By that I mean it is the same at the bottom of the RPM range as it is at the top and every point in between. In practice, that is rarely the case, which means you have to change the slope (and possibly the shape) of the curve. As with the cruise calibration, changing the size of the main circuit high-speed bleed or air corrector jet changes the slope, so if the mixture is leaner at the top end than at the lower end, reducing the size of the air bleed richens the mixture.

To lean the top end compared to the bottom end, increase the size of the air bleed. Do not be surprised to find that the cruise-optimized high-speed bleeds are not exactly what is needed for WOT. If that is the case, a fix must be done later, so for now let us assume that the slope of the mixture curve is good.

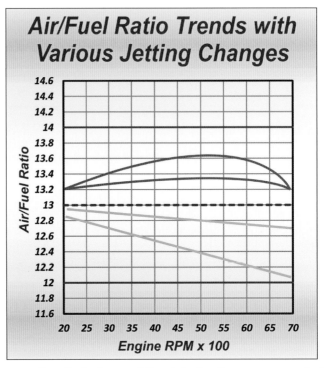

Air/Fuel Ratio Trends with Various Jetting Changes

Fig. 9.12. Here you see changes made to various jets. The blue lines represent the main jet. If the mixture is too rich, reduce the size of the main or PVRC jet. This moves the mixture curve from the lower blue line toward the upper blue line. The curve/slope remains more or less constant.

Next, let us assume that the mixture gets richer as RPM increases, represented by the lower green line. Increasing the size of the high-speed bleed (or air corrector) leans out the top end more than the bottom end thus bringing the curve nearer to the 13:1 horizontal line.

Assuming that the mixture follows the curve represented by the top purple line, trimming the hole pattern of the emulsion tube/well can fix things. Here, the mixture is leanest in the higher mid range. To fix this, reduce the size of the holes in the lower mid part of the length of the emulsion tube/well. (For a review of how the emulsion calibration works, check out Figure 2.9 on page 16.)

One thing often overlooked is that because a race vehicle only uses the top 20 to 40 percent of the engine's RPM range, the air-bleed changes affect the lower part of the used RPM range as well. For example, let us assume that a typical drag race engine's RPM range is from 4,500 to 7,500 rpm. Increasing the size of the high-speed air bleeds leans out the mixture at 4,500 rpm but does so to a greater extent at 7,500 rpm.

What this means is that when an air bleed change is made to alter the fuel curve slope, an accompanying PVRC/main jet change may also be needed. To make the proper calibrations in this situation often requires a great deal of experience. Let me repeat: Without an oxygen system you are hard pressed to discern these small but vital factors.

Target Air/Fuel Ratios

According to my test data and experience, your air/fuel target is about 13.2:1. However, the engine may run at its best with a different ratio, which is dependent on the mixture quality, distribution, and possible unwanted wet-flow issues. For this first round of tests, 13.2:1 is our goal and we adopt it as a base-line. Once achieved, it is the trap speed (not ET) that determines what the jetting and, consequently, the mixture ratio need to be.

So let us assume that the mixture is at about the 13.2:1 mark. Remember, you should have achieved this reading by increasing or decreasing the main jet in the secondary and the PVRC jet in the primary. You need to keep reading the oxygen mixture gauge until you take an average of the readings to arrive at 13.2:1, which requires some interpretation and subjectivity.

Once the required reading is achieved, you can use trap speed as a jetting reference. It is now a question

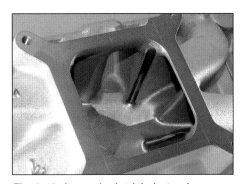

Fig. 9.13. It may look trick, but unless you know otherwise from dyno testing, the floor of this intake manifold should be as rough as the cast finish you see on the outside. When reading the plugs excess wet flow can hide the true mixture.

Fig. 9.14. In 2008, I sat in on the testing of this 500-ci ProStock engine with Dick Maskin of Dart Machine. The task for the day was to see if there was any additional power to be had from some fine tuning of an already finely tuned carburetion system. We started with an output at the low 1,400-hp mark. By the end of the day (some 50 pulls later) an additional 15 hp had been found. It is this attention to detail that wins races.

of increasing or decreasing jet and air bleed size as dictated by the trap speed. Also check the plugs for fuel distribution and stagger jet.

As for the mixture ratio that produces the highest speed for your

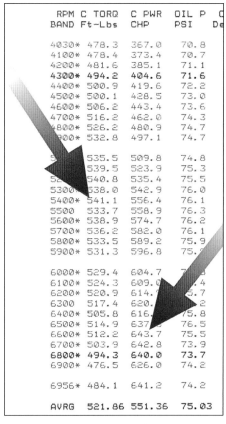

RPM BAND	C TORQ Ft-Lbs	C PWR CHP	OIL P PSI
4030*	478.3	367.0	70.8
4100*	478.4	373.4	70.7
4200*	481.6	385.1	71.1
4300*	494.2	404.6	71.6
4400*	500.9	419.6	72.2
4500*	500.1	428.5	73.0
4600*	506.2	443.4	73.6
4700*	516.2	462.0	74.3
4800*	526.2	480.9	74.7
4900*	532.8	497.1	74.7
5	535.5	509.8	74.8
	539.5	523.9	75.3
52	540.8	535.4	75.5
5300	538.0	542.9	76.0
5400*	541.1	556.4	76.1
5500	533.7	558.9	76.3
5600*	538.9	574.7	76.2
5700*	536.2	582.0	76.1
5800*	533.5	589.2	75.9
5900*	531.3	596.8	75.
6000*	529.4	604.7	7
6100*	524.3	609.0	.4
6200*	520.9	614.	.7
6300	517.4	620.	2
6400*	505.8	616.	75.8
6500*	514.9	637.	76.5
6600*	512.2	643.7	75.5
6700*	503.9	642.8	73.9
6800*	494.3	640.0	73.7
6900*	476.5	626.0	74.2
6956*	484.1	641.2	74.2
AVRG	521.86	551.36	75.03

Fig. 9.15. After calibrating Terry Walter's dyno, we tested my budget-build Chevy 383 race engine with $7,200 in new parts and a stock remachined block. The oxygen readings ranged from 13.1 to 13.3 for best power.

When tested on other dynos, this 12.5:1 engine returned readings as high as 660 hp and 549 ft-lbs. However I believe our dyno calibrations were accurate. This engine employed an out-of-the-box Holley 950 Ultra carb. The readings shown here were produced with only a two-size main jet and air corrector change all around. This engine was installed in a 2-speed Powerglide car that weighed 3,050 pounds and went mid-9s at just under 140 mph.

vehicle, just remember that the more effectively everything works, the nearer to the 13.5:1 mark the best results are. At the other end of the scale if everything (combustion efficiency, atomization, fuel distribution, etc.) is just a shade off the mark, the fastest air/fuel ratio can be 12.8:1. Your job is to find what your engine needs to do its best.

Fuel Curve and Emulsion Wells

We have already looked at the main jets and PVRC jetting to move the air/fuel ratio up and down as a whole. We have also looked at how the high-speed bleed (or air corrector) jets have to change the slope of the fuel curve to optimize it throughout the RPM range.

But you may encounter a mixture trend that does not react in a linear manner. For instance, the mixture could start off at, say, 13:1, go to 14:1, and back to 13:1 at the top end. Obviously, any previous jetting changes do not fix the fact that the mixture is going lean in the mid range only. In such a case, you need to make calibration changes on the main jet emulsion well. (See Chapter 2 and,

Fig. 9.16. Some Holleys, particularly Dominators, have an intermediate transition/ cruise circuit and carbs. These circuits are typically used on carbs that have big venturis in relation to the butterfly diameter.

especially, Figure 2.9 on page 16.)

With the lean mid-range situation in this example, you reduce the size of the holes in the emulsion well at about the mid point in the length of the tube. Here, a race metering block comes in handy because jet size can be manipulated to trim the air/fuel curve as required. To make a measurable difference, a relatively large change in emulsion well jetting is required. To make a whole ratio change in, say, the mid-range RPM, the jetting may have to decrease or increase in area by as much as 50 percent.

Weather and Altitude Changes

Getting the carburetion right on the calibration/test day is important because it gives a working baseline to make corrections due to changes in weather conditions and altitude.

Jetting

The effects of elevation changes and weather conditions cannot be ignored. However, sometimes the need to compensate can be over emphasized. If you are racing in one local event or on a single track, the effects of weather are relatively limited in most cases. However, air density can change dramatically, and that's the time to recognize the value of calibrating to suit the weather.

For example, when I lived in Tucson, Arizona, jetting for the day was worthwhile. During July and August, Tucson went through its wet season. Days could have really high humidity (well in excess of 65 percent) with temperatures over 100 degrees F and the barometer an inch lower than typical. The following week we could be racing on a clear evening

Fig. 9.17. The optimal ignition timing can change from that required on a cool, dry day to that required on a hot, humid day. You can use a thumb wheel to change the timing by one degree without having to loosen the distributor, which is a definite asset.

when temperatures had dropped to 60 degrees F or less, humidity to less than 5 percent, and the barometer high.

Dyno testing could be a nightmare. One day the correction factor might be as high as 25 percent and a couple days later, as low as 5 percent. These correction factors relate directly to the track and jetting. Such a swing in atmospheric conditions resulted in a jetting change of three to four sizes for maximum performance.

Timing

As much as the weather affects optimal jetting, it also affects optimal ignition timing. Most racers completely overlook this factor. That is not good, as with some engines it can have as much effect as getting the jetting right for the day.

As a rule, you can expect the optimum timing to need advancing when the barometer drops or humidity rises. In this respect, it is a good idea to have an ignition system that can be advanced or retarded by a precise increment, rather than having to loosen the distributor and retime it with a timing light.

There are many ways to adjust ignition retard and advance. The simplest, if you are racing a popular Detroit V-8, is to use a Performance Distributors or Professional Products distributor with a manual advance/retard thumb wheel. If you have a high-end race ignition system, such as that produced by MSD, it is easy enough to incorporate an advance/retard control into the system.

There are reasonably well defined trends as to how the optimal ignition timing changes with atmospheric variations, but be aware that these are not set in concrete. Idiosyncrasies of the engine can play a part in countering what might typically be expected.

With that warning in mind you can make certain assumptions with a fair degree of certainty. As air pressure/density rises, the rate of burn increases, which calls for a reduction in advance. If the temperature drops

substantially, the timing may need to be advanced slightly. If the humidity rises substantially, the timing needs to be advanced over that required for dry air. Over a season of racing, you can expect to see as much as 3 degrees difference in optimal timing.

Assuming the jetting was right on the money when initially calibrated, the main jets need to be reduced by one size for every 2,000 feet increase in density altitude.

To figure out the density altitude, you need a weather station to measure the barometric pressure, temperature, and humidity. You also need a calculator to establish, from the readings taken, what the density altitude is. You compare this density altitude number to the one that existed when the carb's jetting was initially calibrated. Change the jets as needed to compensate for the variation.

If you are in the habit of taking your laptop computer to the track, you can purchase and use Performance Trends' Weather Wiz program.

It not only shows the atmospheric figures you need to know but also computes the jet changes required.

Benefits

Jet and ignition timing changes beg the question, What is going to all this trouble worth?

Here's an example: Proper jetting on a North Carolina mid- to high-9-second car going from a cold April setting to a hot-and-humid August setting is worth about 0.1 second. With timing changes that bumps to almost 0.2 second.

That's more than enough for the difference to go from eighth to first place. So the next question is, How badly do you want to win?

Vacuum Secondary Systems

In about 1982 I finally got a state-of-the-art dyno that would do just about any tests that General Motors could do at that time including a drag strip simulation with all the gear changes. I had a stout dyno mule, a 355-ci small-block Chevy (well, what did you expect?) that was representative of a street/strip engine of the day. It utilized a set of factory 186 head castings that I had extensively ported and milled to give (with the pistons used) a 10.5:1 CR. The cam was a flat-tappet hydraulic that had about 278 degrees seat-to-seat duration.

My intent was to test carbs, intakes, and exhausts. Part of the carb testing was to establish the value and the optimal point of opening of the secondary barrels of a 4-barrel carb on a single- and a dual-plane intake. The carb had a much-modified 750 vacuum secondary that ultimately flowed about 920 cfm. The project involved a lot of tests over a period of about a week and several hundred pulls.

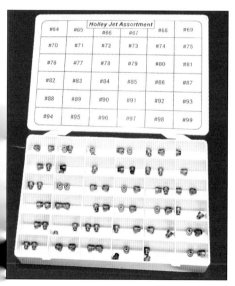

Fig. 9.18. For a dyno operator this comprehensive Holley main jet kit is a must-have item. For the typical racer a set of jets up to four sizes bigger and smaller is often all that is needed to fine tune a Holley.

Fig. 9.19. For a high-performance engine, make sure "picture window" power valves are used, as they flow more fuel than the drilled-hole ones. Note the use of the replaceable PVRC jets where the power valve locates. These are the jets you should be using to tune the WOT mixture.

The point I want to make, though, can be summarized by looking at the results of the tests done on an Edelbrock Victor Jr single-plane intake in Figure 9.20. This shows a test of primary barrels only versus all 4-barrels.

The numbers show that below 3,500 rpm, running with the primaries only, the carb produced more torque and drivability as well as better BSFC. Up to 3,500 there was no downside. Starting at 3,500 rpm, the primary barrel's ability to meet the engine's

air requirement fell off considerably. From 3,500 up, the use of all 4-barrels paid off. Peak power was up by no less than 106 hp and peak torque by 31 ft-lbs. With these numbers in mind, let me ask a question. Why would you want to disable the vacuum secondaries? Opening the secondaries too late reduces power and opening it too soon hinders torque, so this leads to one obvious conclusion. If we open it at the right time and the right rate for the vacuum secondaries, the carb delivers a better power curve as well as considerably enhanced low-speed drivability.

Let's consider drivability. In Figure 9.3, you see torque numbers from just the primaries in operation, and torque is increased by about 43 ft-lbs at 2,200 rpm. What does not show on the graph is the very rough running at that RPM when all 4-barrels are open.

The engine ran very smoothly with just the primaries in operation. Why? Because these 2-barrels were well able to supply the engines air demand and provided a strong booster signal for good fuel atomization.

On the other hand, the fuel atomization at these low RPM with all 4-barrels in operation was very poor. In addition, using the primaries only resulted in a much better BSFC.

Using a vacuum secondary also means that you can size a carb better for both ends of the RPM range. This means the ability to use a larger carb before low-speed drivability becomes an issue. Note that this carb flowed 920 cfm. Ask yourself how many 476-hp 350s could use a mechanical secondary carb with that much CFM without giving away any low-speed output potential. Also because of the better low-speed torque an engine equipped with a vacuum secondary

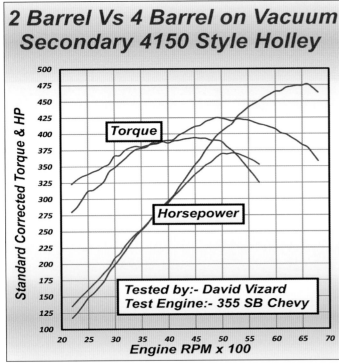

Fig. 9.20. The red curves on this graph show the output on just the primary barrels of a 4-barrel carb. The blue curves show the output with all 4-barrels in operation. Note how much better the output is with just the primaries in use at RPM below 3,500.

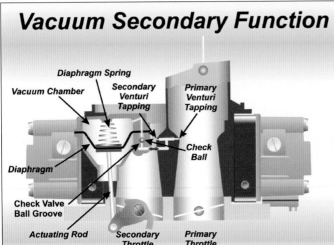

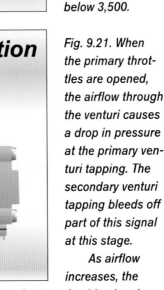

Fig. 9.21. When the primary throttles are opened, the airflow through the venturi causes a drop in pressure at the primary venturi tapping. The secondary venturi tapping bleeds off part of this signal at this stage.

As airflow increases, the partial vacuum at the primary tapping overcomes the secondary tapping bleed and so draws air from the vacuum chamber. This causes the diaphragm to be sucked up and, via the actuating rod, pulls the secondary throttles open.

At this point, the bleed at the secondary venturi tapping becomes an additional source of vacuum and serves to augment the rate at which the secondary is opened.

Fig. 9.22. The red arrow indicates the primary venturi tapping for the operation of the vacuum secondary butterflies. The vacuum signal generated at that tapping is communicated to the vacuum diaphragm housing, indicated by the blue arrow.

has the vacuum diaphragm, situated right at the venturi minor diameter. The one located in the primary barrel senses the pressure drop at the venturi, which increases as the engine's demand for air increases. This primary venturi passage is connected to the space above the vacuum diaphragm and provides the vacuum to lift the diaphragm to open the secondaries. Control of when and how fast it opens is achieved by several means.

A major control factor is a passage smaller than in the primary, which leads to the secondary venturi and is also connected to the primary passage. This passage has two functions. First, it initially bleeds off signal generated by the primary venturi (see Figure 9.21). Just how much it bleeds off is controlled by the relative size of this hole and the one in the primary.

At some point the vacuum signal generated by the primary overcomes the influence of both the secondary barrel bleed and the spring in the diaphragm housing. The secondaries then open. As a result airflow through the secondary barrels causes a vacuum to be generated at the bleed hole.

Second, the bleed hole reverses its function and assists in the delivery of the vacuum signal produced by the primary. Once the secondaries start to open, the bleed hole accelerates the opening process. Also, according to some Holley engineering friends

of mine, this secondary action stops the system from hunting at or close to the transition point.

If you follow the vacuum passage toward the diaphragm housing you come to a ball check valve. (In some newer, smaller CFM carbs this is replaced with a calibrated air bleed but the function is similar.) The seat where the check valve is located is grooved, producing a controlled leak.

The principle purpose of this check valve is to allow the vacuum in the diaphragm housing to build at a controlled rate consistent with a smooth, progressive opening. If the ball is removed, the secondaries open much quicker and, as a result, the manifold vacuum may change fast enough to warrant some accelerator pump action. But there is no accelerator pump on the secondaries unless you build it with one.

The second function of this check valve is tied to rapid throttle closure. When the throttle is closed

Fig. 9.23. Make no mistake, this Holley 750 Ultra Street is a no-holds-barred high-performance carb. Note that it has vacuum secondary barrels! I have run several of these on the dyno and at the track, and they perform excellently.

carb can be paired with a tighter converter, giving the same performance but with better fuel economy.

So, have I convinced you that there is much merit to the use of a vacuum secondary carb? If torque output and fuel efficiency below about 3,000 to 3,500 rpm is important, then a vacuum secondary is the way to go. But consider this: Even if your engine did not really require a vacuum secondary, there is no real downside to a vacuum secondary carb *if optimally calibrated.*

On the other hand, if you used a mechanical secondary, you could be losing a great deal of low-speed torque unless your carb is equipped with very active boosters.

Vacuum Secondary Function

Take a look down the carb's barrels. There is a hole in both primary and secondary barrels on the side that

Fig. 9.24. Holley has a wide range of vacuum secondary springs to suit just about every application. The set you see here is available in Holley's kit (PN 20-13).

Fig. 9.25. If the stock top cover is replaced with this quick-change modification available from Holley (PN 20-59), the vacuum diaphragm spring can be replaced in seconds instead of minutes.

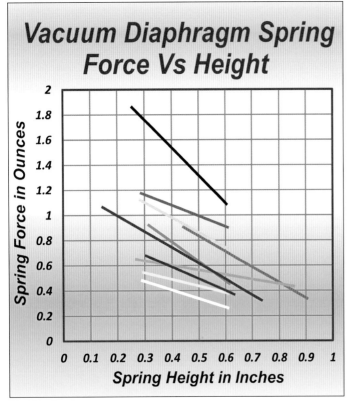

Fig. 9.26. This graph shows the delivered load and stiffness of the springs for tuning in the secondary action on a vacuum secondary carb. The easiest way to get the best spring rate is to start with one that is too stiff and gives clean results, then progressively move to a lighter, weaker spring. When you feel the engine "bog," go back to the last spring that gave a totally smooth transition onto the secondaries.

Fig. 9.27. Here is a typical out-of-the-box Holley vacuum diaphragm housing. Changing the spring contained within this housing is a little more time consuming than you might expect unless the stock cover is replaced.

the vacuum source ceases to produce vacuum. The vacuum existing in the diaphragm housing then causes the ball to lift from its seat, thus rapidly releasing any vacuum in the diaphragm housing. This, in turn, quickly closes the secondary butterflies.

A popular hop-up modification is to remove the ball. Doing so increases the rate of opening but it also reduces control over that opening rate. The only time this works is when the carb is way too small for the job at hand.

In practice, spring selection gives you 90 percent of all control. Holley has a number of color-coded springs ranging in length and stiffness. For the most part you need only concern yourself with five springs: one is white (PN 38R-1195, not included in the PN 20-13 spring kit), two are yellow (one short and one long), one is purple, and one is naturally colored steel. See Figure 9.26 for spring characteristics.

Vacuum Secondary Tuning

Considerable mystery surrounds the tuning of the secondaries on a Holley carb. In fact, it is not at all complex, but it can be time consuming.

As mentioned earlier, by selecting the correct spring for the vacuum chamber, you take care of 90 percent of the tuning of the secondaries. The entire point of a vacuum secondary carb is to eliminate a stumble or hesitation by not presenting the engine

Fig. 9.28. Shown here is the quick-change top cover installed.

Fig. 9.29. The upgraded vacuum secondary housing is reinstalled on the original 390 carb. To change the spring, you only need to remove the two retaining screws holding the bridge part of the cap for access directly to the spring housed inside.

with more carb CFM than it needs. This very issue dictates the way to a good secondary tune.

In essence, you should start with a spring that is too stiff, so it delays the opening longer than necessary. Then test a progressively lighter/shorter spring until you find the lightest one that just causes a stumble. You simply install the previous spring and most of the tuning is done.

To get an idea of the order in which you should try the springs, refer to Figure 9.26. When selecting the lightest spring do not be fooled into thinking that if you can feel the secondaries coming in, it must be better. If you think it is, go to the drag strip and verify that it is happening. The sensation of a secondary surge is usually because, just before the surge, the engine is starting to lay down, giving the impression of more power when the engine recovers. A trip to the strip to test this and a spring that is slightly stiffer and brings the secondaries in smoothly is almost always faster.

Spring Changes

Changing the spring in the diaphragm housing can be difficult. It takes a few minutes to remove the housing and you usually have to take off the electric choke to get at all the screws. In addition, you also need three hands to relocate the diaphragm. The way around this is to use Holley's "quick change" kit (PN 20-59) that allows access to the spring through the top cover without having to touch the diaphragm or its securing screws.

If you want easier adjustment, consider Quick Fuel Technology's externally adjustable vacuum diaphragm housing. It has a vacuum orifice adjusting screw in the cap. This provides the means to make adjustments to the size of the bleed communicating from the carb's barrels to the diaphragm housing. My daughter, who incidentally builds her own race engines, uses a Quick Fuel Technology adjustable vacuum secondary setup as you see in Figure 9.28 on her 525-hp 302, which she runs in a 1969 Boss 302 Mustang bracket car. The car is good for a consistent 6.7 seconds on the 1/8-mile.

The technique to set up one of these secondaries is to adjust the screw right in against the seat. Then turn the screw about 1¼ turns out. Next, select the spring. (Note that for most street and street/strip engines the purple spring in Fig. 9.26 works just fine for probably about 90 percent of applications.)

Once you have chosen a bog-free spring, fine tune the setup at the track by either turning the screw in (slows the secondary opening rate) or back the screw out (speed the opening rate). The ability to adjust the rate of secondary opening is about equal to half the difference between one spring and another so don't expect it to be the solution to an otherwise problematic secondary. It's a fine-tuning tool; no more, no less.

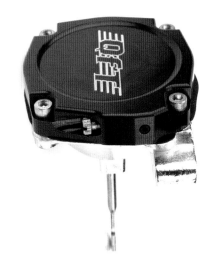

Fig. 9.30. This adjustable secondary diaphragm vacuum housing from Quick Fuel Technology can be the frosting on the cake for serious bracket racers and those wanting the secondary operation as close to optimal as possible.

ACCELERATOR PUMP CIRCUIT CALIBRATION

To understand why you need an accelerator pump, you need to understand the physics of liquids and vapors. The point at which a liquid turns to a vapor is its boiling point, and this is dependent on pressure and temperature. An increase in temperature or a decrease in pressure causes a liquid to boil sooner. As you know, fuels are highly volatile with certain fractions evaporating very easily.

For a well-tuned street engine, you may see 11 to 15 inches of manifold vacuum. Under the sort of running temperatures existing in such an engine at idle, just about all the fuel entering through the carb's idle system evaporates almost the instant it goes by the throttle butterflies. This is good for a smooth idle because it ensures ease of ignition and nearly perfect distribution.

However, opening the throttle at even a moderate rate, momentarily causes the manifold vacuum to drop substantially. When this happens, fuel that is in vapor form within the intake system almost instantly condenses onto the walls of the induction system. This leaves the air within the intake lacking fuel. This lean out is so severe that it is virtually impossible to ignite even when compressed in a hot combustion chamber.

The fix is to inject fuel to "fill in" this lean spot until an appropriate fuel circuit reestablishes the correct steady-state mixture ratio. The circuit that takes care of this transient situation is the accelerator pump.

Accelerator Pump Circuit

The accelerator pump circuit is comprised of a pump situated below the fuel bowl, a throttle shaft mounted metering cam, an actuating arm that transmits the motion from the cam to the pump diaphragm and calibrated pump jets situated just above the venturis.

As the throttle is opened, the fuel metering cam operates the pump

Fig. 10.1. This is the business end of the accelerator pump system. The pump jets, commonly called squirters, are available in a wide range of sizes to calibrate not so much the amount of fuel injected but more the length of time the injection period lasts.

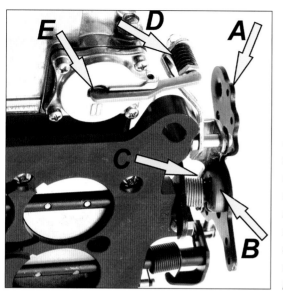

Fig. 10.2. The complete accelerator pump system can best be seen from below the carb flange. When the throttle lever (A) is opened, it rotates the cam (B), which lifts the lever arm (C). That in turn compresses the spring (D), which then pushes the pump diaphragm lever (E).

Fig. 10.3. One, two, or four holes in this location allow the fuel to be drawn into the pump to replenish it after it has been actuated by the opening throttle.

lever arm. This in turn pushes fuel through the metering block to the pump jets and into the engine. The only time the accelerator pump system should supply fuel is during a rapid opening of the throttle. If the throttle is opened slowly, the pump system should not supply extra fuel to the engine.

Steps need to be taken to prevent what is commonly described as pump jet pull-over. This occurs when the airspeed through the carb causes sufficient depression in the vicinity of the pump jets, which activates them and typically delivers unwanted fuel. This fuel is in addition to that supplied by the main and PVRC jets. Although this condition of pull-over is sometimes used as a tuning aid on 2-barrel race carbs, it is generally not useful for a 4-barrel installation.

The accelerator pump system needs to counter the following two situations. So as not to discharge fuel through the squirters when the throttle is opened slowly, in some systems there is a controlled bleed from the pump back into the fuel bowl. Older carbs have a check valve located within the pump. When the

throttle opening rates exceed a certain amount, the check valve closes and the fuel is redirected solely to the squirters.

Also worthy of note is that some aftermarket Holley specialists drill a small bleed-back hole through the pump roof/float bowl floor. This hole needs to be small (about 0.012 inch), but it can be used as a tuning aid for the pump system in much the same way as Weber pump jet float bowl bleed-backs.

To minimize high-speed fuel pull-over, there is a pull-over check valve situated just below the squirters. The intent here is that the weight of the stainless-steel conical-tipped needle closes the valve to the effects of any depression at the squirter discharge point, but is easily lifted off its seat when the pump comes into action.

On carbs with vacuum secondaries, the accelerator pump system is typically installed on the primary side only. That said, I have used a big-CFM vacuum secondary carb with squirters for both primaries and secondaries. But that is more an exception than a rule. A mechanical secondary carb has a complete accel-

erator pump system for both ends of the carb.

As far as tuning the accelerator pump system goes, it is all a question of injecting just enough fuel to compensate for the vapor drop-out and the sudden increase in airflow. The tuning of the accelerator pump system is essentially straightforward so long as you know about the available hardware and what it does.

Accelerator Pump Components

The stock accelerator pump on a 4150-style carb has a capacity of 30 cc for ten strokes of the pump. On Dominator-style carbs, the pump capacity is 50 cc for ten strokes. Although rarely necessary, the bigger pump can be installed on a 4150-style carb by using Holley's conversion kit (PN 20-11). The kit includes a diaphragm and the appropriate linkage to facilitate the swap.

The 30-cc pump is suitable for almost all applications. Just how much pump capacity is required is dependent on the size of the engine, cam duration, and volume of the

Fig. 10.4. The pump comprises the parts shown here. The arrow indicates the discharge port that aligns with the port in the metering block.

Three issues must be considered when tuning the accelerator pump system for optimal results: injection volume, injection rate, and injection duration. The cam on the throttle shaft combined with the pump's size (30 or 50 cc) largely controls the volume injected during an idle to WOT situation. At part-throttle operation, the cam profile and the size of the squirter control the rate at which fuel is injected. Last, squirter size largely controls the duration.

Preliminary System Tune

After the engine is warmed up and you are satisfied that the idle speed is properly set up, your first step is setting the pump arm preload spring. To do this, tighten the nut/bolt assembly that compresses the spring until there is a slight amount of clearance (0.001 to 0.005 inch) between the head of the adjusting bolt and the pump arm. Next, undo the adjusting nut until the bolt head is just in contact with the pump arm. At this point, turn the adjusting nut two flats to lightly preload the spring against the pump arm. With that done, it is set.

Now is the time to check those provisional settings. To do this give

Fig. 10.5. Fuel from the accelerator pump enters the metering block (A), moves through the passage in the casting (B), and into the carb body on the other side of the metering block (C).

intake manifold. Tall intakes with large ports and a spacer usually need a lot of pump shot, so they may be a candidate for a 50-cc pump on a 4150 carb. Again, if you order a carb spec'd for the job at hand, chances are that you have very little to do in terms of dialing in the accelerator pump system.

Pump volume is a measure of the amount of fuel available for one shot only. This volume obviously always needs to be somewhat bigger than the engine needs from the carb during the most demanding situation. The fuel cam on the throttle shaft dictates the amount of fuel and the rate it is injected into the engine. The size of the squirters mostly dictates the length of time of the injection phase.

When the throttle is opened, the spring on the end of the fuel cam arm activates the pump arm. Rapid opening causes the spring to become compressed and injection continues until the spring has returned to its normal length.

Fig. 10.6. A check valve that's a weighted conical-tipped needle below the squirters counters the effects of high-speed "pull-over."

the engine a quick "blip" of the throttle. It should, without hesitation, respond in a nearly instantaneous fashion. If the engine stumbles when given a sharp blip of the throttle, increase the pump jet size until the hesitation is gone.

If you are easing up to the size and no hesitation is experienced, you need to recognize what is needed when the engine is given throttle under load. It may need 0.002 to 0.004 inch bigger than required for a clean pull in neutral. This is especially

Fig. 10.7. If squirters more than 0.035 are used, the hollow securing screw must be used to avoid restriction at the screw location.

true if the engine is equipped with a light flywheel or a small-diameter high-stall-speed converter.

If a blip on the throttle shows black smoke in the exhaust, drop the squirter size by a couple of numbers at a time until the black smoke disappears. If the response is sharp and no black smoke is seen, you can go on the road or track to check out the pump action over the anticipated operating range.

Final System Tune

For the accelerator pump action to be optimal, you need to consider those three factors mentioned earlier: volume, rate, and duration. As a matter of reference heavy vehicles pulling from low RPM and gaining RPM relatively slowly require smaller pump jets and a longer duration. On the other hand, engines in light vehicles that pick up RPM fast need bigger pump jets and usually less duration.

With all that in mind, let's look at what may happen at the track and determine the possible fixes. Let's assume that the pump action is not delivering sufficient fuel at some point during the injection phase. If this is the case, there are a couple possible problem symptoms.

First, if when given full throttle from an idle (or near idle), the engine just bogs and never recovers, you can be assured that the accelerator pump is delivering substantially less than the engine wants. The cure is to increase the pump jet by at least 0.005 inch. Continue to increase it until no bog exists.

In extreme cases, the entire capacity of a 30-cc pump may be completely used up. If so, the carb needs a 50-cc pump. However, this is only the case on some seriously high out-

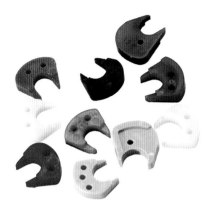

Fig. 10.8. Here is a variety of accelerator pump cams. Refer to the charts in Figure 10.11 for the opening rate and lift characteristics.

put engines. Typically a single 4150 on an engine up to about 700 hp is fine on 30-cc pumps.

Second, the vehicle initially launches then takes a dive for a moment before recovering. When this happens it is a sure sign of insufficient fuel due to a pump shot duration that is too short. Your first move is to use a slightly smaller set of squirters to see if there is any improvement. The smaller squirters extend the duration but reduce the rate.

If the problem is a little better, continue to reduce squirter size until no more improvements are seen, but the problem still exists. If this is the case, you need to look at changing the pump actuating cams on the throttle shafts to ones that have a longer stroke.

At this point, refer to the pump cam characteristics in Figure 10.11 so you can make an educated choice of a cam. You need to primarily choose a cam that produces more stroke to deliver a greater quantity of fuel over a longer period. The rate at which the cam lifts is of no consequence if the throttle action is from idle or some relatively low RPM to wide open. Slamming to WOT rotates the cam instantly to its full-

Fig. 10.9. To convert a 30-cc pump to a 50-cc pump, you need this Holley conversion kit (PN 20-11).

stroke position, so the slope on the cam does not figure into the equation. Experiment with cams giving increasingly greater stroke until the throttle response is sharp and fast.

Part-Throttle Response

During typical street driving, there are countless instances where the driver calls for a little more power. In doing so, the throttle moves a relatively small amount. This is when

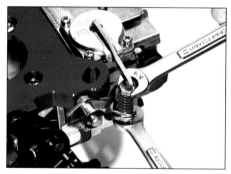

Fig. 10.10. Some controversy exists within the Holley community as to how the accelerator pump preload spring should be adjusted. Most technical guides state that additional pump arm travel of 0.015 inch is suitable when the throttle plates are wide open. This sometimes puts things at odds at the other end of the pump stroke. I have not seen the need for additional pump arm travel, especially on Holleys made after about 2005.

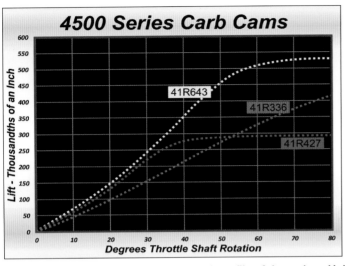

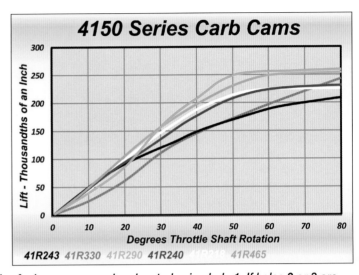

Fig. 10.11. These two charts show the lift profile of the various Holley fuel pump cams when located using hole 1. If holes 2 or 3 are used, the motion is retarded (moved to the right on the graph by about 5 to 8 degrees).

the shape of the cam and the location hole used to secure it to the throttle shaft comes into play.

Location Holes

All cams have two or three location holes that can be used to position and secure the cam to the throttle shaft. The hole 1 location puts the cam in its most advanced position while hole 2 retards the action by about 5 degrees of throttle shaft opening.

For most applications, where the idle speed screws are nearly closed and idle speeds are in the 550 to 750 range, securing the cam via hole 1 is best. When a big cam is used and idle speeds are in the range of 950 to

1,200 rpm, use of the hole 2 or 3 is usually more appropriate.

Part of the reason for retarding the cam when a high idle speed exists is the throttle shaft has rotated more at the higher idle speed. It has, therefore, used up some of the pump cam's lift, unless it was retarded some.

Profiles

If the engine has been extensively tuned for the street and uses a short-duration high-lift camshaft and a healthy amount of compression, it

should exhibit a high-idle vacuum. Under these conditions even a small opening of the throttle at low RPM causes the intake vacuum to drop sharply for an instant. This is when the most aggressive fuel dropout occurs, and for that, the setup for the pump action needs to come on fast.

If the engine has a relatively big cam and idle vacuum is low, the rate of change of idle vacuum is less and usually slower so a cam with an initially slower opening rate could well be what is needed.

If the engine is a large-displacement high-output unit, a high-lift cam to deliver more fuel is needed.

If it is a relatively small engine less fuel (and consequently less cam lift) is required.

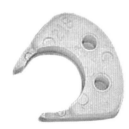

Fig. 10.12. Most pump cams have two or three locating holes. They retard pump action and are normally used for big-cam engines.

Fig. 10.13. This Holley kit (PN 36-184) is useful when setting up accelerator pumps.

Fig. 10.14. The difference between a 50-cc diaphragm (left) and a 30-cc one (right) is very obvious. On a well set up engine, a 30-cc accelerator pump should be able to deal with anything up to about 700 hp.

RAM AIR AND HEAT MANAGEMENT

Ramming air into the induction system for greater output looks like an easy return on time and money invested. In the real world, it is not that simple. Although lowering the intake charge temperature is generally considered a guaranteed way to increase engine output, it also is not without potential problems. Indeed, in some extreme cases, lowering the charge temperature by a substantial amount such as, say, 50 degrees F, can actually lead to reduced output. It is important to understand the factors that can work in opposi-

Fig. 11.1. A power-producing element is very obvious on this 580-hp Chevy 355. However, the fact that it contributes to output is far from obvious. If you have not guessed, it is the polished exterior surface on the intake manifold.

tion to the potential positive effects of ram air and charge temperature reduction.

Air Temperature

Any moves to reduce intake charge temperature must start with attention to the amount of heat the outside source of air is likely to pick up prior to its entry into the engine's induction system. Feeding the engine underhood air at the elevated temperatures seen is not a good plan for performance.

Some tests on my 1980 Pontiac Trans Am fully illustrate just how much loss the engine can experience when fed underhood air at typically more than 170 degrees F. This California-spec car had

to meet emissions standards and was equipped with a rather anemic 305 small-block Chevy, which cranked out a supposed 190 hp. The hood shaker induction was just a dummy setup, but it could be easily converted to a functional system drawing on outside air instead of underhood air.

The tests were done on a 100-degree day at the drag strip in Tucson, Arizona. On such a day, it was typically a low-17-second high-70-mph car. When the back of the hood shaker air scoop was opened up and the underhood air sealed from entering the induction system, the car picked up a little more than 2 mph and dropped about 0.2 second from the ET, making it a high-16-second low-80-mph car.

You may have noticed that the air inlet on the scoop faces backward (see Fig. 7.1). This has undoubtedly raised the question among some readers as to whether the car would have been quicker with the scoop turned around to face forward. The thinking here is that a forward-facing hood scoop should have the benefit of "ram air."

Simple theory tells us that the system should ram more air into the intake and, therefore, make more power. Sure, gains can be had from ram air. However, in reality, possible gains from ram air are overestimated and often poorly executed.

Figure 11.2 shows the increase in air pressure at the mouth of a closed tube. We are looking at the pressure head generated by bringing air to a standstill at the mouth of a scoop. Of course, it works equally well by assuming that the air is stationary and that it is suddenly accelerated to speed by the motion of the air scoop on the car moving through it.

Figure 11.2 shows that the pressure head developed is relatively small until the speed increases to about 100 mph. For instance, at 75 mph, the pressure head due to the forward motion is only 0.1 psi. At sea level, where the air pressure is typically 14.7 psi, the percentage increase in air density at the intake is 0.68 percent. At 100 mph, the air density increase is a little better at 1.2 percent and better yet at 2.7 percent at 150 mph.

Putting a big hood scoop on your racer may look fast, but it is far easier to increase the drag than the power. Sure, power may increase, but the drag can increase even faster. If it does, performance drops rather than increases. So a serious effort at ram air needs to take into account the aero drag involved as this could more than cancel out efforts to increase the vehicle's performance.

Also, in practice, the pressure head that the system should develop is not met. The reason for this is that as fast as air is fed into the scoop, the engine is drawing it out at the other end.

The only performance aspect that can be guaranteed is that the air entering the hood scoop is at the ambient (outside) air temperature. From that aspect, a hood scoop is a good idea.

Before we finish with the problem of additional drag from a hood scoop, I should mention that there is a way to get most of the benefits of ram air and actually cut the aerodynamic drag of a vehicle. Instead of a hood scoop, try drawing the engine's air supply from directly behind the grille or a headlight opening. Routing the air from these location reduces the stagnant pressure head a the vehicle is pushed through the air Additionally it also delivers air at the lowest temperature possible.

Something you must conside and deal with is pressure equalization between the fuel bowl and the amount of air fed to the venturis. I this is not taken into account, the mixture leans out as speed increases You need to make sure the fuel bow vent tubes experience the sam pressurized air that is feeding th venturis.

On a Holley carb this is a com mon consequence of installing an ai filter/ram air system mounted on th carb's air filter ring. Doing so leave the float bowl vent tubes within th confines of the air filter/ram induc tion system.

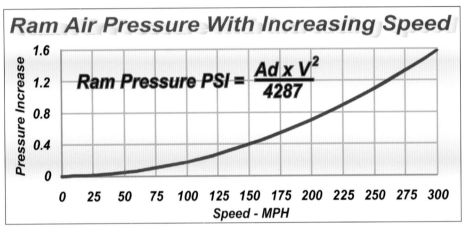

Fig. 11.2. As can be seen here, ram air does not amount to much until speeds are relatively high. If the car has the capability of topping about 125 mph in the 1/4-mile, a well-designed hood scoop installation starts to measurably pay off.

Fig. 11.3. This setup is ideal if you want the benefits of cold air and ramming. With this setup not only is the engine being fed with cool air above ambient pressure, but the car also becomes slightly more aerodynamic. This is due to it feeding from the stagnating high-pressure zone built up at the front of the car. Because this front is virtually flat, the benefits of drawing air from that location are measurable. This installation is from Air Inlet Systems.

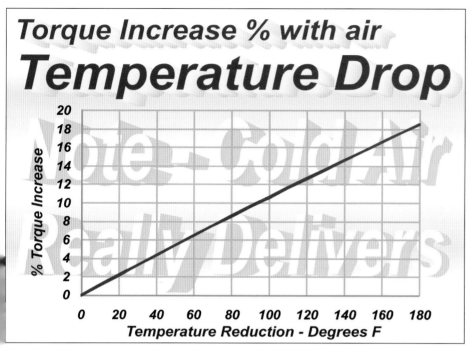

Fig. 11.4. If the air is not excessively heated downstream of the point of induction, feeding the engine cool air can produce significant output gains.

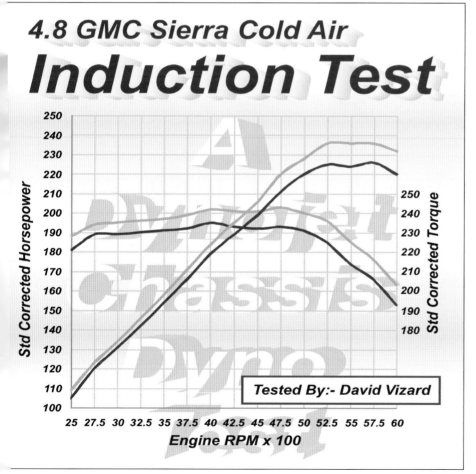

Temperature Control

There are systems on the market intended to cool the air fed to the carb. Some are pretty exotic and use the cooling effect of compressed gases to cool the ducting to the carb. While such systems work, they are somewhat expensive.

I have tried cooling the air to an engine via ice water in a long aluminum tube inserted into a large-diameter plastic tube. While it did offer a performance advantage (about 4 hp on a highly tuned 2-barrel Pinto 2-liter engine), it was cumbersome. However, if the race regulations don't specifically ban air temperature control, if a suitable simple system can be devised, it's worth some serious thought.

Fuel and Charge Temperatures

In the late 1980s, I built an octane-fuel test engine that looked at fuel detonation limits in a different fashion to that of the CFR research engine normally used for octane evaluation. Instead of having a variable CR, my test engine (a Chevy 355-ci small-block with iron heads) used ignition advance to evaluate the effects of intake charge temperature on the detonation limits of a number of service-station pump fuels.

The test engine was a 14:1 unit with a set of ported factory iron heads.

Fig. 11.5. Although this test was on a fuel-injected engine, it is a good example of what can be achieved by drawing cold air from behind the radiator grille. On average, the temperature reduction was about 38 degrees F. This corresponded to 8 to 10 ft-lbs of additional torque as measured at the rear wheels. The cold-air kit for this test is from K&N.

Fig. 11.6. A dual-plane intake was selected for the apparent octane tests.

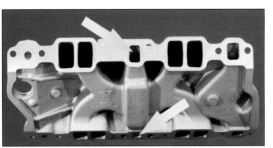

Fig. 11.7. The heat cross-over passage on a typical street dual-plane V-8 intake manifold is indicated by the arrows. For the "hot" tests, the exhaust was allowed to pass through this passage to heat the intake. For the second series of tests, this passage was simply blocked off. For the cold-intake tests, the passage exits were welded shut and, via two tappings on the top side, fed city water at about 40 to 42 degrees F.

Three thermally different intake manifolds were used; all Edelbrock Performer RPM dual-plane intakes. The first had the usual exhaust cross-over passage operative so it was heated by the exhaust. In the second unit, the heat cross-over was welded shut to block it off, and to minimize heat conducted into the manifold from the cross-over port in the heads. Also, an intake manifold gasket, which was made of an insulating material, blocked off the cross-over port in the heads. The third intake had the cross-over blocked from the exhaust, but the passage itself was drilled into and a water fitting installed. This allowed the manifold to be water cooled by the city water supply, which at that time of year was around 40 degrees F. The intent was to see how much power a fuel could produce at whatever advance it could tolerate before detonation set in.

It is quite reasonable to expect two fuels of the same octane to produce the same results. That proved to be far from the case. These tests established several important factors that are often discussed among racers, or conversely, completely overlooked. For these tests, eight different brands of fuel were used. For a given octane, the difference between the worst and the best for any given octane was well over 30 hp.

Although things have undoubtedly changed since I performed these tests, it is worth noting that, at that time, the worst fuels in terms of output were the cheap off-the-wall brands. Another factor that was amply demonstrated was that a fuel that may be best at one temperature was not necessarily best at another temperature. For instance the best 90-octane fuel in the water-cooled intake test was Sunoco. However, when run with the exhaust-heated intake, it was far from the best.

The difference in a fuel's resistance to detonation over a varying temperature range is called the fuel's sensitivity. When fuels are tested in a variable-compression CFR research engine, they are tested for "motor" octane and "research" octane. The motor octane is tested with the intake air temperature about 150 degrees F hotter than with the research value. As of 2012, the difference between these two shows up as about eight octane numbers. If a fuel is rated at 90 octane on the R+M/2 system typically used in the U.S., we can reasonably assume that the research octane is 94 (which is one of the most often quoted on the service-station pumps in Europe) and the motor octane is 86. The difference is 8.

Another point worth mentioning is that a higher octane (as measured on a CFR engine) does not always translate into greater resistance to detonation in a real-world race engine. However, with these tests, one aspect was apparent across the board: Intake charge temperature played a big role in the final results.

The first temperature-related factor you need to take into account is that, on average, for every 8 degrees F increase in induction temperature your engine needs one more octane number to stay out of detonation. Every time a charge temperature reduction can be made the fuel gains an apparent increase in octane value. For example, if an engine just detonates on, say, 100 octane when the intake charge temperature is 90 degrees F, the same detonation point is reached at 97 octane if the charge temperature is reduced to 76 degrees F.

There are other factors that increase octane other than reducing the charge temperature. One is an increase in charge density, which has the potential to produce more power. My test engine showed that the difference between an exhaust-heated intake and one with the exhaust heat deleted was, on a typical performance street 350-ci engine, typically 5 to 7 ft-lbs throughout the RPM range. The water-cooled intake delivered a further 5 to 7 ft-lbs.

I discovered another interesting point. The water-cooled intake was fed water at the same 90 degrees F air temperature that existed in the dyno cell. The charge temperature as measured at the intake manifold to head interface, was about 35 degrees F lower due to the evaporative cooling effect of the fuel. When the intake air temperature increased, the evaporative cooling increased, although it did not keep pace with the intake inlet temperature. When the intake temperature dropped, the charge temperature (due to evaporative cooling from the fuel) was reduced. These are important points to remember in relation to the subject of artificial fuel/charge cooling.

Fuel Temperature Problems

The fuel temperature in the carb's fuel bowl can have a significant effect on the engine's output. When underhood temperatures have stabilized under fast driving conditions, fuel in the bowls is typically 130 to 140 degrees F, but on a hot day, the temperature can rise to as high as 190 to 200 degrees F and this is the borderline of a problem area.

If the vehicle has poor underhood air circulation on a hot day, the fuel temperature can rise to extreme temperatures and certain fractions of the fuel actually boil. Boiling fuel is far less dense than fuel at a typical temperature. This allows the fuel bowl float to drop so more fuel floods in. This causes the carb to go seriously rich or even flood. In extreme cases this leads to a complete engine cut out. Such a situation is referred to as percolation.

Another phenomenon due to excess heat is vapor lock. This is when the fuel feeding the fuel pump is starting to boil. This leads to the pump not delivering the fuel it should, thus causing the engine to severely lean out due to lack of fuel. Vapor lock is far less likely to occur if the fuel pump is of the immersed type. Next best thing is to have the pump situated immediately adjacent to the fuel tank and as low as possible.

All the forgoing points to one inescapable fact: If maximum performance is the goal, being conscious of fuel temperature at every stage of its handling is necessary and that starts at the point of storage.

Here are a couple racing tips. The day before a race, put all of your fuel into containers and then into a large ice chest with as much ice as space allows. Also make sure the vehicle's fuel tank is as far as possible from any heat source, such as the exhaust system. If a heat source is close some insulation work is required. The fuel line must be insulated when it comes from a rear-mounted fuel tank with fuel pump, or from a tank with a mechanical fuel pump mounted on the engine. The plumbing department of any big home improvement store has split foam tubing that's typically used to stop water pipes from freezing, and it's suitable for installation on the lines from the tank. The split line is coated with adhesive so it can be sealed onto the fuel line.

Artificial Charge Cooling

Now I want to delve more deeply into the subject of artificial charge cooling (ACC) by means of super-cooled fuel and its effect on output.

The simplest and most common way to cool the fuel entering the carb is via a "cool can." A cool can is a simple heat exchanger. As such, it can function effectively and, if it is used correctly, the power gains can be substantial. Figure 11.10 shows the air temperature reduction produced by fuel in the fuel

Fig. 11.8. Gone are the days when a cool can was literally a tin can with a copper tube coiled inside and soldered into place. This unit from Moroso has a large ice/coolant capacity and a good amount of surface area on the finned-aluminum center section. The can itself is made of reinforced expanded foam that has great insulating properties. This means more of the ice absorbs heat from the fuel rather than from the underhood environment.

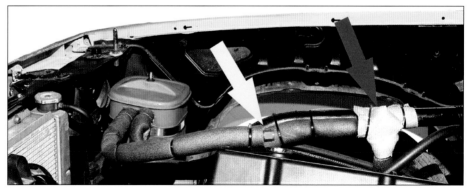

Fig. 11.9. This Moroso cool can was used in the Malibu that I race with my partner David McCoig. It is positioned as close to the carb as conveniently possible to minimize additional heat absorption. Note also that all the fuel lines are insulated with foam-rubber tubing originally intended for protecting household plumbing from freezing.

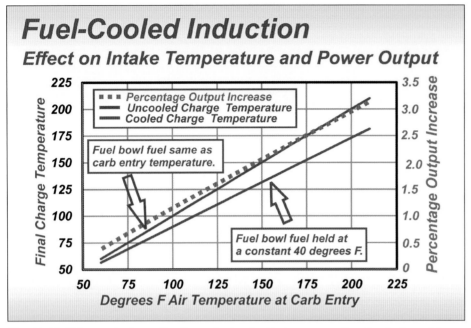

Fuel-Cooled Induction
Effect on Intake Temperature and Power Output

Fig. 11.10. This graph shows the theoretical gains that super cooling the fuel provides before the fuel enters the carb. The red line represents a typical situation in which no artificial cooling of the fuel is used. The blue line indicates the charge temperature after the air has been mixed at a 13:1 ratio with fuel at 40 degrees F.

The higher the ambient temperature, the greater the effect of super-cooled fuel. The super-cooled fuel affects output by increasing torque. When racing in hot weather, super-cooled fuel produces a distinct advantage over a vehicle not so equipped.

bowl held at 40 degrees F while carb entry temperature rises from 60 to 210. Assuming a typical race blend and a 13:1 air/fuel ratio, every 5.6 degrees F the fuel entering the carb is reduced results in the potential to reduce the charge temperature as a whole by 1 degree.

Ignoring, for the moment, any aspects concerning fuel evaporation, mixture quality, and effects of carb body temperature on the charge itself, the reduced charge temperature is worth a sufficient power increase to easily make the difference between winning and finishing several places down the field. The hotter the weather, the greater the difference made by cooling the fuel. However, installing a cool can alone is unlikely to deliver the full benefits of a fuel-cooled charge.

Here it is worth mentioning a test I did with a fellow California racer in the 1980s. On a very hot afternoon in midsummer the effect of a cool can on a 468-inch big-block Chevy Camaro was worth about 0.1 second on what was essentially a low-11- to high-10-second car depending on track and weather conditions. But this was an extreme case. Simply installing a cool can (especially on a 1/8-mile drag car) can be far less productive unless the setup is suitably refined.

The biggest problem here is that, unless steps are taken to the contrary, the cooler fuel does not begin to have a significant effect until the vehicle is about 150 to 200 yards off the start line. That is because the fuel bowl is initially full of warm/hot fuel and the carb body is hot. This means quite a

lot of cooled fuel must pass through the system for it to cool the carb body and the air by any significant amount. Testing a cool can system on the dyno showed that the engine did not produce its best output until the cooler fuel had run through the system for at least 20 seconds. If you are drag racing, the run is long over with at the point the system gets into full swing.

Before utilizing a cooled fuel system I first drain the fuel from the tank and the fuel bowls. Previously cooled fuel is then poured into the fuel tank. The fuel line is disconnected at the carb and the cooler fuel from the tank is pumped through an already ice filled cool can through the pressure regulator, the carb fuel log, and into a spare gas can. This cooled the fuel system as a whole and the lines from the cool can to the carb even more so.

Next the carb is sprayed with a mixture of 25-percent water and 75-percent alcohol. The high latent heat of evaporation of the alcohol takes all the excess heat out of the carb. With the carb now cold to the touch the insulated fuel lines are reconnected.

When all is buttoned up the car is pushed (or towed) to the staging area.

On my 1/8-mile restricted-spec (had to run a stock out-of-the-box dual-plane intake) Malibu, the cool fuel tactics paid off (as tested on a 75 to 80 degree F day) to the tune of about 0.004 second on a 6.3-second car (that's about 9.7 for the 1/4-mile). Going to all this trouble on a 1/4-mile car typically produces proportionately better results. For a 1/4-mile car in the same speed and ET range you can expect to see an ET reduction of 0.010 to 0.015 second.

So why did I see such a small gain on the Malibu compared to a big-block Camaro? The answer here is that prior to installing the cool can I was already fuel-temperature conscious in as much as I always use cooler fuel from an ice box and all the fuel lines were insulated right up to the carb's fuel rail.

Super-Cooling Cool Can

When Holley introduced the center-drain fuel bowl it opened the door to a straightforward way to pre-cool the fuel system right up to and including the carb. Figures 11.11, 11.12, and 11.3 show an installation on one of my dyno mule engines. Here is how it works.

Previously cooled fuel is fed into the Moroso cool can where it is cooled considerably by a mixture of ice and antifreeze. In addition to this a little dry ice for a super-cooling effect (does not need much) is usually added to the mix. Paying attention here has produced fuel temperatures exiting the cool can as low as 20 degrees F. This fuel is then pumped into the carb's fuel bowl where it cools everything as it passes through and out of the fuel bowl drain. A small scavenge pump connected to the drain hose ensures a fast fuel throughput and

Fig. 11.11. This thermally controlled carb setup is not yet covered with insulating foam. Depending on the type of fuel-pressure regulator being used (see Chapter 12), fuel either enters at the standard regulator or returns to the tank from the bypass regulator.

If a standard regulator is used a fitting (red/white arrow) plugs the outlet. If a bypass regulator is used this is the "fuel in" port via the cool can from the fuel pump. Although either type of regulator works, the best choice should be a standard regulator. Used in this manner the standard regulator never dead-heads the fuel pump because fuel is always being bypassed by virtue of the flow out of the fuel bowls. From the regulator, fuel is fed into the carb's fuel log and into the fuel bowls.

returns the fuel to the fuel tank.

With this system everything downstream of the carb is fully cooled prior to making a pass down the track.

Cool Fuel Compromises

So, it looks as if fuel cooling of the induction system is a slam-dunk procedure for achieving greater power output. As is so often the case, however, things are not quite that simple. There are some factors that actually add to the potential power increases but there is also a major factor that, unless satisfactorily

addressed, conspires to reduce the chance of really positive results. Let us first look at what is potentially a major pitfall in the quest for maximum output.

When fuel is cooled, less of it vaporizes. If the cooling is carried out to an extreme as is being proposed here, there may be insufficient

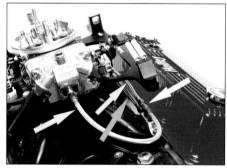

Fig. 11.13. Using an Ultra HP carb center-drain bowl makes it easy to plumb in a super-cooled fuel system. The fuel lines (yellow arrows) lead from the fuel bowl drains. These are connected to a tee junction (white arrow) that is in turn fitted into a junction block. Leading from this junction block is a fuel line (green arrow) that is connected to the suction side of a small electric fuel pump with a capacity of 30 gallons per hour.

Fig. 11.12. The two red arrows at either end of the carb show where the fuel is being drained from the fuel bowls. From there each line enters a distribution block via a T junction (blue arrow). The red arrow leaving the fuel distribution block indicates the direction of fuel flow to the scavenge pump. This pump returns the fuel to the fuel tank.

fuel vaporization for a good start to the combustion event. This results in a reduced output even though the charge is cooler.

If, after installing a super-cooling cool can system, the vehicle shows no performance improvement, it is a sure-fire bet that the mixture characteristics (other than air/fuel ratios) need to be investigated. When a thermally managed induction system or a super-cooled fuel system or both is used, the usual problem is that the booster, if optimal for a conventional induction system, now delivers fuel that is insufficiently atomized.

The preferable fix is the reevaluation of the booster style employed and if possible changing to a design having superior atomization characteristics. Typically this can mean going from a stepped dog-leg booster to an annular discharge booster. Sounds like a lot of work but you can take some solace in the fact that if the carb is marginally too small under normal conditions it may be okay with the booster when a super-cooled fuel system is used.

If you are already using a race-blend fuel, ask your fuel supplier for a blend with more light, front-end hydrocarbons in the fuel than whatever you are currently using. If they don't have one, order some straight toluene and try progressively adding that to the fuel. Up to a point the extra toluene acts as an ignition enhancer in most fuels. It is also lighter and evaporates easier than most other fuel formulations.

As long as the CR is not over about 13.5:1 you can also add small quantities (up to about 5 percent) of acetone or methyl ethyl ketone (MEK). Both evaporate very easily and can make up for the reduced vaporization experienced by the cooler charge. Do not use more than about 5 percent as it may lead to an earlier onset of detonation.

If you decide to run either of these compounds as additives in your fuel be aware that, as hydrocarbons, they do not register as illegal in a fuel check. Also, since they ignite very easily you may need to back out the ignition timing by a few degrees. If you are running an alcohol-based fuel, in colder weather the addition of up to 5-percent acetone or MEK makes for easier starting and more power.

Evaporative Cooling

The more you cool the fuel to reduce overall charge temperature, the less the charge is cooled by the effect of evaporative cooling. The truth of the matter is that, at least with gasoline, the effect evaporative cooling has on power is usually over-rated. In practice, the fuel's evaporative cooling makes the air denser, but the fact that fuel had to be evaporated to do so is largely offset by the fact that a portion of the fuel has turned from a liquid to a gas.

The evaporated fuel takes up about as much space in the manifold as the difference it created by cooling the air in the first place. The volumetric efficiency then changes very little. My experience is that most dyno tests to establish the effect of evaporative charge cooling are actually mixture-quality tests. The extra vaporized fuel in the charge has led to a better combustion process and this is where the extra power comes from.

Because the cool fuel reduces the amount of fuel evaporated, finer fuel atomization takes on greater meaning. Ideally, the best situation is to have a very large portion of the mixture in the form of fine fuel droplets (5 to 10 microns) and have minimal fuel evaporation while in the intake manifold. These fine fuel droplets react, at the time of combustion, about the same as vaporized fuel. Tests indicate that minimizing the amount of fuel vaporized in the intake and optimizing the average fuel droplet size produces the best volumetric efficiency from the engine. The optimal droplet size can vary from engine to engine.

Fig. 11.14. This AFR Titan plastic intake manifold is made for a Chevy small-block. It keeps the intake charge between 20 and 40 degrees F cooler than with a typical aluminum intake. Also it usually works best with one or more of the supplied spacers.

Fig. 11.15. The Titan is actually a multi-piece intake. Apart from its thermal virtues the fact you can see clearly down each of the runners makes it much easier to port match.

Another small effect that works in your favor is that the significantly cooler carb body actually flows more air as well as further cools the incoming charge. I did some simple tests with a pair of 650 carb bodies and a pair of 850s; they both showed some interesting differences.

One carb body of each model was put in a freezer at 20 degrees F for a few hours while an identical carb body was kept at room temperature of 75 degrees F. Each body was then tested for flow at 1.5 inches of mercury. Each of the carb's four-barrels was tested separately. The bodies were then reversed and the room-temperature bodies put in the freezer while the others were allowed to warm up.

The tests were repeated and measured before and after flow and exit temperatures averaged out. The 650, with its smaller venturis, responded slightly better that the 850 to the cooling procedure. The exit air temperature dropped close to 4 degrees F, compared to the exit temperature of the uncooled body. Airflow was up by about 2.5 cfm per barrel. The 850

delivered a reduced exit temperature just shy of 3 degrees F and was up on flow by about 1.8 cfm per barrel.

ACC in Practice

My first serious dyno test of ACC potential was in my dyno shop with the late Brad Urbane of the Carb Shop in California. We used a modified 650 mechanical secondary carb that produced a flow of about 715 cfm with the stock main venturis. The increased flow was the result of slimmed-down butterflies and shafts and a quick polish job on the otherwise stock venturis intended only to remove any slight casting imperfections. Brad had modified the carb body to allow a booster swap without having to remove the carb from the engine. The fuel bowls were drilled at the floor so a scavenge tube could

be connected to a small electric fuel pump to return fuel to a small dyno fuel tank. An antifreeze/dry ice heat exchanger cooled the fuel in the tank.

The test engine was a mildly modified Chevy small-block 350 with a 12:1 CR that cranked out a nominal 430 or so hp. The heads were a set of factory iron 186 castings, which I had previously ported to a decent race spec. An Edelbrock Victor Jr intake was used. The cam was a single-pattern, hydraulic flat-tappet grind of about 218 degrees at 0.050-inch lift. The ignition was an MSD unit with advance/retard control right on the dyno console. This allowed for nearly instant ignition timing changes, as I anticipated that different fuel temperatures probably needed slight timing changes to show the best of a cooler-running induction.

Fig. 11.16. Note the brackets and throttle linkages on this installation of a cooled-fuel setup. These are only as far away as your Holley on-line catalog and they make for a much better functioning system.

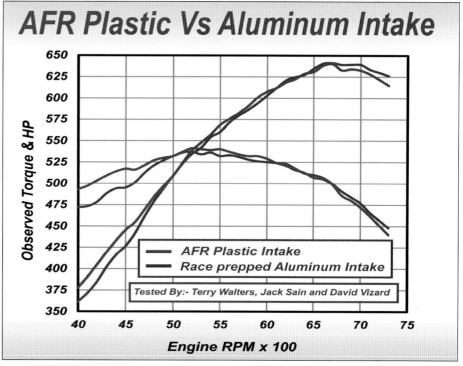

Fig. 11.17. This graph shows the difference in output of one of my tricked-out small-block Chevy aluminum race intakes versus AFR's plastic Titan intake. Not only is this manifold a featherweight, but also its cooler-running characteristics are worth the sort of power increases seen here.

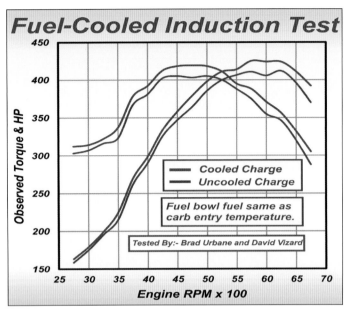

Fuel-Cooled Induction Test

Cooled Charge
Uncooled Charge

Fuel bowl fuel same as carb entry temperature.

Tested By:- Brad Urbane and David Vizard

Fig. 11.18. For these tests, I wanted to simulate track conditions. Therefore, observed figures were used (not corrected ones, as would be seen in early summer in Southern California). The dyno cell room was at about 100 degrees F and the fuel hovered around the 90-degree mark for the uncooled baseline tests (red curves). By the time this fuel had been in the carb body a short while, it had heated to about 100 degrees F. By circulating cooled fuel at about 25 degrees F, it was possible to hold the fuel bowl temperature around 30 to 32 degrees. After reoptimization of the boosters and ignition timing, the engine produced the figures shown by the blue curves.

Figure 11.18 shows the results of this test. Note that they are uncorrected observed figures. The purpose of showing the observed figures, which were done as A-B-A tests just minutes apart, is that this is what would have been seen at the track under running conditions. Just for the record, the correction factor for the day of the test was 1.076 so the corrected fuel-cooled output was 451 ft-lbs and 442 hp.

The gains make for interesting reading. First, peak torque climbed by 13.3 ft-lbs and occurred about 100 rpm sooner. Peak power rose by 12 horses, but the output rose by 17 ft-lbs and 22 hp at 6,750 rpm. This ability to hang on to the power at the top end pays off by allowing the upshift to be made at higher RPM.

These results did not come from a fuel temperature change only. The test fuel was from Daeco Fuels in California. To arrive at the best combination, the carb was run with three different booster styles. It was found that,

with uncooled fuel, a stepped dog-leg booster was the best, with the straight-leg and annular discharge boosters producing measurably inferior results.

With the cooled fuel tests, the straight-leg booster, which was designed for use with a heated intake as per a stock production vehicle, had dramatically less output. However, the annular discharge booster's performance was markedly better than when used with the uncooled fuel. So much so that it was a close call between it and the stepped dog-leg booster's performance. At the lower RPM, the annular discharge booster was marginally better, but at high RPM it was marginally worse.

Another point to note is that (on the test engine, at least) the cooler charge needed a degree or so of additional timing. The need for more advance, though, doesn't seem to be a universal thing, so some experimenting with timing is almost certainly needed.

Performance Conclusions

As you can see, there is more to making full use of super-cooled fuel than just doing a good job of actually cooling the fuel. Having covered the most likely problem areas, let me sum up the conditions under which super-cooled fuel works best. First, as expected, such a system works best when the weather is hot.

Second, it works better when the induction is restricted somewhat. For instance, if you are running a 750-cfm carb, but the engine makes just a shade more on an 850, then the cooled system delivers better performance. If the class of racing you run calls for a severe restriction, such as the mandated use of a 2-barrel carb or a restrictor plate, this system can pay off big time.

If you are using a thermal-barrier-coated intake manifold or manifold and intake ports, be aware it's more difficult for the boosters to produce a sufficiently atomized charge. The chances are you may have to use every trick in the book to get a good charge light off but it will be worth it!

The visually obvious, but not often seen as such, aspect of the engine shown on page 99 is the shiny exterior finish on the Edelbrock Victor Jr intake. Such a finish reflects heat that otherwise heats the intake manifold. The benefits are hard to realize on the dyno because cell conditions are vastly different than those for an engine installed in a vehicle. Also the benefits on a drag race car are most likely minimal, but for a high-performance vehicle that is run hard for long periods (such as a road racer), the benefits of a highly reflective intake are, on some vehicles, actually measurable in reduced lap times.

FUEL SYSTEMS

I realize that the fuel typically flows from the fuel tank to the carb. But I am going to handle the fuel system from the main jet back. I am starting with fuel slosh and attempts to control it. Fuel control problems are largely a case of out of sight, out of mind. However, if fuel control and delivery problems are not dealt with, a lot of power can be lost.

A point I really need to drive home here concerns the bowl's fuel level stability and its ability to combat fuel foaming. The problem in appreciating resistance to foaming and fuel level is that for the most part they are only ever seen (and rarely, at that) while the engine is on a dyno. That is an artificial environment and suffers zero effect from g

forces. It is largely out of sight, out of mind. In practice g-induced fuel-level changes and foaming of the fuel occur to a far greater extent than most racers suppose.

Let me give you an example. Just after oxygen sensors became a fixture in the automotive world, I did some mixture tests measuring all eight cylinders while on a dyno then at the track. On the dyno, the engine ran with a consistent 12.9 to 13.2:1 air/fuel ratio throughout the RPM range. However, the g forces at launch down the strip caused most of the front cylinders to run as rich as 9:1 while some of the back cylinders leaned out off the scale at an inferred

Fig. 12.1. To make the metering and atomization functions of a carb work as intended fuel pressure, flow, slosh, and foaming management are all critical. The design of the fuel system from the tank to the carb's jets dictates successful operation.

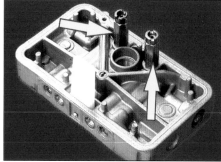

Fig. 12.2. Shown here are the main jet extensions used to compensate for fuel-bowl surge during high-g operation.

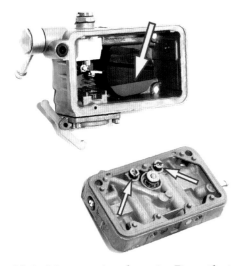

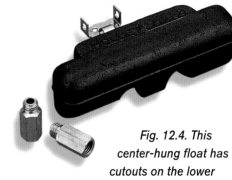

Fig. 12.3. Clearance between the jets (lower photo) and the float (upper photo) of a side-hung float bowl is about 0.300. Jet extensions in this shorter bowl need only be half the length of those in a center-hung bowl, so a 0.250 jet extension produces the necessary results. To install jet extensions, use a nitrophyl float and cut away about 1/4 inch deep section of the float (shaded area in top photo) and reseal the float with epoxy.

Fig. 12.4. This center-hung float has cutouts on the lower surface used to clear the jet extensions.

18:1. My question here is: Does that sound like acceptable fuel control? No, it certainly does not. Your first job is to set the fuel level as discussed below in "Fuel Level Adjustment."

Jet Extensions, Fuel Slosh and Fuel Level

Under hard acceleration, the fuel piles up at the back of the fuel bowls. On the drag strip, the fuel surface can be 45 degrees or more than what it is at static when the car is stationary. Video of a Plexiglas-windowed fuel bowl shows, on a pass down the drag strip, fuel foaming far beyond what you may have expected. Indeed there is some fuel foaming on the dyno when the engine reaches a certain RPM and strikes a vibration frequency that coincides with a frequency multiple of the fuel in the bowl.

The first move in fixing back-cylinder launch lean out is to equip the rear float bowl's main jets with jet extensions. If you are road or circle track racing, go ahead and fit jet extensions all around. These jet extensions can be of varying length. For drag racing, they can be long, but for road or circle track a mid-length setup is better. It puts the fuel pickup about in the middle of the fuel bowl, so it is able to handle braking as well as acceleration fuel surge.

When using jet extensions, you need a float with cutouts that clears the jet extensions. But there are some exceptions, such as AED jet extensions,

---

Fuel Level Adjustment

To raise or lower the fuel level in the fuel bowl is a straightforward job.

First loosen the slotted lock screw on the top of the float bowl. Then, using a 5/8-inch open-end wrench, turn the adjusting nut clockwise to lower the fuel level or counterclockwise to raise it.

At the track, raising the fuel level to slightly enrichen the mixture or lowering it to lean it provides little fine-tuning capability. Changing the fuel level by about 0.100 inch is worth about one main jet size. ■

If the fuel bowl has a sight plug, adjust the fuel level until fuel just starts to spill from the sight plug hole. If the fuel bowl has a clear window, adjust the fuel level to the middle of the window.

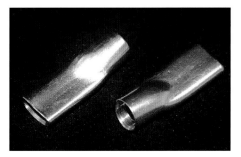

Fig. 12.5. These AED jet extensions have oval-shaped ends, which can be used without cutouts in the float.

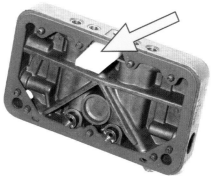

Fig. 12.6. This is an anti-spill device for the fuel bowl, popularly known as a "vent whistle."

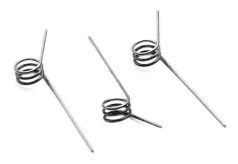

Fig. 12.7. Sometimes a float that bounces around too much, such as in off-road use, can be tamed somewhat by using a stronger bumper spring. Braswell Carburetion makes a 0.016 and a 0.017 spring for replacement of the stock 0.015 springs.

because they are oval at the open end and they clear most floats.

Another problem you are likely to see in high-g circumstances is that the float can bounce around and lose much of its control over the fuel level. This is especially true with off-road use. For better fuel control the bowl should be equipped with a whistle vent (Holley PN 26-89). Holley's high-performance carbs, such as those in the HP line, come with a whistle vent in the bowl. (An alternate to the vent whistle is a vent screen [Holley PN 26-39] but the vent whistle is the preferred choice in most cases.) Also, to better control

the float motion during high-g vertical motion, a stronger bumper spring is often a help. Braswell, for example, has two springs stronger than stock.

If fuel slosh/surge proves to be a problem, part of the reason for the engine stalling could be that the fuel has sloshed out the vent tube and gone into the engine. When this fuel enters the engine, it makes it very rich. For some vehicles it's a persistent problem and for a hard-charging off-road vehicle it is always a problem. To prevent this, attach a hose to the vent tubes to extend them while still keeping the open end within the confines of the air filter.

Floats and Bowls

A number of modifications can be made to floats to better deal with g-induced fuel slosh and foaming.

A variety of floats are available, but for the performance 4150–4160 and 4500 carbs, some are designed to work better than others. Before you modify any float, check out the offerings from Holley or Braswell Carburetion; there is a good chance you can buy what you need rather than making it.

Most Holley carbs for high-performance single-carb applications utilize a center-hung float and float bowl. Typically, these carbs are mounted with the fuel bowl aligned with the axis of the vehicle. During high-speed cornering, the fuel migrates toward the outside of the

Fig. 12.8. A center-hung fuel bowl is installed on most high-performance 4150- and 4500-style carbs. If you are drag racing, you almost certainly need to use jet extensions and the appropriate cutaway float.

Fig. 12.9. When fuel stacks up on the outside of the bowl during cornering on a circle track, it causes the needle valve to shut off the fuel supply earlier. To combat this, Holley offers this wedged float.

Fig. 12.10. In road racing, autocrossing, or other forms of competition with left and right turns, a double-wedged float can be used, such as this one from Braswell.

Quick Change Fuel Bowls

Not long ago, Holley introduced the Quick Change fuel bowl. As you can see from the photo, they have two plugs in the end of the fuel bowl that align with the main jets. Removing these plugs allows access directly to the jets without having to remove the fuel bowl itself.

All looks good here, but you need to make a shortened version of the special screwdriver shown so you can insert it between the float bowl and the distributor on Chevy applications.

Also, these bowls are best used with Holley screw-in jet extensions. It is a good idea to apply a small dab of Loctite (222 purple or 243 blue). Also be sure to tighten the jet extensions just a little more than the jets so during removal, only the jet comes out, not the jet and the jet extension.

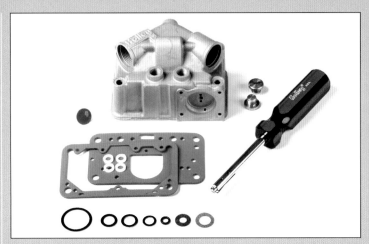

These are a "quick change" fuel bowl and the special jet screwdriver to access the jets. This setup allows you to change jets without removing the fuel bowl.

turn. This can cause the float to shut off the needle a little earlier than normal. This reduces the amount of fuel entering the float bowl and thus reduces the fuel height and availability for at least one of the jets in each bowl.

For a circle track car Holley offers wedged nitrophyl floats, one designed for the front float bowl and one for the rear.

If the application is for a road racer, the floats may need to be wedged on both sides. A Holley float can be used as a pattern, or you can check out Braswell's range of floats.

Holley's carbs can have white plastic, brass, or nitrophyl floats. The most popular for high-performance applications is the nitrophyl version. In terms of flotation, they are no better or worse than either of the other types, but they are alcohol compatible and their shape can be altered to suit certain parameters.

When modifying a nitrophyl floats to the shape required, you cut through the non-porous outer skin of the float into the foam inner structure. Once the float has been reshaped, a thin smear of epoxy can be used to reseal it. Note that having a float that does not leak is vital. Whether modified or not, you should check that the float does not leak or has not developed any porosity. For a nitrophyl float porosity can be determined by weighing the float on a gram scale then immersing it in fuel for a couple of hours and then reweighing. The tolerance for leakage/porosity is zero!

Needles and Seats

Fuel bowl needles and seats can be an area in which issues that lead to fuel foaming and loss of fuel level control start. On top of that, you need to select a needle and seat

assembly that flows sufficient fuel to meet the engine's demand.

The fuel flow per float bowl needs to be in the region of 0.5 lb/hour/hp for gasoline, about 0.8 for ethanol or E85, and 1.3 for alcohol. It's not difficult to hook up a pump and regulator to a fuel bowl with the float

Fig. 12.11. This is a typical Holley Viton needle valve. The same material and conical shape is used on virtually all gasoline needles.

Fig. 12.12. *This is the needle shape I came up with in the 1970s while working with Holley guru David Braswell. It has become the most popular as it overcomes significant flow limitations of a conical needle.*

dropped just shy of its full travel and weigh what passes through it in one minute. Water can be used; it weighs about 25 percent more than fuel. But for most practical purposes, you don't need to take these measures.

Typically for smaller carbs, say up to about 650 cfm, Holley's 0.97 needle and seat generally does the job. For anything up to 750 cfm, a 0.110 assembly should be just fine. Beyond that, a larger assembly might be needed. Holley and several other manufacturers make them up to 0.150-inch needle.

Most needles for gasoline applications are Viton tipped and conical in shape. For alcohol applications the needle needs to be made of a material that's compatible with alcohol as many types of plastic/Viton mixes degrade with alcohol. Your best bet is a steel needle, which is unaffected by alcohol. However, don't use a non-Viton-tipped needle just for the sake of it. A Viton needle does seal better at low fuel demands.

The shape of the needle is also a factor in fuel flow. A conical-point needle is convenient to make, but a correctly designed spherical form provides for more sensitive fuel level control at idle and low speed. In addition, this type of needle has the

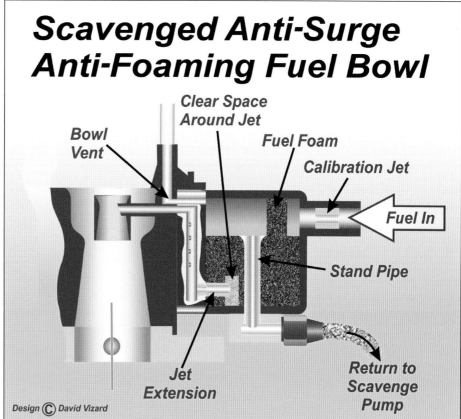

Fig. 12.13. *This schematic is helpful for fixing fuel slosh and foaming. Fuel control in the bowl is so steady that the carb runs over any terrain at any speed in much the same manner as fuel injection. Let's discuss the components, starting at the fuel input.*

Fuel to the calibration jet must be fed from a fuel pump capable of at least 10 psi at the jet. Output from the pump must be via a pressure regulator situated near the fuel bowl as this is a calibration factor. Fuel pressure is initially set on the pressure regulator (I used 9 psi).

The fuel is fed to a jet that allows just enough fuel to flow to meet the engine's needs at maximum demand. This flow value can be calculated from the fuel flow figures seen on a dyno or can be estimated by assuming 0.45 pounds of fuel per horsepower per hour are used. In practice the fuel pressure is backed off until the oxygen sensors indicate the mixture is just starting to go lean and then increased by about 1/4 psi.

The type of pressure regulator to use is one that references intake manifold pressure so at idle the fuel pressure is only about 3 to 4 psi.

The fuel coming from the jet should first enter an open volume and then flow onto fuel foam to dissipate its energy. The standpipe height can be adjusted. It works just fine if the top of it is set at the stock Holley fuel height but it's worth knowing that fuel control is so good that the stock fuel level to jet spill height is way more than needed. The fuel level can be raised without penalty if it proves to be beneficial to have the main system pull in sooner.

The scavenge pump must be able to pull out all the excess fuel when the engine is at less than WOT so its capacity needs to be about as big as the inlet pump.

Jet extensions should reach to about the middle of the fuel bowl. The area around them needs to be clear of foam so as not to impede flow to the jets themselves.

Fig. 12.14. This is Moroso's bowl extension and fuel tank foam fuel control conversion kit. A number of successful off-road racers use this system and report positive results.

capability of significantly more flow for WOT usage. Other than Braswell, BLP makes a spherical-ended, high-flow alcohol needle. Any of these spherical needles flow enough alcohol for a substantial four-figure power output.

Most needle and seat assemblies are either of "picture window" design or what is popularly known as, but misnamed, a "bottom feeder." What this actually means is that the needle/seat assembly has a bottom discharge capability by virtue of a sculpted needle so that fuel can discharge via the windows and the bottom of the brass body.

For a conventional needle and seat to work at its best use as little fuel pressure as possible along with the biggest needle possible so that the fuel has less tendency to enter as a high-speed jet, which may lead to foaming. A bottom-feeding needle and seat assembly is a little better than a regular window assembly, but it is still far from optimal when high-gs and vibration are involved.

At the time of writing, Bo Laws Performance is developing a true "bottom-feeding" needle and seat assembly that actually feeds the bottom of the float bowl. The fact that this needle and seat assembly feeds within 1/8 inch of the bottom of the fuel bowl makes a huge difference in the ability of the system as a whole to avoid fuel foaming.

Many off-road racers use the Moroso fuel foam/bowl extension kit in Figure 12.14. I have no personal experience with this anti-slosh kit, but it looks as if it should work, and that's an opinion supported by a couple of off-road racers, who have reported their successful results back to me.

If your application needs a fix for fuel surge, there is one. I got the idea from the late Sig Erson of Erson Cams while he was visiting me in England in 1974. The weekend he was with me he volunteered his services as a crew member for my British Touring Car Championship race at Thruxton. We had suffered minor fuel surge problems with our Weber carbs and Sig claimed the following solution to be a 100-percent fix. As our off-road Holleys later proved it was a 100-percent fix, and Figure 12.13 shows how it was done. As you can see the system uses fuel foam, a standpipe that acts as a weir setting the fuel level, and a scavenge pump.

Although it may seem as if the standpipe is plumbed in and everything is done, we could still do a measure of tuning. In practice, for a carb equipped with a regular float bowl, there is a calibration element in the fact that as the fuel demand increases, the fuel level drops. This means that there is a leaning-out process countered by the jetting. When making a change to the standpipe/scavenge system, the fuel level stays essentially unchanged so the top end can be richer than with the float assembly metering to the fuel bowl.

The way around this is to start with a restrictor jet that is just a little bigger at, say, 7 to 8 psi pump pres-sure, and then turn down the pressure in small increments until a lean out simulates the float assembly. At this point your jetting is back where it was with a float setup.

Pressure Regulators

Running just the right fuel pressure is important. Indeed, mino adjustments to find optimal pressure can be a tuning aid. You are looking for sufficient fuel pressure to supply a little more fuel than the engine needs at the lowest pressure possible because this minimizes fuel foaming (aeration). While this seemingly delicate situation may not be of much consequence to the street performance, bracket, or amateur racer, a 3- or 4-hp increase for a pro could make the difference between winning and losing.

So this little revelation now begs the question, "What pressure should I use for my application?" Let's start with what you may need to build a good but inexpensive setup for your street machine. It's common for a fuel pump with no more than 8-psi output pressure to be used without a pressure regulator. Holley states that a pump of 9 or more psi (as per their high performance pumps) should be used with a pressure regulator. For the price of a simple, low-cost pressure regulator it is worth installing anytime fuel pump pressure is more than 6 psi.

For an entry-level installation you need little more than a basic two-port inline regulator. This is a

Fig. 12.15. This is Holley's non-bypass regulator (PN 12-803). It is a real workhorse at an affordable price. If you want to build a better but still basic fuel system this is the unit to install.

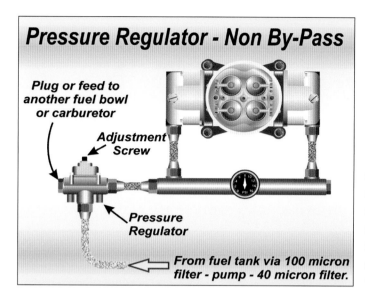

Pressure Regulator - Non By-Pass

Plug or feed to another fuel bowl or carburetor

Adjustment Screw

Pressure Regulator

From fuel tank via 100 micron filter - pump - 40 micron filter.

Fig. 12.16. Here is how you plumb in Holley's (or any other similar type) non-bypass pressure regulator (PN 12-803).

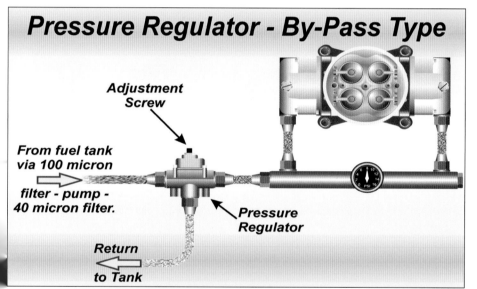

Pressure Regulator - By-Pass Type

Adjustment Screw

From fuel tank via 100 micron filter - pump - 40 micron filter.

Pressure Regulator

Return to Tank

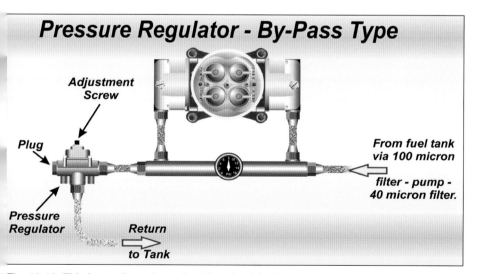

Pressure Regulator - By-Pass Type

Adjustment Screw

Plug

Pressure Regulator

Return to Tank

From fuel tank via 100 micron filter - pump - 40 micron filter.

Fig. 12.18. This is an alternate method for plumbing in a bypass pressure regulator.

Fig. 12.17. If you are using a bypass regulator the pressure is controlled not by dead-heading the fuel to limit the pressure but by bypassing excess fuel back to the tank. This requires a return line and the plumbing routing seen here.

simple as it gets. You just install the regulator in the line and adjust the pressure to about 6 psi.

A high-output fuel pump, typically pumps at pressures up to 14 psi with some going as high as 25 psi. These pressures overwhelm the needle and seat assembly in the fuel bowl. Here a typical inline regulator (such as Holley's 12-803 unit) works. However, you can install a bypass regulator to improve control and increase pump life.

If there is a return line from the front of the vehicle to the tank or you are prepared to install one, it is a better choice to go with a bypass regulator (such as Holley's 12-803BP). With this system, pressure is held at the set value by allowing the fuel to bleed off back to the tank. This means the pump is not "dead headed," which means it is not trying to pump fuel pressure against a closed or nearly closed output that is virtually stalling it.

Fig. 12.19. This is Holley's bypass pressure regulator (PN 12-803BP). A unit like this is about twice the cost of a non-bypass unit (PN 12-803) and requires a return line. However, the extra cost does buy you better fuel pressure stability.

Fig. 12.20. Holley sells these billet pressure regulators: model 12-840 (left) and the bigger, higher-capacity 12-843 unit (right). Both have a refined, precision, non-bypass design intended to maximize fuel pressure stability when a non-return system is used. Holley also has equivalent billet-style units in bypass configurations.

Fig. 12.21. Although Holley's billet regulators cost a little more they do provide the ideal place to locate the virtually mandatory pressure gauge.

Fig. 12.22. Setting the idle fuel pressure is just one aspect of optimizing the prevailing fuel pressure. Equally important is to know how the fuel pressure may vary as the vehicle travels down the track. To see this you need a dash-mounted fuel pressure gauge. Do not use a mechanical one as this can be dangerous in the event of a crash. Shown here is the Holley electric unit. It isolates fuel from the driver's compartment.

Fig. 12.23. This Holley pressure regulator mount locates on the carb. This is not only convenient but also makes for a smart-looking installation.

Fig. 12.24. This four-outlet port regulator is set up for a pair of 4-barrel carbs. The fitting allows braided lines to be used to each fuel bowl. The regulator itself needs to be mounted centrally fore and aft of the carbs and laterally at a point that minimizes fuel line length yet also avoids exhaust system heat.

Under these conditions, the pump runs hotter and the fuel heats up. Neither is what you want. The bypass regulator circulates excess fuel from the tank to the regulator and back to the tank. Plumbing for both types of regulators is shown in Figures 12.16, 12.17, and 12.18.

If you are building a super-cooled fuel system as described in Chapter 11, you can use an inline pressure regulator and the system will, to an extent, act as a bypass regulator (as

fuel is continually drawn from the fuel bowl by the system's scavenge pump). Therefore, the main fuel-supply pump is never dead headed.

If you are going to use E85 or alcohol as a fuel, you need a fuel-compatible pressure regulator. Holley's selection is a good place to start, but if you want to expand your range, check out Summit's large selection.

When alcohol is used, you need a large needle valve and adequate fuel pressure to flow enough fuel for maximum power. Fuel pressures need to be adequate at WOT and maximum RPM, but these higher pressures are often too much for the float to accurately control the fuel

flow at idle. If the pressures are set for idle, the engine starves of fuel at the top end. This situation is by no means universal, so it depends on the design of needle and seat used in the fuel bowl as well as its effective diameter. I have a friend who has just wrapped up a championship with his dragster and has not run a single pound over 3 psi all season. Therefore, if the needle and seat geometry is good enough, high pressures are not needed. However, it may take a while to sort

Fig. 12.26. Aeromotive makes a nice range of manifold referenced fuel pressure regulators. My experience with this company's products has only been positive.

Fig. 12.25. This Mallory pressure regulator can be boost or manifold-vacuum pressure referenced. This allows a reduction in fuel pressure to be made at idle. This is especially useful for alcohol-fed engines where the pressure at maximum output may need to be as high as 9 psi. If more pressure than this is required, investigate the needle/seat flow as it may be questionable.

through your fuel system to get to this happy state.

The best way to run strong while still in the process of making adjustments is to have a vacuum-referenced pressure regulator, such as one made by Mallory. A few other companies, such as Aeromotive, also make vacuum/boost-referenced, fuel-pressure regulators worthy of consideration. All these regulators compensate linearly, and that means for every 1 psi the intake pressure changes, the regulated fuel pressure changes the same amount.

Here is how this works for an alcohol-fueled engine. If, at idle, there are 6 inches of vacuum (3 psi), the pressure regulator reduces the pressure delivered by 3 psi. So if the base pressure is set at, say, 6 psi, then, at idle, it is 3 psi.

Using one of these pressure regulators makes it much easier to sort out an alcohol carb, especially if it's a big-block with a Holley Dominator or two. Summit Racing's website

includes the function and application of about three dozen brands.

Fuel Lines and Filters

The carburetor can be considered the end of the fuel system where the real business is conducted. The fuel supply must exceed the engine's demand. Therefore, you need to select an adequate pump and make

Fig. 12.27. If your carb has a sintered bronze filter, replace it with a higher-flow regular filter. The sintered units are only good to about 375 hp.

Fig. 12.29. If you are building a fuel system using braided hose with aero-style fittings, Earl's sells cost-effective in-line filters. These have replaceable filter elements that makes checking and refurbishing easy.

sure the system losses, as fuel is pumped from the tank to the carb, are minimized.

When building an effective low-loss fuel line, the first concern is to route the line as far from heat sources as possible. Should you think such a move is unnecessary, I suggest you read Chapter 11 on system thermal management again.

Once a viable route is established, you need to determine the ideal fuel-line diameter. Most factory fuel systems use 5/16-inch diameters. At about 6 psi, a stock pump does not deliver sufficient fuel volume for an engine that produces real power. Some fuel lines are complex to replace but if pump pressure is increased, the pipe's restriction is partially offset by the higher

Fig. 12.28. Holley has two versions of this type of canister fuel filter. One is 5/16 (PN 162-524), the other 3/8. The 3/8 (PN 162-523) version is good to about 500 hp.

Fig. 12.30. You need Holley's pro-quality billet-case fuel filters if you plan on building a top-of-the-line fuel supply system.

flow. Doubling the pump pressure results in an approximate 40-percent increase in flow at the carb.

If you'd rather not replace the fuel line, you can explore the use of one of Holley's 14-psi electric pumps and a pressure regulator. You can test the flow of your setup by running the pressure regulator outlet into a graduated can. In round numbers 1 quart per minute is good for 180 hp. If your 14-psi electric Holley pump in conjunction with a regulator cutting the pressure to 7 psi meets your needs, you can go with a 5/16-inch line.

If that's not enough, you need to increase the line to a minimum of 3/8 inch (-6 hose). This meets the needs of most street and street/strip vehicles that produce up to about 600 hp, although that figure is dependent on just how many sharp, right-angle fittings are used. If it is a race application, 1/2-inch diameter (-8 hose) should be considered a must.

The type of hose material is another factor that can come into play. Although a rubber hose spec'd for gasoline may provide adequate performance, it does present more resistance to flow than a purpose-made braided fuel line, such as produced by Earl's Performance Products (a division of Holley). Also, as a safety issue, you should use steel or vinyl braided hose for higher pressures, such as those delivered when Holley's top-performance pumps are in use.

Fuel filtration can be a big obstacle in cutting flow losses. First, if your Holley carb has the sintered fuel filter housed at the fuel bowl's inlet fitting, you should replace it if your engine makes more than about 375 to 400 hp.

Use a high-quality, in-line, free-flow, coarse fuel filter at the pump inlet. Use a fine fuel filter anywhere after the pump and prior to the pressure regulator.

Mechanical Fuel Pumps

The style of mechanical fuel pump you most often see on a production V-8 is used because it is quiet, cost effective, and reliable. It is also the style of pump mandated for use by a number of premier NASCAR series. To meet the demand, Holley developed high-performance versions.

Having an engine-mounted pump up front means sucking fuel from a tank as far away as 10 feet. When the vehicle accelerates, the pump has a much harder time sucking fuel than a pump that pushes it from the rear forward. Also, an engine-mounted pump gathers much heat and consequently unnecessarily warms the fuel. OE-type mechanical pumps, for the most part, have a good flow rate so they can supply engines up to 500 hp.

My advice: Only use a mechanical pump if it is adequate for your engine or the race sanctioning body requires it. If a mechanical fuel pump is required, use a really stout one with a high gallons-per-hour (gph) rating. The fuel is sucked forward from the tank to the carb, which is harder to do under high-g acceleration.

An electric pump at the back pushes fuel forward and these pumps are typically very consistent. Here, some numbers might help you make your decision. For a 10-foot tank-to-pump line and a 1-g start line launch, the pressure starts at the input side of the pressure regulator, and drops by 3.3 psi when it reaches the regulator. Since most vehicles can launch at more than 2 g, you can see that a pump sucking from the tank is at a disadvantage. The most suction that can be applied is equal to the atmospheric pressure (14.7 psi at sea level). If the fuel tank is mounted in the engine compartment just ahead of the engine, a mechanical pump works just fine.

Where a conventional pump, such as a high-flow Holley Ultra unit, has advantages is in a circle track situation where an alcohol carb is used. The gs pulled off the corner are not as high as at the start of a drag strip pass so the loss of pressure at the pressure regulator is not the big issue. Using a conventional cam-lobe-driven pump is a good way to get an effective high-flow fuel system. If you need a top-of-the-line performance

Fig. 12.31. Stock mechanical pumps are generally good for 50 to 80 gallons per hour. By the time installation losses are taken into account, this equates to 375 to 600 hp. This Holley pump, for a small-block Chevy (PN 12-327-13), is good for 130 gallons per hour.

Fig. 12.32. This is Holley's pump for a small-block Chevy (PN 12-327-30). At 200 gallons per hour it can accommodate about anything you can throw at it, such as more than a 1,500-hp fuel demand.

pump, Holley is sure to have one for you. When installing a mechanical pump, be sure to check the type of pressure regulator needed for it.

Alcohol Applications

A whole class of belt-driven mechanical pumps are offered for high-performance use with alcohol applications. The belt is installed on the nose of the cam or remotely mounted (fuel tank, usually) and cable driven. These pumps are expensive, and many are intended primarily for alcohol fuel-injection systems. However, the increasing usage of alcohol carbs has brought about the production of many pumps specifically aimed at meeting the needs of an alcohol-carbureted engine. If you are intent on a high-tech fuel delivery system for your alcohol-fueled engine, you can get specific information from companies such as Bo Laws Performance, Enderle Fuel injection, Hilbourne Fuel Injection, Kinsler Fuel Injection, Ron's Fuel Injection systems, and Waterman Pumps.

My experience in this area has been limited to a couple of drag race

Fig. 12.33. A belt-driven fuel pump for an alcohol carb, such as this Bo Laws unit, is well thought of by many professional Holley carb specialists.

applications and a half dozen or so circle track applications. What I can tell you is that the Bo Laws alcohol pump is highly recommended by a number of top carburetor specialists. I have also used Ron's Fuel Injection alcohol pumps to good effect. And I know that Waterman has a very large number of choices.

Electric Pumps

In conjunction with Holley carbs, most performance applications are likely to use an electric pump.

Flow Capability

Before making your selection, it is wise to have some idea of how big a pump your engine is likely to need. Looking at the fuel flow ratings is your starting point. Holley's performance fuel pumps are primarily rated by their free-flow capability.

This number can be misleading. You need to be aware that the greater the restriction, the lower the flow. For that reason, Holley gives a second number that provides the flow volume at a given pressure. You should have at least 7 psi for high-pressure pumps, and no more than 14 psi. And you should have at least 4 psi for low-pressure pumps, and no more than 7 psi. The figure you need to work

Fig. 12.34. This Holley's blue-top high-output pump. It has been favored by enthusiasts for probably 30 years. About 90 percent of engines I build make use of this versatile and cost-effective pump.

with is the second, smaller figure. At the end of the day, just how suitable your pump is can be greatly affected by how free flowing the plumbing is from the pump to the carb.

As an example, Holley's perennially popular "blue top" pump delivers 88 gph at 9 psi. If there is no loss in the system, this pump can support a 1,300-hp output of a well-tuned race engine. That looks good in theory, but what about in the real world?

Such an output means that each gallon the pump moves per hour supports 15 hp. But that does not take into account fuel-system losses. The reality is that some systems are a plumbing nightmare: For each gallon per hour of its rated flow at the quoted pressure, a given pump may only support 8 to 9 hp for every GPH of rated flow. If you build a good fuel system, that figure can go to 10 hp per gallon of rated flow per hour. If you build a reasonable system, that Holly "blue top" meets the needs of a 750-hp engine. But if you build a *really* good fuel system, it supports 880 hp.

Holley's "red top" pump can be used without a regulator. Its output at the pump is 7 psi and even at idle this is a little less at the fuel-bowl needle valve. This sort of pressure is acceptable but I still use a regulator to reduce that to about 5 psi. With high-output pressure pumps (14 psi) a regulator is virtually mandatory.

Fig. 12.35. This Holley pump (PN 12-150) looks good and is still all business when it comes to flow. This unit moves 140 gallons per hour at 7 psi.

Fig. 12.36. This Holley inline high-performance pump is smaller than average, but it has low-current consumption. It's operationally quiet and pumps enough fuel for a 900-hp carbureted engine.

Fig. 12.37. Building engines for magazine projects as I do means building good looking engines. Here are some of Holley's high-performance pumps, regulators, and filters that make my job just that much easier.

Pressure Output

Next, you need to learn whether the pump should be used with a bypass regulator or a non-bypass regulator.

An excess pressure limiting recirculatory bypass valve is installed within Holley's electric pumps. The pump's output-side pressure acts upon a spring-loaded pressure relief valve. When that pressure exceeds the set limit (14 psi for high-pressure pumps), the valve opens against the spring and feeds the fuel back to the inlet side of the pump. Although this is an effective way to control maximum pressure, it does mean the electric motor powering the pump can become hot and the action of recirculating fuel causes the fuel to heat up. The way to minimize this is to use a pump compatible with a bypass regulator rather than a dead-head regula-

tor as with a non-bypass unit.

When it comes to plumbing your fuel pump into the system there are a half dozen or so options depending on the number of carbs, the type of fuel used, etc. Holley has all the layouts you are likely to use as shown in Figure 12.38.

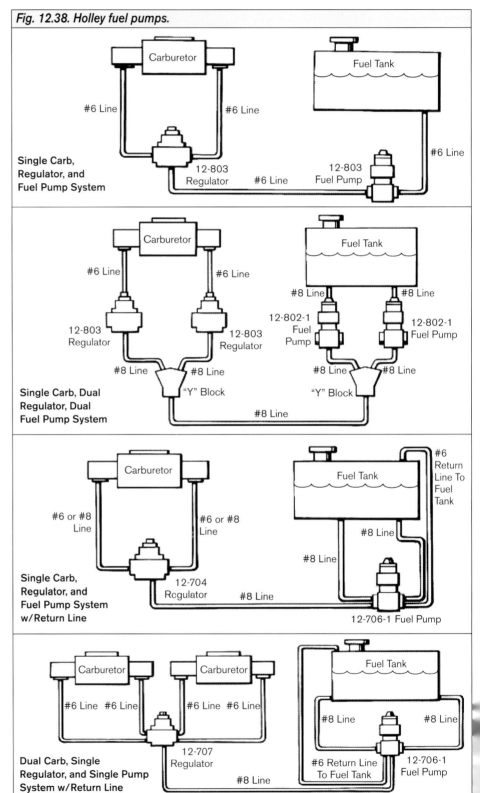

Fig. 12.38. Holley fuel pumps.

Single Carb, Regulator, and Fuel Pump System

Single Carb, Dual Regulator, Dual Fuel Pump System

Single Carb, Regulator, and Fuel Pump System w/Return Line

Dual Carb, Single Regulator, and Single Pump System w/Return Line

CALIBRATING FOR VARIOUS FUELS

In most cases, a fuel's octane value is the performance enthusiast's primary focus. But I must be absolutely clear here: There is no performance value in a high-octane fuel unless the engine's compression ratio and thermal-operating conditions dictate its need to stave off detonation. An 8.5:1 compression ratio engine will, as often as not, produce a better output on a quality 87-octane fuel than a costly 110-octane race fuel.

Today, various sanctioning bodies allow a wide range of fuel specs. Some allow only gas-station pump fuel while others specify a certain brand of race-grade gasoline, oxygenated gasoline, methanol, or ethanol/gasoline mixes such as E85. At the end of the day, you need to understand that an optimal result depends on knowing the best air/fuel ratio required for that particular fuel, so you can successfully increase output. In some cases, such as with methanol and E85, mixture quality is also important. A simple thing, such as a really effective booster, can easily be 30 hp and 30 ft-lbs on a typical 350-inch racer over one that is not.

Almost everything covered so far about the selecting, modifying, building, and calibrating your Holley has been for the use of a conventional non-oxygenated gasoline. This chapter focuses on some of the need-to-know factors of other fuels you might want to use.

Fig. 13.2. Racer David McCoig says, "If you know what your fuel likes in the way of engine specs, then you will like what your fuel delivers." That's the viewpoint of every pro fuel blender.

Fig. 13.1. A Ford 4.6-liter Modular engine is not endowed with a lot of cubes. However, this Mustang came alive and posted low-10s for the quarter when a Holley carb replaced the stock fuel injection and it was run on E85.

Fig. 13.3. This 950-cfm Holley was built from the parts bin and specifically spec'd to suit a particular induction system and fuel type. In this instance the carb was used on a single-plane race manifold and to feed the engine oxygenated gasoline. This meant appropriately larger jets in the main system.

Fig. 13.4. Optimizing the booster spec for a given fuel can mean a lot of dyno testing. Heed the booster advice if a predominantly alcohol blend of fuel is going to be used.

Oxygenated Fuels

Probably more than 99 percent of those reading this book have used oxygenated fuels in their daily driver. Next time you fill up, check the labels on the pump. Many have a notice stating that the fuel could have up to 10-percent ethanol blended into it.

Ethanol is an oxygen-bearing compound, which calls for a much greater amount of fuel per pound of air to achieve the stoichiometric air/fuel ratio. An engine equipped with an oxygen sensor feedback fuel-injection system compensates for the fact that a gasoline may contain up to 10-percent ethanol.

That, however, is not true for a carbureted engine. For complete use during combustion of both air and ethanol, the mixture ratio has to be exactly 9:1. (For methanol, the ratio is 6.5:1.)

To get to the stoichiometric ratio for station pump fuel with a 10-percent ethanol mix requires a jet area increase is necessary, as shown in Figure 13.5.

If you are blending gasoline with methanol, the jetting increase needed is greater. Figure 13.6 gives you the details.

When using the numbers in Figure 13.5 or Figure 13.6 for a jet size increase, there are a couple of factors you should be aware of. One is that the percentage of jet increase refers to the total increase in jet area. Remember, at WOT about 25 to 30 percent of the fuel goes through the power valve jetting, so if you are going to calibrate solely with the carb's main jet, it has to be a proportionally bigger increase than shown.

I prefer to rejet the power-valve restriction channel, because when going from mid to wide-open throttle, the response is usually cleaner and sharper. The difference is not very significant with small amounts of alcohol in the fuel; you get a more significant difference when E85 or near-100-percent alcohol is used. The improved transitional throttle response may not be important for the drag racer, but it

Tuning for Ethanol	
Percentage of Ethanol	Percent of Increase in Jet Area
2	0.6
4	1.2
6	1.8
8	2.4
10	3.0
12	3.5
14	4.1
15	4.4

Fig. 13.5. You need to run the correct size jets for the percentage of ethanol used.

Tuning for Methanol	
Percentage of Methanol	Percent of Increase in Jet Area
2	1.3
4	2.5
6	3.8
8	5.0
10	6.2
12	7.4
14	8.6
15	9.2

Fig. 13.6. Jet size needs to be calibrated for the amount or percent of methanol used.

Fig. 13.7. Since the early 1990s, 87-octane fuel has improved greatly. This is one of my "regular gas" Chevy 383 small-block builds. It has a 550-rpm idle and 14 inches of vacuum, yet it makes 503 ft-lbs and 482 hp.

is important for a circle track racer on a short track.

Another factor to consider is the cooling effect due to a high latent heat of evaporation. Also, the best power with alcohol-type fuels happens at a much richer mixture than stoichiometric. Therefore, all the jetting increases in Figure 13.5 and Figure 13.6 are the minimum increase you should use. Among all that has been said so far, there has been no mention of how you would know just what percentage of ethanol is in the gas-station pump fuel you bought. It is far from a consistent amount. This is yet one more example of why the installation of a wide-band oxygen mixture ratio gauge makes so much sense.

Power Increase

Now let's address the subject of potential power increase with a fuel mixed with up to, say, 10-percent ethanol or methanol. By weight, ethanol is 35-percent oxygen and methanol is 50-percent oxygen, which makes them appealing as means of power enhancement.

But this simplistic viewpoint is somewhat misleading. By the time you take into account all the other factors involved the theoretical power improvement at stoichiometric between straight gasoline and a gasoline/alcohol mix is very small. In fact, the difference is usually in favor of the straight gasoline.

So why use an alcohol/gasoline mix? Well, small power gains are realized mostly because the latent heat of evaporation of alcohols is considerably higher than that with straight gasoline.

Also, ethanol and methanol produce the best power when they are richer than straight gasoline. This means the jetting changes indicated in Figure 13.5 and Figure 13.6 need to be bigger than shown. Just how much bigger is a question of trial-and-error testing; a job to do at the track.

While attempting to get the best trap speed be sure to take note of the air temperature, humidity, and barometric pressure. When the weather is very hot or cold the use of an alcohol additive produces very little improvement over a straight, non-additized gasoline. This is because at high ambient temperatures the alcohol evaporates and uses up intake manifold volume, thus reducing the volumetric efficiency by more than the cooling effect increases it. At low temperatures the ignitability of the alcohol is compromised and offsets the possible gains from other aspects.

A low-percentage alcohol blend works best when ambient temperatures are between about 70 and 90 degrees F. This is true even though this blend is also

Fig. 13.8. This big-block Chevy 496 engine is on the Terry Walters dyno in Roanoke. It was used for the VP fuels test. The oxygen sensor data logging system allowed us to quickly home in on the best air/fuel ratio required. Usually when converting to an oxygenated fuel the fuel manufacturer advises what ratios are likely to be optimal.

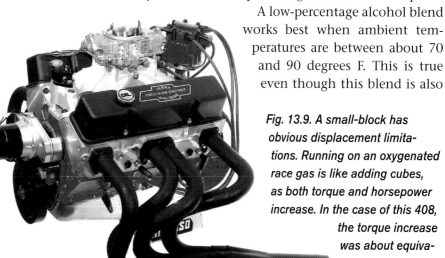

Fig. 13.9. A small-block has obvious displacement limitations. Running on an oxygenated race gas is like adding cubes, as both torque and horsepower increase. In the case of this 408, the torque increase was about equivalent to having 422 inches.

dependent on the engine's underhood and coolant temperatures.

Note that the potential to increase the octane value of a straight gasoline is reduced as the temperature increases where the mixture enters the cylinder. So in practice, high air and coolant temperatures nearly nullify any octane benefits you get from alcohol additives. At the end of the day only fine tuning of the system can show benefits at the track.

Oxygenated Race Gasoline

For many years, sanctioning bodies banned oxygenated fuels, but beginning about 2000, oxygenated fuels began gaining in popularity as a means of increased output. Although race fuel blenders don't talk about the contents of their fuel, you can assume that for the most part, oxygenated fuels contain compounds such as propylene oxide (up to 2 percent) and nitro paraffin (including nitro methane).

These compounds may also be used with methanol and ethanol. The alcohol content added to a mixture tames the combustion process, reduces peak temperatures, and adds some octane value. As a result, the fuel is more "compression friendly."

The first question that most hot rod skeptics ask is, "Does oxygenated fuel work?" The answer is "Yes," as long as you know what you are doing.

Because part of the content of the fuel flowing through the jets is oxygen, it is necessary to increase jet size. The stoichiometric ratio of a typical oxygenated fuel is a couple of ratio numbers richer than a non-oxygenated fuel. To bring the

Fig. 13.10. The amount of ethanol in E85 varies greatly with the season. To get the jetting right means being able to correct the ratio of ethanol to gasoline. This Echecker from Quick Fuel Technology does just that.

TECH TIP

Vizard/Walters Fuel Test

One of my big-block Chevys was used to test VP oxy fuel against VP non-oxy fuel for power gains at Terry Walters Precision Engines. This engine, which is featured in a YouTube.com video, was not a race engine but a 10.5:1 street engine with a 650-rpm lope-free idle.

In most, but not all, instances a high-octane oxygenated race fuel is much better suited to a high compression ratio. This engine did not need the octane value of either of the test fuels. Indeed, prior to the test it made a tad more power on 93-octane unleaded fuel.

The bottom line here is that if oxygenated fuel produces 27 extra hp in what is essentially a street engine, you can assume it will do even a shade better in your high-compression race engine. ■

Fig. 13.11. This 750-cfm Holley HP and intake manifold replaced the fuel injection induction on the 4.6 Mod Motor Mustang shown in Figure 13.1. The result was an increase of more than 60 hp!

Fig. 13.12. Here is the carbureted 4.6 Mustang induction ready to run. This setup was used to test output with gas and E85.

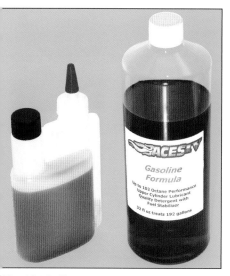

Fig. 13.13. If you are running gasoline you need this ACES gasoline formula. If the fuel is an alcohol or ethanol blend, you really need to use ACES alcohol formula.

mixture up to what is required usually takes jetting 4 to 7 numbers up from what is already being used either in the main jet or the power valve restriction channel.

Also, the ignition timing may need some attention, depending on what was used prior to the fuel changeover. Usually flame speed is higher with oxy fuels so the timing may need to be retarded by a degree or two.

E85

E85 is theoretically defined as a blend of 85-percent ethanol and 15-percent gasoline with a great potential to be a very cost effective power-producing race fuel. In practice, the label E85 encompasses a mix of ethanol and gasoline ranging from 51- to 87-percent ethanol. This wide range is to ensure good startup characteristics from summer to winter. The more ethanol there is in a blend, the harder it is to start under cold conditions. The problem for the racer is that this big variation means that jetting must suit the blend of the day.

Vehicles made to run either gasoline or E85 are designed around the output of an oxygen sensor, which corrects the injector open time to produce the correct air/fuel ratio. With a Holley carb, you don't have that luxury. So, while running E85 promises performance similar to a high-dollar oxygenated race gas, it is not without problems.

As long as it is not too cold, running a true E85 (85-percent ethanol, 15-percent gasoline) is about your best bet for output. To ensure that this is what you are actually feeding your engine, you need an Echecker from Quick Fuel Technology. This ingeniously simple device allows you to measure, within close limits, the ethanol/gasoline ratio. Most E85 contains 87-percent ethanol. But you may need to buy some straight ethanol to boost an ethanol-shy E85 mix to the 87-percent mark.

E85 Home-Blend

Another option is to brew your own E85. I have found that a mix of good 87-octane fuel and acetone or methyl ethyl ketone (MEK), plus ethanol in a ratio of 13/2/85 produces good results.

You may be asking yourself if using 93-octane would be better in your home brew. The answer is that you could barely notice a difference, so 87 is as good as any—and cheaper.

Also be aware that tetraethyl lead as used in race gas does little for increasing the octane value of alcohols. This usually means that mixing ethanol or methanol with leaded race fuel is a waste of money.

Fig. 13.14. This E85 conversion kit from raceone85.com was tested on the 4.6 Mustang shown in Figure 13.1.

Fig. 13.15. Shown here are the parts in the conversion kit from raceone85.com was quick and simple. Dyno results in this high-compression engine were slightly better than with a straight 105-octane race gas.

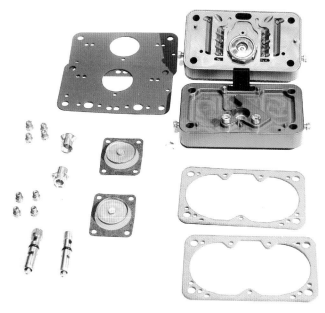

If you want to hop up your E85 blend for a power/torque increase of at least 1 percent (but usually nearer 1.5 percent), try this: Add the appropriate dose of ACES IV-A Alcohol Formula from American Clean Energy Systems. I have personally run dyno and wear tests on this product over many years. Many top racers who know about it absolutely do not want me to tell you about it because they do not want to lose the edge it gives them over those who are not using it.

So what does ACES IV-A do? First, it totally counters an alcohol-based fuel's lubrication stripping bore wash effect. From my own tests (to the point that bore and ring life are improved) wear is reduced by a minimum of 300 percent. That means if the bores wore 0.003 before then it would be a maximum of 0.001 after ACES IV-A is used.

Second, the typical top ring ridge is not seen even with a full season's circle track racing. The upper cylinder lubrication decreases friction and increases power.

Fig. 13.16. This is a very comprehensive alcohol conversion kit for a Dominator from Quick Fuel Technology. The bowl extenders (arrows) increase the volume of the fuel bowls.

Fig. 13.17. If you are starting from scratch with a new alcohol engine, a cost-effective route is to get one of Holley's alcohol carbs. My experience, although limited to just a few examples, has indicated close out-of-the-box calibrations and good dyno results.

Fig. 13.18. Because of their limited breathing, Chevy big-blocks love high-compression ratios. This, and the added cooling effect of alcohol, makes them more responsive to alcohol-based fuels than might be expected.

Fig. 13.19. Poor atomization and induction system wet-flow characteristics produce equally poor output results. An intake manifold with a more direct shot to the head port and high-port velocities pay off in this respect.

Third, ACES IV-A includes an ignition enhancer. This helps toward a cleaner burn and usually less of a need to run quite as rich a mixture.

Last, there are corrosion inhibitors in the formula. Ethanol and substantially more so methanol attack many of the component materials of a fuel system made for straight gasoline. Those corrosion inhibitors also act as a lube for fuel pumps, considerably extending their lives. For all practical purposes, using ACES IV-A totally eliminates fuel system corrosion of an alcohol-fueled engine. An effective dosage amount can be as little as 1/2 ounce per gallon.

If your regular street driver is a flex-fuel vehicle, you can save yourself some dirty varnished injector problems down the road by running regular gasoline/alcohol fuels blended with ACES IV-A.

Legislation cutting the amount of sulphur allowed in gasoline and Diesel fuels for the road has been introduced. This means that in the near future we will see the number

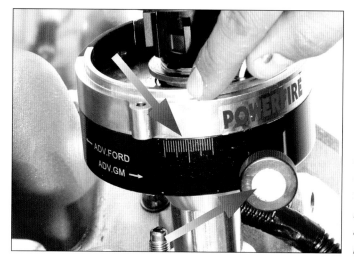

Fig. 13.20. If, with alcohol-based fuels, the engine is not awash with an overly rich mixture, the ignition timing becomes more of a tune-up factor. Being able to adjust in increments of 1 degree as with this Professional Products distributor is a positive aid in finding maximum output.

of problems with varnished injectors and in-tank pumps continue to increase. The use of ACES IV-A is a 100-percent corrective fix!

Metering Blocks

If your intent is to use ethanol or methanol, the design of the metering blocks needs to be drastically revised as to fuel volume handling capability. It is possible to modify gasoline metering blocks to get the job done. Heck, back when, if you wanted to run alcohol fuels, there were no real options other than using highly modified production metering blocks. These days things are a lot different. Holley and many aftermarket Holley specialists offer metering blocks specifically for ethanol- and methanol-based fuels. If you have the budget this is the painless way to go.

Flowing enough alcohol fuel into the induction system means

Alcohol Conversions

The first alcohol (methanol) Holley I built was when I was living in Tucson in the 1970s. I was able to shortcut the route to success with some good guidance from David Braswell and Bill "Buckwheat" Wheatly, now of CV Products. The following is a quick rundown on how to build your own alcohol carb from a typical mechanical secondary performance-orientated Holley. I must warn you, however, that a mistake here could void the economics of doing the job yourself.

Modify Carb Body

Use metering blocks with a power valve and drill the PVRCs to 0.100 inch. (This is about the limit of flow for this circuit).

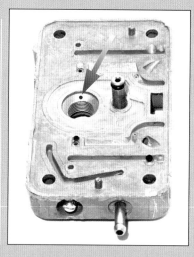

Drill both power valve restriction channels to about 0.100 inch.

Alcohol Conversions *continued*

Pull the plugs on the main jet emulsion wells and drill the wells to about 0.25-inch diameter. These need to be replugged when done.

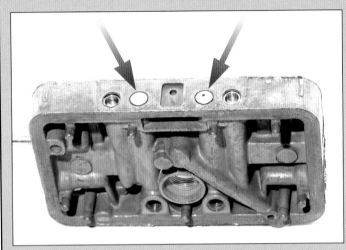

Remove the main well plugs and drill the well to 0.250 all the way to the bottom of the existing hole. Holley has replacement plugs for this location.

Suitably enlarge the angled holes that connect the boosters in the carb body to the main jet emulsion wells.

Drill a 0.075-inch hole (use a #48 or #49 drill) directly above the main jet hole. This acts as an auxiliary jet so you can use jets you already have.

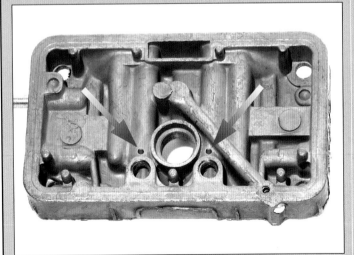

Drill auxiliary main jets to 0.075 inch.

Drill out the idle jets with a #60 (0.040-inch) drill. This is your starting size. When tuning you may have to open these up to as much as 0.060-inch in diameter.

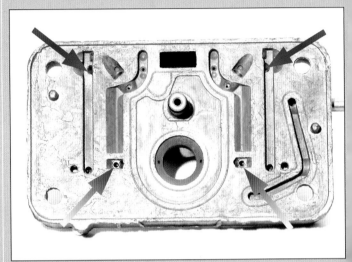

Drill idle jets to 0.040-inch diameter. Remember they can be located in a number of different places. The most common locations are shown here, which are either toward the bottom of the metering block (yellow/red arrows) or at the top (blue/red arrows).

Enlarge Booster Passage

Your next move is to enlarge the booster's internal passage and this is where your first big obstacle can lie. For alcohol fuels, the best results are seen with high-gain boosters that have a stronger pull on the main jet and provide better fuel atomization (see Chapter 7 for more detail). In order of performance, this means annular boosters are followed by dog-leg boosters and then straight-leg boosters.

If you are using a straight-leg booster don't use a 1.5-inch venturi in a 4150 carb because the combination produces a very poor signal. However, enlarging the hole in the booster is easy and can be done without removing the booster from the carb body.

For an annular discharge booster enlarging the hole in the booster can also be done without removing the booster from the carb body.

You need to remove the dog-leg booster to get to the angled-down leg part before you can enlarge the passage to about 0.190 inch. Removing the booster from the body involves destroying the swaged retention. This means you need an alternative retention method when refitting unless you purchase a booster fitting tool (from AED or BLP, for example).

Reinstall Booster

A professional carb shop can reinstall boosters but the best bet (and least expensive?) is to modify new boosters yourself.

Drill some holes in the body just above the booster's location.

Tap the holes to take a small Allen screw to lock the booster in place.

Apply epoxy to glue in the boosters and seal them. If you do not use a securing/lock screw here and the boosters fall out they jam the butterflies wide open and that has dire consequences.

Adjust Air Correctors

Drill the idle air correctors (outer ones) to 0.075-inch diameter (a #49 drill works well). Also, when you set up the idle make sure that both the primary and secondary butterflies are open about the same amount. During setup

the idle air bleed size probably doesn't need much resizing. If it does, it can go larger by up to about 0.015 inch. (Most idle-mixture calibration is done on the idle jet.)

For the main circuit air correctors (high-speed bleeds), what works depends somewhat on the booster signal. If you have a straight-leg booster in a big venturi (low signal), an air corrector diameter around 0.025 inch is a good place to start. If you are at the other end of the scale with a high-gain annular booster, an air corrector diameter about 0.035 inch is a good starting point.

Accelerator Pump System

On engines up to about 650 to 700 hp you are probably fine with a 30-cc accelerator pump. On engines over that you should start thinking in terms of a 50-cc pump.

As for squirters, get a jet drill set from Holley and start with a 40 to 45 for size.

Also be sure to use the hollow pump jet securing screw.

As for pump-arm cams, start with a #41R465 on both ends and tame things down as indicated by track testing. Initial tune-up procedures are the same as for gasoline use.

The last of the mods for alcohol are in the float bowl and are discussed in Chapter 12.

not only having jets with 60 percent more area (ethanol) or 260 percent more area (methanol), but also having the relevant passages suitably enlarged. Another consideration is the volume of the accelerator pump system.

At first, you would think that this also needs to be enlarged in the same proportions as the jets but this proves not to be so. In fact, the system runs very rich for best results with alcohol-based fuels, and the amount of vaporized fuel in the intake manifold is substantially less. In turn, the demands on the accelerator pump system are not proportionally greater,

but they do, nonetheless, need to be enlarged.

When you make the swap from gasoline to alcohol be sure to get alcohol-resistant pump diaphragms, fuel bowl needles, check valves, etc. Also be aware that at high power levels the amount of fuel that is required to pass through the booster passage becomes limited by the size of that hole. Make sure this is not a limitation, as running into a lean mixture with either ethanol or methanol is bad news for pistons.

Fig. 13.21. Holley's Alcohol Dominator on a big-block engine proves to be a very effective power/torque generator with results similar to those of oxygenated race fuel.

IMPROVING AIRFLOW

Maximizing airflow to the engine helps ensure your engine produces the maximum horsepower and torque. Selecting a carb too big for the job is really all about making sure that whatever it flows in the way of CFM is done while meeting the demands for a sufficiently strong booster signal. Even without having the entire range of rebuild/modification equipment of a full-blown carb shop there is a lot you can do to a stock Holley to increase airflow without incurring any penalties.

Even simple mods produce increased airflow as well as enhance the all-important booster gain/signal.

In this chapter I use an 850 vacuum secondary Holley to show how to bump it to almost 960 cfm, and actually increase the booster signal in a proportion slightly greater than the airflow increase. In practice, this means the low-speed output of this carb is as per its original CFM rating, but the high-speed output is as per the modified CFM rating.

Now you may ask, If I can do this in my shop at home, why can't Holley engineers with all their resources do it? The answer is, They can. Everything I discuss here is known to Holley engineers. The reason they don't incorporate most

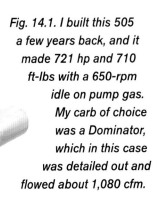

Fig. 14.1. I built this 505 a few years back, and it made 721 hp and 710 ft-lbs with a 650-rpm idle on pump gas. My carb of choice was a Dominator, which in this case was detailed out and flowed about 1,080 cfm.

of what I am about to show you is simply a matter of production cost.

The Source of all Induction

Whether induction is brought about by the exhaust pulse or the downward motion of the piston during the induction stroke, its source is the cylinder. When selecting a carb, make sure that the induction demand originating at the cylinder is allowed to communicate as effectively as possible with the carb. This means that whatever intake manifold you choose needs to be as flow efficient as possible.

Runners must be the right size for good port velocity and they must be shaped to be efficient in terms of flow. A runner too big for the job does not produce anywhere near the best torque curve. The better the intake, the better your engine responds to a thoughtfully selected carb CFM.

Also bear in mind that as far as the boosters are concerned, their job of atomizing the fuel is better served by a pulsating flow as each individual cylinder draws. An inefficiently flowing manifold or one with too much volume (due to big runners or big plenum or a combination of both) damps the pulsing flow seen by the boosters and low-speed output suffers while showing no gain at high speed. Part of the reason a large carb can work so well on a good (emphasize *good*) dual-plane is the fact that the boosters see a much stronger induction pulse from any given cylinder.

Making More Air

There are plenty of reasons for wanting more air from a Holley carb without spoiling its low-speed capability. Just as I was about to write this chapter, I prepped a carb for a couple of big-block Chevy test applications. Both were true street-performance engines, and as such, a vacuum secondary carb was appropriate. One was a low-buck 468 engine built to demonstrate the results from a set of Edelbrock's entry-level E heads. The other engine was for a GM 572 update project.

The goal was to retain total streetability while extracting maximum output within a certain cost range. Any decent-size big-block really deserves the services of a Dominator in terms of WOT output, but in this case cost and fuel economy meant utilizing a 4150-platform carb. Because a big-block needs Dominator airflow you can see the need to make the most of any increased airflow potential a 4150-style carb may have.

Because a choke was a prime ingredient, an 850 vacuum secondary

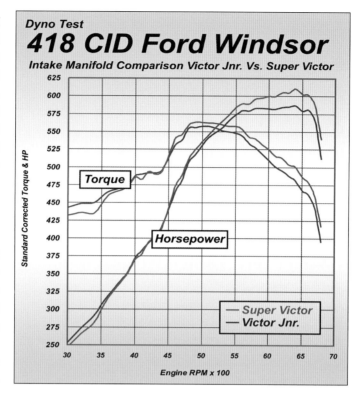

Fig. 14.2. Selecting the right manifold can often be difficult. Here is a test of an Edelbrock Victor Jr versus a Super Victor. If the build is targeting more than about 600 hp and it needs a top end, the Super Victor is the best choice. The carb on this build is a 950 Ultra.

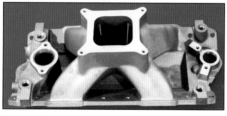

Fig. 14.3. You should consider the Holley 300-110 if you have a small-block build that is targeting the 550- to 650-hp range and needs a wide powerband for street/ strip use. Designed by Keith Dorton, my tests show it runs well in the top end and better than you might expect down in the lower range. I used it with a 950 Ultra on a 383 that made 641 hp and 542 ft-lbs.

Fig. 14.4. Laz Mesa of Mesa Balancing and I have worked on several very successful project engines together. This street 425 Ford Windsor small-block was one of them. For this build, Laz did all the machining while I ported the heads.

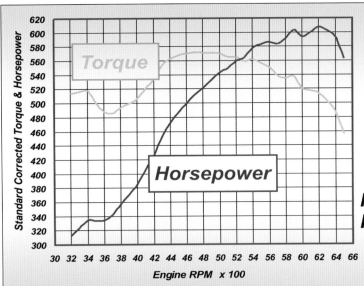

Dyno Test
425 CID Pro Power/RHS equipped Ford Windsor built by Mesa Balancing

Performance Specification:
Peak Horsepower - 607 @ 6,200 rpm
Peak Torque - 572 ft-lbs @ 4,500 rpm

Fig. 14.5. The Mesa/Vizard 425 was a true street unit in that it utilized a hydraulic roller cam (Comp Cams ground to my spec). It idled at about 700 to 720 rpm and ran on pump gas. The carb was a detailed 850.

carb was chosen for the series of flow tests. These tests also help you better understand and appreciate where major flow losses occur and where they might look as if they occur but don't.

Flow Mods: Phase One

Mounting the carb directly into the flow bench and blowing air through the carb is no different than mounting it the other way around and drawing air through it. The advantage of blowing air is that the exiting flow path can be easily plotted with the aid of a pitot tube velocity probe.

Refer to Phase One shown in "Airflow Test Results" on page 134. Test 1 is the stock carb's flow capability. Test 2 is about as simple as it gets for more airflow through a Holley carb, especially one that must have a choke and, consequently, a choke horn.

Test 2 is also with a K&N Stub Stack installed. Note the baseline airflow went from 849 to 872 cfm and it took much longer to unpack the Stub Stack than it did to install it.

Fig. 14.6. Holley's most versatile high-performance carb probably is the 750 HP Ultra. Right out of the box, it can really deliver the goods on any engine that is intended to produce between 475 and 600 hp. It does this while delivering great torque and good driving manners.

Fig. 14.7. The 850 vacuum secondary test cab was mounted on the flow bench and the air was blown through it for most of the flow tests in this book. On the bench, this 850, in stock form, delivered 849 cfm.

Fig. 14.8. A K&N Stub Stack is the fastest way to add 25 or more CFM to your street Holley. Where flow is limiting output it can show a really useful power increase.

Fig. 14.9. The two K&N Stub Stacks at the top are for Dominators and the two on the outside of the middle row are for 4150s and 4160s. The one in the middle is for 4150 carbs with a milled choke horn. The one on the bottom fits the popular 5-inch air horn that so many racers believe increases airflow. The bad news here is that they do nothing other than add aero drag unless used with that Stub Stack insert.

Incidentally, I have had a number of successful engine builders express surprise when they see a Stub Stack on one of my Holley-equipped engines. The usual comment is along the lines of, "They don't actually work, do they?" That is sort of a statement and a question all rolled into one. Well, here is the bottom line: The reason I designed the original Stub Stack and took it to K&N was because I felt there was a need for such a system.

My business is making more horsepower, so if it did not work, I would have dropped the idea. When I demonstrated a prototype to K&N engineers on my dyno, it showed a 5- to 6-hp increase on a 400-horse small-block Chevy. On the popular 496 (1/4-stroked 454 with 0.060-inch oversize bore) a big-block Chevy Stub Stack can be worth up to 9 hp, depending on the rest of the engine's spec.

Flow Mods: Phase Two

On the subject of Stub Stacks and spacers and how they affect flow and power potential is where mounting the carb upside down and blowing through it shows just what a spacer can do for flow.

In Phase Two tests, the baseline is once again 849 cfm for a bare carb. The first spacer to be flow tested is of a not-so-common 2-inch-thick, "four round to two oval" hole design. Note the flow went from 849 to 937 for a whopping 88 cfm increase. If that sounds almost unbelievable, let

Fig. 14.11. The open spacer (left) and the four-hole tapered spacer (top) are the most common types available. The only source I know of for the not-so-common 2-inch-thick, "four round to two oval hole" design (lower right) is from Terry Walters Precision Engines. This spacer works well with a dual-plane when blended into the high-plenum turn shown in Figure 14.10.

me explain why the gain was so substantial.

It's far more important how the air *leaves* an object in its flow path than how the air *arrives* at it, unless supersonic speeds are involved. In this instance the spacer allows the discharge from the base plate to be tidied up along its exit path. That is good, but what you see here is something of an artificial situation. With no manifold downstream of the spacer, the spacer itself acts as if the manifold is perfect in terms of allowing an uninterrupted flow.

In practice the presence of the intake manifold can seriously interrupt the discharge flow pattern out of the spacer. With a well-designed

Fig. 14.10. The upper plenum of a dual-plane intake can suffer a significant flow loss because the casting takes a tight turn immediately after the air exits the carb barrels. By using a 4 into 2 spacer and applying a much larger radius to the corners (yellow arrows) and blending it into the bottom of the spacer this situation can be considerably reduced. Enlarging the radius at the bottom of the deep plenum (blue arrow) can also contribute measurably to the output seen with a dual-plane intake.

single-plane intake having steeply inclined ports for a more direct carb-to-runner path, things are not too bad. Where problems arise is when the hood-to-carb clearance may be an issue, especially with a dual-plane intake and, specifically, with the higher of the two plenums.

On the high plenum of a dual-plane without a spacer, the air exiting the carb has to make an almost immediate right-angle turn upon

Airflow Test Results

These are the results of the flow tests discussed in the main text. As you read through follow up by referencing the results here.

Test	CFM	Conditions
Phase One: K & N Stub Stack		
1	849	Baseline: stock carb, bare
2	872	As above but with K&N Stub Stack air entry
Phase Two: Spacer Test		
1	849	Baseline: stock carb, bare
2	937	2-inch 4-hole spacer into two oval holes for two-plane intake
3	954	2-inch open spacer
4	969	2-inch 4-hole tapered spacer
5	550	1-inch reverse-taper-restrictor spacer, 1.75 to 1.25
6	563	2-inch reverse-taper-restrictor spacer, 1.75 to 1.25
7	470	1.25 restrictor plate
Phase Three: Carb Modification Tests		
1	849	Baseline: stock carb, bare
2	993	Stock body, less base plate
3	853	Removed choke plate and shaft
4	874	Removed screw ends
5	861	Slab cut throttle shaft
6	916	Aero cut throttle shaft
7	922	Dome cut screw heads
8	924	Knife-edged butterflies
9	935	Dressed venturis and boosters
10	956	Added K&N Stub stack
11	1,004	Modified body, less base plate

Fig. 14.12. For such a simple change, a spacer can be worth a surprising amount of extra power, particularly on a large or high-RPM engine or an engine with too small a carb. The place to find out if your engine needs one is on the dyno or at the track.

Fig. 14.13. When it come to boosting flow, the four-hole tapered spacer is definitely the best. However, the place to determine if that is what the engine wants is still the dyno.

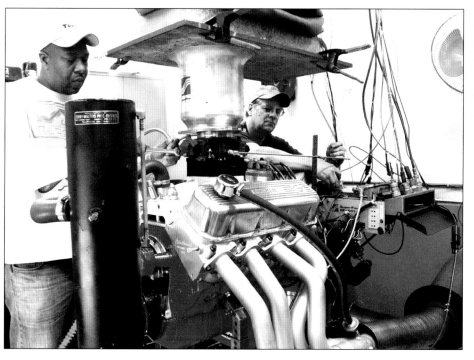

Fig. 14.14. This low-buck big-block was built to test Edelbrock E heads. Even with a small flat-tappet hydraulic cam this 468 was, with the aid of an open-plenum intake and a black 950 Ultra carb, cranking out nearly 600 hp and 600 ft-lbs.

exiting the carb (see Figure 14.10). That, as you can imagine, is not good for flow. By using a "four round to two oval" hole spacer as shown in Figure 14.11, you can dress out the typically tight radius seen at the top turn of the high plenum on a dual-plane to good effect.

With this as part of the power recipe, I have seen as much as 570 hp from a dual-plane, bored and stroked

small-block Chevy. This design of spacer maintains the integrity of the dual-plane 180-degree induction pulse separation concept. In other words, you are not making a poor single-plane intake from a dual-plane concept.

Test 3 shows the result of using the most common of all spacers: the 2-inch open design. In this instance flow increased from 849 to 954, a 105-cfm increase.

Test 4 shows the effect of a four-hole tapered spacer. This type of spacer (sometimes referred to as a "super sucker") seeks to streamline the exit as far as possible within the 2 inches it occupies between the carb and the intake. On single-plane race intakes these are the spacers most likely to work.

On some occasions race rules or race conditions may call for a spacer whose sole purpose is to reduce engine output to one more appropriate to the track. Test 5 and

Fig. 14.15. Filing the projecting ends of the butterfly securing screws is an easy and worthwhile flow mod. Be sure to use thread-locking compound on the screws to prevent the engine from eating them.

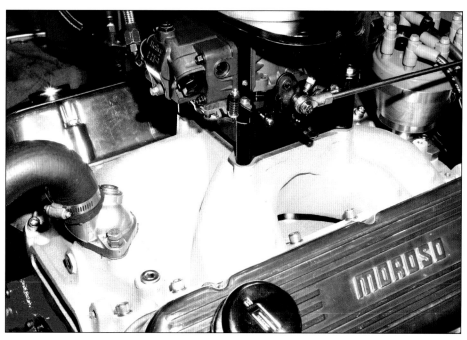

Fig. 14.16. To make your carb work its best, be sure to select an efficient intake manifold. A single-plane on any big-block of 454 inches or more works fine for the street, as a correctly built engine still has the low-speed output to overpower street tires.

Fig. 14.17. Although intended for a race application, this 950 Ultra on a Chevy 572 big-block allowed a street-spec engine to handsomely surpass the 700-hp mark while running 87-octane fuel. It did this with impeccable manners, and the only work done on the carb consisted of jetting for the application.

Test 6 show the results of using two reverse-tapered spacers (one is 1 inch thick and one is 2 inches thick) and a restrictor plate.

The interesting factor here is that when flow is reduced like this on the bench, you see it mirrored when the engine is on the dyno, unless the intake manifold is incredibly bad. The point is that you can destroy flow potential a lot more easily than you can generate it.

Flow Mods: Phase Three

The next step is to physically modify the carb in an effort to obtain extra flow. It took me about a day to modify the 850 unit in Figure 14.24, and the only tools I used were a set of needle files, a die grinder with a speed reducer for about 2,000 rpm, and some nearly worn-out 100-grit emery rolls.

In Test 1, the baseline flow is once again 849. For Test 2, and to demon-strate a point, I removed the base plate completely. This resulted in 993 cfm. This big increase indicates that the butterflies in the base plate con-stitute a major flow restriction.

I so often hear, "Well why didn't you simply bore out the venturis?" The answer is that with any flow development project you start by improving the worst flow restrictions. The venturis of a carb are already super-efficient in terms of flow for a given area. The butterflies, on the other hand, are not as efficient. The butterflies and shaft assembly cause the 144-cfm flow loss.

For Test 3, I reinstalled the base plate and performed the first simple flow mod. This entailed removing the choke plate and its shaft from the choke horn. This move provided a 3.5-cfm flow increase (but because I am rounding to the nearest whole number it is recorded as 4 cfm). That is probably a lot less than you might have thought.

In just a few minutes working with a file, you can augment this mod by applying a radius to the top edges of the choke horn. This increases the flow about 3 to 5 more cfm.

You may see carbs that have been reworked for a higher performance by milling off the choke horn. If the edges of the milled surface have been given only a cursory de-burr, these sharp edges actually detract from the carb's flow potential.

If you have the choke horn milled from your carb, be sure to install a K&N Stub Stack made specifically for milled horns (see Figure 14.9).

For Test 4, the form of the flow-restrictive butterfly and shaft assem-bly is addressed. The first move is to simply file off the excess and aerody-namically disastrous material from the ends of the butterfly securing screws. Note that as the carb leaves the factory these screw ends are staked to spread them so they don't back out and get eaten by the engine. To guard against this after the screws have been filed off, they need to be removed one at a time and "locked in" with blue Loc-Tite.

The airflow test results on page 134 shows that simple move was worth 19 cfm. A point to note here is that each time you increase airflow by using a more efficient butterfly and shaft assembly you actually increase the booster activity. That means all this extra airflow has no downside as far as low-speed output is concerned.

Test 5 involves slabbing the throttle shafts to reduce the cross-sectional area presented to the incoming airstream. This is a popu-lar move and is done on many high-performance carbs, either built by Holly or an aftermarket carb com-pany. As the airflow tests show a loss of 13 cfm, you can safely conclude

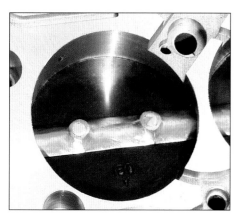

Fig. 14.18. Here is the installed aero shaft ready for flow testing. As the results show it was worth a few CFM.

Fig. 14.19. The simple job of aero forming the screw heads into a dome can result in an increase of up to 6-cfm.

Fig. 14.20. Knife-edging the butterflies to better streamline them can also aid flow. Just how much depend on the type of butterfly. The brass ones are less efficient than the steel ones so show a greater gain when modified.

it is not all it's supposed to be. This move reduces the area presented to the airstream but the introduction of corners has increased the shaft's drag coefficient by a greater amount. The net result is a loss.

In Test 6, the shafts are aero formed (see Figure 14.18 and Figure 14.19). In doing so we are not only reducing the area presented to the airstream but also decreasing its drag coefficient. The numbers tell the story: an increase over Test 4 (stock shafts) of no less than 32 cfm!

Holley employs a number of different styles of butterfly securing screws. On the more basic, street-

oriented carbs (such as our 850) the Phillips screw head is not particularly streamlined. Loading them in a lathe (or a securely held drill gun) and filing the heads to a dome helps. Reshaping the screw heads in Test 7 resulted in another 6 cfm of airflow.

Can you streamline the butterflies as done with the shafts? In this context, it's called knife edging, which can make a big difference depending on the type of butterfly. Early Holleys had 1/16-inch-thick brass butterflies but the current models mostly have a steel butterfly about 0.030 inch thick. Knife edging is worth about 6 cfm on the earlier, thicker butterflies.

For Test 8, the butterflies were knife edged, which left about 0.010

of the original edge so as to still fit the bore. Fit is not an issue if you have time with a needle file so you can cut the knife edge right to the minimum. Test 8 shows that the half hour or so I spent knife edging the butterflies only paid off to the tune of 2 cfm. The only consolation is that it is 2 cfm in the right direction.

It is clear that we have pretty much exhausted any gains to be had by simple grinding and/or filing. But I've shown the potential for improvement in flow without touching the boosters or enlarging the venturi.

Fig. 14.21. Here is a steel knife-edged butterfly. The gain was only 2 cfm.

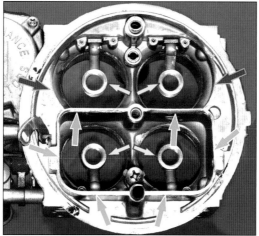

Fig. 14.22. In a home workshop, you can use a die grinder and some 100-grit emery rolls to do all the work on this body. The points of note are the detailed boosters with a sharp edge (yellow arrows), the rounding of the edges leading into the secondary barrels (blue arrows), and the radiusing of the edges on the choke horn (green arrows).

Fig. 14.23. This is what the underside of a detailed booster should look like.

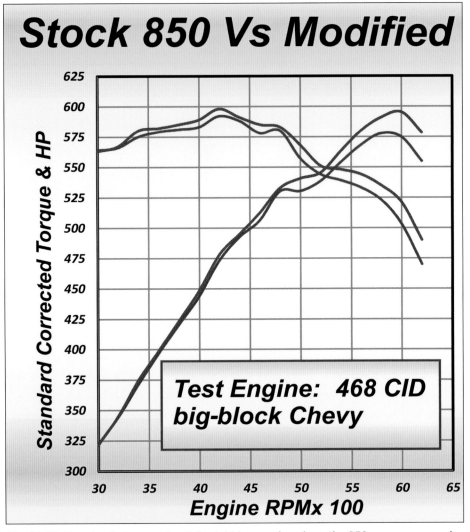

Fig. 14.24. Here is what approximately eight hours of work on the 850 vacuum secondary was worth on a test Chevy 468 big-block engine. Peak power increased by 17.6 hp while the output at 6,200 rose by 24 hp but only after the regular dog-leg booster was reworked to a stepped version (see Chapter 7).

The next question is, How much more can you can get if machining is an option? If you have a lathe or small mill, it is possible to machine the 1.75-inch butterflies on our 850 to take a 1.80-inch butterfly. On the 850 this can add about another 10 to 15 cfm.

Let's also consider using a smaller carb, such as a 750 with a 1¹¹⁄₁₆-inch throttle blade bore instead of the 850's 1¾-inch bore. By taking an 850 base plate and adapting it to a 750 it is possible, with nothing more than some cleanup on the venturis and boosters, to have a 750 flowing about 920 cfm. In so doing you can have all the low speed a 750 can deliver but with the top end of a 920. This is a move that many carb specialists make in the bid for more air without incurring a compromised low-speed output.

Once you have reduced restrictions caused by the butterfly/shaft assembly you can look at the venturis and boosters to see what improvements can be made. I am not talking about a big enlargement of the venturis because the 850's 1.5-inch venturi is almost as big as you can go in a conventional 4150 casting. Any bigger and the signal (which is already

marginal with a 1.5-inch venturi) just goes completely down the drain.

Test 9 was confined to executing a good blend and cleanup job on both the venturis and the boosters. The results show what can be done without removing the boosters from the body. This is a situation that most people can relate to. Sure, removing the boosters can produce better results, but the tool to reinstall them costs about $300.

Figure 14.22 shows a steady hand with a die grinder can elimi-

nate any venturi casting mismatch and clean up the booster venturis to produce a sharp edge at both leading and trailing edges. The result is 935 cfm. That's an overall increase of 10 percent. The booster signal also rose by more than 5 percent.

The installation of a Stub Stack for Test 10 pushed the flow to 956 cfm. That is an increase in flow of more than 12.5 percent.

Test 11 and Test 2 are of the body alone. If you compare them you see that the gains made were very small.

That alone is a prime indicator that the hardware in the airflow is the prime restriction, not the venturi size.

Power Increase

So how much power increase can we expect from an increase in airflow with the modifications to our 850 carb? The answer to that depends almost entirely on how starved of air the engine is. I found dyno test results for our 850 that were also dependent on modifying a regular dog-leg booster to a stepped dog-leg version.

On 450- to 550-hp small-blocks using a good dual-plane making gains of between 5 and 15 hp are common. A big-block with a dual-plane intake can show gains as much as 30 hp but 15 hp is more common. If the manifold is a single-plane, however, the effect of a carb that is too small is a little less pronounced. After a rework of a stepped dog-leg booster, it produces better results as proven in Figure 14.24.

Figure 14.24 shows a stock 850 versus a modified 850 (956 cfm in this particular case). Peak power rose by about 17.6 hp but the power hung on longer so there was an increase of almost 24 hp at 6,200 rpm. All the additional power came with no loss at any other part of the RPM range.

Fig. 14.25. K&N pioneered the oiled cotton/gauze-type filter about 50 years ago and has made it the leading performance filter in the industry. Few have been able to come close to it, but it is often copied. Some do it well while others fail. The result is a filter that neither flows nor filters very well. To avoid buying a filter that is below par, stick with K&N.

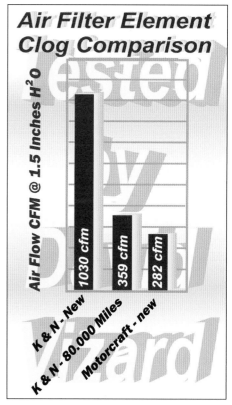

Fig. 14.26. If you are running an off-road vehicle, this is a very important graph. It shows that not only can a K&N effectively filter heavily dust-laden air, such as during the Baja 500 and 1000 events, but it can also hold far more dirt before it becomes overly restrictive. These were not K&N tests, they were mine!

Keep It Clean

There is little point in spending time and money to improve the output of an engine and then allowing it to breathe dirt-laden air because of the lack of a filter or the use of a restrictive filter. Unfortunately the filter industry is rife with manufacturers claiming much but when put to the test just don't deliver in one or other vital area. I have heard top pro engine builders say, "We all know that the use of a filter costs power." The good news is that if you know what you are doing, that is not actually true.

My advice is that you run a filter and, unless you are an expert on all the different brands, I recommend a K&N.

Sure, there are some filters that look like a K&N but they either don't flow or filter the same. Certainly there are a few brands from smaller companies that produce a filter as good as a K&N but without a flow bench and a dust-arresting test machine you won't know the difference until it's too late.

One last thought: I have found that at least 50 percent of counter staff and even shop owners are insufficiently informed on filter selection. You won't go far wrong if you follow my advice.

As far as power loss is concerned, if the filter is correctly sized there is no power loss and possibly a small gain.

INTAKE PORT MATCHING

When looking through engines for sale in classified ads, it doesn't take too long to find one that says the heads and intake manifold have been "gasket matched." That is shorthand for reworking the entrance of the head ports and the exit of the manifold ports (runners) so that they (hopefully) match.

The intent is to give the impression that the ports are truly aligned to aid power production. Two things to note here are: Just because the ports in each of these components have been matched to an intake gasket it is no guarantee that, when installed, the inlet manifold ports are aligned to those in the heads to respectably close limits. Also, you can be absolutely sure that the guy who designed the intake gasket did not use a cylinder head and flow bench to arrive at the gasket's port shape.

In reality a gasket match is nothing more than a way to suggest to a potential buyer that the engine is a little more special. Trust me, you often pay for something that is simply cosmetic or out of sight until the next time the engine is torn down. Not only that, but often it actually reduces engine output.

Given enough dyno time and engine building experience, you come to realize that we should be calling what we are looking at here as "dyno-developed port mismatching."

Simple Port Matching

Most intakes are cast with a taper over the last inch or so to facilitate intake matching. Port matching a tunnel ram's intake runners to the cylinder heads is about as straightforward as it can get. It is usually just a case of looking down the runners to visually check and fix the mismatch. To a degree the same applies to a single-plane intake although usually not all the edges of the manifold's port can be seen.

The first step is to attach the intake manifold gasket to the cylinder heads with sufficient glue (I use contact adhesive) to hold it in place. Do not use so much that you have to

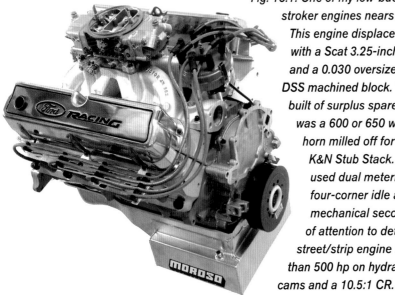

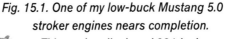
Fig. 15.1. One of my low-buck Mustang 5.0 stroker engines nears completion. This engine displaced 331 inches with a Scat 3.25-inch stroke crank and a 0.030 oversized bore in the DSS machined block. The carb was built of surplus spares. The body was a 600 or 650 with the choke horn milled off for use with a short K&N Stub Stack. The build also used dual metering blocks and four-corner idle as well as a mechanical secondary. With a lot of attention to detail, this budget street/strip engine returned more than 500 hp on hydraulic street roller cams and a 10.5:1 CR.

Fig. 15.2. With the use of a flashlight, positioning the visible edges of the manifold runners becomes simple. Once the edges of the manifold runners have been cut to align with the port runners they can be used as a reference to cut the unseen edges of the runners.

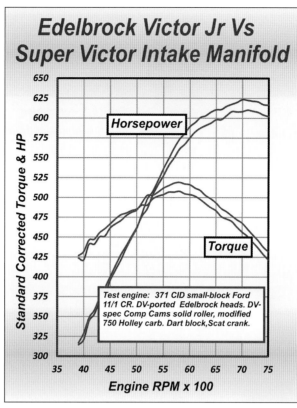

Fig. 15.3. Picking the right manifold is a challenge, let alone having to do the right port match. With Ford and Chevy small-blocks, if I think the engine could make around 600 hp, I use that as a yardstick and go with a Super Victor. As can be seen here the payoff is greater output above the 5,000-rpm mark and usually less below.

scrape gasket and glue off the heads for half a day when it comes time to replace the gasket.

Next, apply a generous amount of heavy grease over the gasket and the mating faces of the intake manifold. At this stage, leave out the lifter valley gaskets at each end of the block. You do this because the head's block may have been machined to increase compression so it makes the manifold sit lower on the block. If this is the case, the end gaskets aren't thick enough. If the manifold has been machined to compensate, the use of a regular valley end gasket could be holding the intake off the point it otherwise fully seats.

Place the intake accurately on the block to ensure it is as near as

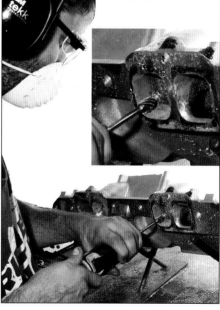

Fig. 15.6. Because of the taper toward the manifold's face, quite a lot of material can be removed from the port over the first inch or so. This means a lot of metal chips flying around. Safety must be your number-one concern here. Note the safety glasses, mask, and ear protectors being worn here. Be sure to follow suit!

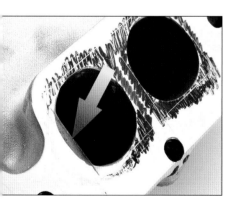

Fig. 15.4. Sometimes the intake is missing material at a location where it actually needs it (arrow). A two-part epoxy resin was used here to fill the port to achieve alignment.

Fig. 15.5. I have tried a variety of port fillers with varying degrees of success. This Goodson type of filler worked well and is very popular with high-end professional head shops.

Fig. 15.7. Port matching or mismatching can not only increase the airflow into the engine but can also help reduce or eliminate any wet flow problems. Airflow tests show an effective port match is worth about 3 percent more induction flow at full valve lift.

you can get it to being aligned. You don't want to slide the intake along the length of the block to align it. (You can use the imprint of the gasket on the grease to give you a rough idea where the port runners are in relation to the head's ports.) Using a flashlight is a good way to check the alignment.

Now, with well-greased manifold securing bolts, progressively torque down the intake.

Next, blue up a patch on the intake and a head. This is the position you return the intake manifold to each time you reinstall it to check alignment.

Take a look down the ports and assess how much metal needs to come off the runner edges in order to align them.

Remove the intake and cut the visible parts of the port to achieve a satisfactory alignment. It is a good idea to have the port in the intake just a little smaller than that in the heads. When you remove the intake, you see an imprint of the runners in the grease. You can use this as a guide to see where metal might need to be added to or

removed from the manifold to achieve alignment. It often takes a number of trial installations of the intake to get all the visible edges aligned.

Once all the visible edges have been cut and aligned (in most cases, the floor and the sides on the outside turn wall), you can match up the unseen edges. To do this, measure the height and width of the ports in the heads and use this measurement less, say, 0.025 to mark the manifold runners' unseen edges from the edges you have just cut.

You should now have an intake that is sufficiently well aligned to get the job done.

Complex Port Matching

So much for the easy way of port matching. The following technique is used by most professional head and engine shops that build serious race engines. This procedure is not the fastest but it gets the job done if sufficient care is taken to maintain the best accuracy possible.

Essentially, you mark a set of reference lines on the heads so you can

transfer them to the intake manifold itself. After transferring the lines from the head to the ends and top of the intake, remove the intake from the engine assembly and ready it for the final phase of the mark up. At this point you should be fully acquainted with techniques to port match any intake to any head.

If you have a dual-plane intake, the complex port match technique is about the only one that works, other than cutting an intake gasket to the exact port shape and transferring an imprint from the assembly grease.

Intentional Port Mismatching

A precision port match may not be what's best for the engine. Sometimes a precision port match actually cuts power. Why? In effect, power is dependent on how well the manifold runners and head ports manage wet flow. If there is a small step at the manifold/head face junction with the intake runner being slightly smaller, the power is likely be as good as, or better than, an absolutely perfect match.

Fig. 15.8. Align a long straightedge with the tops and bottoms of the port and scribe along it to the ends of the cylinder head. Repeat the process for the sides of the ports.

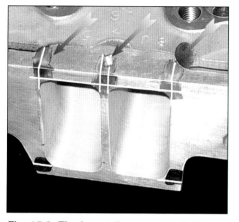

Fig. 15.9. The layout lines now look like this on the top face of the heads.

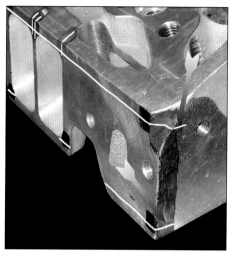

Fig. 15.10. On the ends of the heads the layout lines look like this (arrows).

The straighter the port runner's approach to the head, the greater efficiency it has. For a tunnel ram intake, I generally attempt to match the roof and sides as closely as possible without making them too large. On the bottom of the port in which wet fuel flow often occurs, I leave a step of about 0.03 inch. For most single-plane intakes, I target a small step on the floor and the edge of the outside turn of the port runner.

If you are using a heated dual-plane intake, the chance of a wet fuel problem is minimized, but it still does not hurt to do the matches as I have described so you don't have wet flow issues that foil your realization of maximize power.

If you have some idea where the wet fuel flow path is, some redirecting grooves can be cut into the manifold to move the fuel from a low-flow area to a high-flow area. This brings the raw fuel into close proximity to high-speed airflow and the fuel is mostly shredded back into the main airstream.

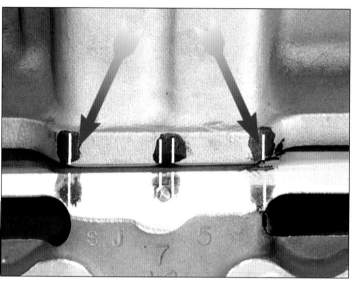

Fig. 15.11. With the manifold bolted and torqued into place, the layout lines on the cylinder heads are transferred to the intake manifold that was previously blued in the relevant areas.

Fig. 15.12. The lines from the end of the head are being transferred to the end of the intake manifold.

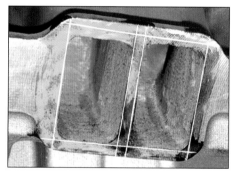

Fig. 15.13. The lines are then transferred to the manifold face as seen here. I cut the sides and bottom of this tunnel ram intake to within about 0.015 to 0.020 inch of the layout lines. The top lines have not been cut yet. The remaining amount required to be cut to align the top of the port is about typical for a big-port Chevy small-block.

Fig. 15.14. The port runners on an Edelbrock Super Victor intake for the Ford small-block are matched to the head's ports. A 60-grit emery roll was used for the finish. The final operation on this intake is to shot blast the port floors with a course-grit media to give a cast-like finish.

SOURCE GUIDE

Advanced Product Design
3025 N. Genoa-Clay Center Rd.
Genoa, OH 43430
419-855-3073
www.apdracing.com

AED Performance
2530 Willis Rd.
Richmond, VA 23237
804-271-9107
www.aedperformance.com

Air Inlet Systems
177 Grace Ave.
Hamilton, Ont, Canada L8H-3X1
905-549-6135
www.ramairbox.com

BLP Racing Products
1015 West Church St.
Orlando, FL 32805
407-422-0394
www.blp.com

Braswell Carburetion
7671 N. Business Park Dr.
Tucson, AZ 85743-9622
520-579-9177
www.braswell.com

Brodix Cylinders Heads
301 Maple Ave./P.O. Box 1347
Mena, AR 71953
479-394-1075
www.brodix.com

CFM Performance Carburetors
3337 Yost Rd.
Litchfield, OH 44253
330-723-5688
www.cfmperfcarbs.com

Dart Machinery
353 Oliver St.
Troy, MI 48084
248-362-1188
www.dartheads.com

DeVane Carbs
1007 E. Flora St.
Tampa, FL
813-546-3423
www.devanecarbs.com

Edelbrock, LLC
2700 California St.
Torrance, CA 90503
310-781-2222
www.edelbrock.com

Holley & Weiand
    Performance Products
1801 Russellville Rd.
Bowling Green, KY 42101
270 782-2900
www.holley.com

KB Carburetors
7009 Monclova Rd.
Maumee, OH, 43537
419-866-5722
www.kbcarburetors.com

K&N Air Filters
P.O. Box 1329
Riverside, CA 92502
800-858-3333
www.knfilters.com

Pro Systems Racing
1879 S. Wolf Lake Rd.
Muskegon, MI 49442
727-490-5717
www.prosystemsracing.com

Professional Products
2205 W. El Segundo Blvd.
Hawthorne, CA 90250
323-779-2020
www.professional-products.com

Profiler Performance Products
P.O. Box 217
New Carlisle, OH 45344
937-846-1333
www.profilerperformance.com

Quick Fuel Technology
129 Dishman Ln.
Bowling Green, KY 42101
270-793-0900
www.quickfueltechnology.com

Summit Racing Equipment
1200 Southeast Ave.
Tallmadge, OH 44278
800-230-3030
www.summitracing.com

Trick Flow Specialties
285 West Ave.
Tallmadge, OH 44278
330-630-1555
www.trickflow.com